HEADING TOWARD
OMEGA

· · · · · · · · · · · · · · · ·

÷

HEADING TOWARD
OMEGA

*In Search of the Meaning of
the Near-Death Experience*

KENNETH RING

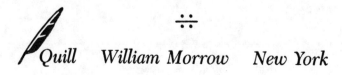

Quill   *William Morrow*   *New York*

To Norma Kraenzle,
mistress of the Near-Death Hotel
and its heart

Library of Congress Catalog Card Number: 85-62560

ISBN: 0-688-06268-7

Printed in the United States of America

First Quill Edition

1 2 3 4 5 6 7 8 9 10

BOOK DESIGN BY MARIA EPES

Preface

Year round in my part of the United States, and maybe in yours, many of us awaken from our nightly slumber to a beautiful mixed chorus of bird songs. This is not because I live in Big Sur country, where avian melodies can be heard winter and summer; my birds instead come out of a box on my night table. The box, of course, is my clock radio, and the bird songs I awaken to are the recorded opening theme music of a favorite classical music program, *Morning Pro Musica*. It pleases me to imagine that the many inhabitants of New England, where I do live, stir comfortably underneath their bedcovers and are thus collectively roused gently to full wakefulness by these same morning calls, which serve as a prelude to some easy Vivaldi (after the news). It is, in any case, quite a delight to awaken in this fashion.

This book, too, is about awakening, though the call to do so comes, of course, from a different species altogether and has, I think, a greater urgency to it. I am alluding here not to human beings in general but, as you may have supposed, to those human beings in particular I have made it my professional business to study and ruminate about over the past six years—namely, individuals who have survived a near- or clinical-death incident and who claim to recall what it was like to die. Nevertheless, I must hasten to add that *Heading Toward Omega* is not just another one of those books crammed with more firsthand accounts of "near-death experiences." Rather it is, as I have already said and now wish to emphasize, a book about *awakening*.

But whose awakening? And awakening to *what*, exactly?

To answer these questions, some background comments are first necessary. In my initial work on the near-death experience (NDE), which I reported in my book *Life at Death*, I was mainly concerned to describe the specific features of this experience. From that research and from the abundant research of others it was clear that the NDE not only followed a certain common pattern but also that it could be understood as representing an individual's direct personal realization of a higher spiritual reality. The NDE, then, seemed to be a glimpse, albeit a brief one, of a transcendental domain of preternatural peace and beauty. It is in this sense that the NDE may be spoken of as an awakening.

Omega follows the trail charted by *Life at Death* but takes it much farther by drawing on an entirely new set of findings related to NDEs: aftereffects. We are now in a position to describe in depth and in detail what happens afterward to people who have survived an NDE. And it turns out that this new material actually holds the key to the meaning of these experiences and to the significance they have for each one of us, whether we have had an NDE or not. *Life at Death*, then, attempted to say what NDEs are; *Omega*, by tracing their effects and estimating their incidence, shows why NDEs are arguably phenomena whose evolutionary implications must be grasped if one is fully to understand what they *mean*.

Although *Omega*, like *Life at Death*, is based on my own empirical research, I have tried to write this book in a more personal vein since it reflects and, I now believe, concludes my own search for a deeper understanding of these extraordinary experiences. And while I have stuffed the statistics describing some of my findings in Appendix III, I have this time introduced into my chapters many of the remarkable people I have met in the course of my travels on the way to Omega. These individuals really provide the substance to my story, and their words will convey what statistics never can, so I hope you will enjoy these NDEr friends of mine and find it as easy and instructive as I have to listen to them. It may be that in speaking of their own awakenings and of the transformations that followed, they will awaken something in you.

So we return, then, to the questions I posed earlier: Whose

awakening are we discussing here? What is being awakened to?

Although the meaning of the phrase "heading toward Omega" will be fully explained in the last chapter, suffice it to say here that I believe and argue in this book that humanity as a whole is collectively struggling to awaken to a new and higher mode of consciousness, which many have already called "planetary consciousness." Furthermore, I believe that a significant number of persons have already evolved or are evolving toward that form of consciousness and that the NDE can be viewed as an *evolutionary device* to bring about this transformation, over a period of years, in millions of persons. In my judgment, this transformation is already taking place and it is likely to accelerate and spread. My thesis is, in short, that we ourselves are witnesses to a major evolutionary metamorphosis in the human race and that many NDErs—as well as others who have had functionally similar awakenings—are on the leading edge of this evolutionary wave.

That I am not guilty of facile visionary speculations or of having read too much science fiction will I hope be demonstrated by the data I have marshaled from my *Omega* sample of NDErs to support my thesis. I will not, of course, claim here or elsewhere that these data *prove* my thesis, but I do believe that they clearly point to its plausibility and that my interpretation of the NDE at least provides the most cogent overall framework within which to understand its great significance. In any case, I hope that interested scholars and researchers will find my data and conclusions useful in promoting further inquiry into the NDE and its implications.

Does it strain credulity too much to suppose that such an emergent form of consciousness is already in evidence and that it is now starting to diffuse over the planet? Did fourteenth-century Italians, steeped in their medieval world view, appreciate the spirit of the Renaissance as it was making itself manifest? In an age such as ours, where the nightly news bombards us with the ephemera of world and national occurrences and with the doings of the latest celebrities, it is understandable that in our fascination with quotidian events we might lose our sensitivity to the larger, more subtle rhythms of evolutionary trends that are nevertheless there to perceive. Is it not just possible that in all the din, fear, and confusion of modern life there is a faint chorus somewhere raised in song auguring a new dawn for the human race and calling us all forth to participate in the grand awakening?

Listen to the voices in this book joined in common song and determine for yourself what you hear.

Preface to the Paperback Edition

In the short time since the publication of *Heading Toward Omega*, it has become clear that the most provocative—and certainly controversial—aspect of the book concerns my thesis that the NDE may represent a major catalyst for human evolution and planetary transformation. Accordingly, in this new Preface, I would like to address briefly a few points that you should bear in mind when considering this argument.

First, it should be evident that the NDE is by no means the only or even the principal sign of the possible next stage in humanity's slow progression toward higher consciousness; rather, it is but one facet in the jewel of transcendental experience to whose radiance we as a species seem increasingly to be drawn. There are many other ways to know what the NDEr has come to learn through a near-death crisis and, similarly, the pattern of transformation that tends to follow an NDE is not unique to NDErs.

Second, I need to clarify the meaning of the term *Homo noeticus*, which, on the basis of previous usage, I appropriated to characterize an emergent form of humanity foreshadowed, I believe, by modern NDErs. Of course, by using this phrase, I did not intend to imply that *Homo noeticus* signifies a new *species* of man, for that would be ludicrous biologically. Instead, this designation should be understood to refer to a human being whose potential for higher consciousness has been awakened to such a degree that he/she unmistakably manifests the qualities traditionally associated with the most spiritually advanced persons. (These attributes are discussed in Chapters 9 and 10.)

Finally, despite the wisdom and love that many NDErs exude, and even while noting that collectively they may be harbingers of humanity's psychospiritual evolution, I want to caution against exalting NDErs as a class of persons. NDErs are usually the first to concede that they "are all too human" and that the NDE itself is just the beginning of a long initiation into life's highest mysteries. Indeed, anyone who starts to explore the implications of the NDE will soon find that, though this experience may well house an evolutionary thrust whose full effect only the future can disclose, its legacy can be traced back to the secret ceremonies of antiquity. From this perspective—which has come to inform my work since the publication of *Omega*—what we have in the contemporary NDE is a modern version, cloaked in the symbols of our own time, of the ancient mystery teachings concerning life, death, and regeneration. I will leave it to the reader to ponder the possible significance of the re-emergence of these teachings in a form and on a scale unprecedented, so far as we know, in the sometimes faltering and wayward history of our light-seeking species. In any event, NDErs, whatever their evolutionary role, ought not to be thought of as offering the final word on the meaning of their experience, nor should they be set apart from or above others. *All* of us are made of the light NDErs have experienced, and though they may help to illuminate the way, it is still up to each of us to find and follow that way for ourselves.

Storrs, Connecticut
July 1985

Foreword

It is a great honor and pleasure to write a few words of introduction to Kenneth Ring's new book *Heading Toward Omega*, which has been eagerly awaited by people who are familiar with his research.

For two decades many of us have been diligently collecting cases of what are now called near-death experiences. Not until Raymond Moody's book *Life After Life* became a best seller did this term become familiar to professionals as well as laypeople. More and more serious researchers and clinicians became interested in this phenomenon, which has been known for centuries but was very rarely studied seriously.

Until those bold enough started to speak about it publicly and publish some of their findings, my patients were very reluctant to have their material revealed in any identifiable fashion. Most of those who shared their own personal experiences of this near-death phenomenon initiated their story with statements such as "I am happy to tell you what occurred to me if you promise not to tell my doctor, my family, etc." The common fear was that they would be labeled as psychotic, as hallucinating or "being of Satan" if they revealed their encounters.

With the publication of books on this subject by such authorities as Moody, Karlis Osis, and Michael Sabom—as well as Kenneth Ring's previous book *Life at Death*—this phenomenon has gained credibility and can now be openly discussed.

I will never forget when I had my own personal experience after a busy and exhausting workshop. I was lifted out into a realm of such love and care, floating and uplifted as by invisible, tender arms and experienced a rejuvenation and a recharging of my energies as if half a dozen mechanics had lovingly fixed up an old car and made it new. When I returned to my physical body I felt refreshed and strong again and had a conviction that we are truly looked after beyond all our comprehension.

It was many years later, during a much more intense experience of this nature, that I was allowed to experience and become part of that light that so many people try to explain in words. Anyone who has been blessed enough to see this light will never again be afraid to die. The unconditional love, the understanding and compassion in the presence of this light are beyond any human description.

And this is perhaps the greatest contribution of Kenneth's new book. It tries to comprehend the ensuing changes that persons undergo once they have been in the presence of this light. It is a spiritual, sacred experience, which leaves the person profoundly transformed. The near-death experience also gives new dimensions to living and to the understanding of human life and its purpose.

It is my belief that with the beginning of the New Age, more and more people are being given this gift and this knowledge. It will be, as Kenneth shows, a great contributing factor to the changes in consciousness—to the comprehension and experience of unconditional love—not only on the other side but also here on earth, where it is so sorely needed to heal the wounds of people and of nations.

Once enough people have experienced this love, maybe we will be able to bring about peace on earth.

Thank you, Kenneth, for your masterful work and for the objectivity and openness of this new book.

—ELISABETH KÜBLER-ROSS
Escondido, California
September 30, 1983

Acknowledgments

Every book is a collaborative enterprise, no matter who is listed as its author, and this book is no exception. Here I wish to acknowledge just a few of the many who have, knowingly or otherwise, helped me on my way to Omega.

First in line have to be my companions at "the Near-Death Hotel"—what that is will be explained in the first chapter—who supported me in so many ways before and during the composition of this book. And first in that line must be Norma Kraenzle, whose love and criticisms were both sometimes more than I felt I deserved, though I took more of the former than the latter in any case. I am indebted also to Steve Straight for our many stimulating dinner (and after-dinner) discussions of NDEs. To Maria Castedo, I give my thanks not only for her loving tolerance of my brutish ways but also for her painstaking tabulation and double-checking of some of my data. She was of inestimable help in culling materials from my files for me, too.

I wrote most of this while on leave from the University of Connecticut, during which time I was also relieved of my administrative responsibilities for IANDS, the International Association for Near-Death Studies (see Appendix IV). This was possible only through the kindness of two individuals in particular: Nancy Evans Bush, our executive director, whose capacity for misleading callers concerning my whereabouts is beyond praise, and Bruce Greyson of the University of Michigan, who assumed the presidency of IANDS while I hid out writing.

Bruce, in fact, is only one—though perhaps he is foremost—of my many colleagues with whom I was able to discuss my work and writing in the course of their development and to whom I wish to give thanks in this regard. Others I wish to mention here, though it is far from a complete list, are Michael Grosso, Charles Flynn, Raymond Moody, John Audette, Mineda McCleave, and Boyce Batey. In addition, I'd like to thank Caroline Myss for her careful reading of the manuscript and for her useful criticisms of it. And finally here to my friend Tom Penrose, who has influenced me more than he knows, my thanks and my love.

For some reason, it isn't customary to thank one's agent for services rendered, but I don't know why not. I happen to have a gem, and I want her to know it. So to Sallie Gouverneur for all her support and encouragement, my deep gratitude. My editor, Alison Brown Cerier, also has my sincere thanks for the many ways she has found to improve the manuscript. And for still another kind of assistance, my appreciation to the Academy of Religion and Psychical Research for a small grant to cover clerical expenses for some of the research reported in this book.

No book would ever see the light—and dark—of print without the indispensable labors of typists and (these days) word processors (I mean the people who use them, not the machines themselves). So I salute them, too, here: Sandy English, who typed the original draft of *Omega*, and the always competent and friendly staff at Parousia Press: Carolyn Lemire and Dara Palmer, who did the typing, and Elaine Venti, who prepared the figures in Appendix III.

I have saved for last, of course, the hundreds of near-death experiencers whose lives have been my life for the past six years. Many of them you will come to meet and know through this book and you will thereby come to appreciate the special bond that exists between them and me. I have learned more from them than I could ever possibly acknowledge here, and I will be, at least figuratively speaking, many lifetimes repaying them for what they have taught me in this one. I only hope that they will feel that I have adequately transmitted to you in this book the insights they have entrusted to me during the past several years. To attempt to be the vehicle through which they speak—at least for those who do not write books themselves—has been the privilege of my life.

Storrs, Connecticut
July 1983

Contents

CHAPTER 1

· · · · · · ·

NDEs on the Road to Omega

÷

A *New View of Death*

More than six years have now passed since I began my own research into the near-death experience, and in that time much of the Western world has come to look at death with open eyes unclouded by fear. What has happened to bring about this new view of death?

Although there are clearly many developments within the field of thanatology, the study of death and dying, that have helped to shape this new perspective, it seems evident that the primary one stems from research during the past few years in the field of *near-death studies*.[1] This area of scientific and medical investigation focuses on the near-death experience and now includes scores of researchers and scholars in this country alone who have, since 1977, made substantial contributions to our understanding of what it is like to die. And what these students of the near-death experience have been telling us seems destined to move us collectively into a positive and fear-free attitude toward death on a scale scarcely imaginable even a decade ago.

Of course, at a popular level, it has not been near-death studies so much as the subjects of that research that have been responsible for articulating this new point of view about death to the public at large. In an age dominated by talk shows and other forms of entertainment-as-education, it has been the near-death experiencer who has become the chief spokesperson in the field of death education. On literally hundreds of radio and television programs over the past five years, scores of men and women—sometimes accompanied by researchers to add a note of professional authority—have described for mass audiences the experience of dying. And, with few exceptions, their accounts of their near- or clinical-death experiences have shown striking commonalities in stressing the great peace and beauty and all-pervading sense of love that they report characterized their close brush with death. Moreover, both popular magazines and tabloids have printed many similar narratives based on direct interviews with near-death experiencers. When you add to these sources of information the spate of books (see the Bibliography) dealing with near-death experiences that have been published since the mid-seventies—and that usually quote copiously from the testimony of near-death experiencers—it seems safe to infer that only a person who made a dedicated effort to avoid exposure to all popular media and professional literature in the past few years might still be unaware of these reports. And even then the person probably couldn't go for long without encountering someone else who had heard of them.

In short, in America now, the level of popular if sometimes superficial familiarity with near-death experiences appears to have reached a very high mark. Although familiarity does not necessarily imply acceptance, the available evidence[2] suggests that the latter is also appreciable. In all of this, the direct testimony of hundreds of near-death experiencers has, in my opinion, probably been the most significant influence on public opinion.

However that may be, we now need to ask: What precisely is this new view of death that has developed mainly as a result of the widespread acceptance of near-death experiences?

The answer here might best be indicated by way of contrast. Consider the way most of us over the age of thirty were socialized, consciously or otherwise, to think about death. Perhaps our first exposure to human death was overhearing the whispered conversation of our parents as they discussed the death of a beloved family member. For many of us that conversation would eventually be followed by a viewing of the corpse at a family wake or some other preburial public ceremony. In other cases, we might ourselves have been involved in an automobile accident where one of our companions was killed. As a result, the memory of this person's shattered and bloodied body, lying partially covered by a blanket on the roadside, might thereafter be the source of a powerfully charged image of death. In still other instances, it may be not an actual death but a prospective one that significantly shapes our view of death. For example, we may visit an elderly relative in a nursing home and be shocked by the degree of physical decrepitude and loss of function that appear to be the precursors of death. To see the vacant stare of one's grandmother, now incontinent and speechless as well, with a body ravaged by degenerative disease, can have a devastating effect on a young person—for that matter, on anyone. One's elderly relative may appear to be only a caricature of a human being and her personality may be nowhere in evidence. Under such circumstances—if this were our grandmother—what impressions would we tend to form of death?

It is hardly necessary to resort to further situations involving contact with the dying or dead to appreciate how we are typically educated to understand death. Plainly, we learn to view *death from the outside*. We are always spectators to death; obviously, we think, we can never experience our own. When we conceive of death from this perspective, we may have images of physical deterioration and feelings of the pain of separation from the dying person. Thinking of death in this way, it is natural to fear it, even to be repulsed by it, and to avoid the subject of death as if it were still under some cultural taboo. Even persons who take some nominal comfort in religious doctrines regarding what is supposed to happen following death are not altogether immune from the particular kind of uneasiness that comes from viewing death from the position of a witness.

Consider next, however, the understanding of death suggested by near-death research. This is an *interior* view of death. It is based on the direct experiences that thousands of people have when they almost die, or when they do die clinically. The great unanimity of these reports means that there is a consensus among near-death experiencers concerning what it is like to die. This collective testimony, which will be further supported by the research reported in this book, states that the experience of death is exceedingly pleasant. Indeed, the word "pleasant" is far too mild; "ecstatic" would be chosen by many survivors of this experience. No words are truly adequate to describe the sense of ultimate perfection that appears to characterize the entry into death.

What do these experiences teach us about death? First, they demonstrate that the appearance of death is not at all like the *experience* of death. What death looks like is not what it feels like. Indeed, what it feels like is in many ways the opposite of what it appears to be to someone witnessing the onset of death in another. Second, it teaches us not to fear death. One of the most consistent findings to emerge from the body of near-death research is that people who have had NDEs[3] do not as a rule fear death at all; furthermore, their loss of the fear of death appears to be permanent following an NDE. The virtual universality of this finding and the conviction with which near-death experiencers have been able to express their fearlessness about death are two of the reasons why those who have been exposed to near-death research or experiencers can be expected to have their own fear of death diminished.[4]

Take a minute or two to reflect on the significance of these implications. Imagine a mother whose young daughter has recently been struck and killed by a driver who lost control of his car. The mother may have seen the impact and a few seconds later may have held her daughter's broken body in her arms hoping she would at least regain consciousness before she died. Think what it would mean to this mother to know or believe that her child did not feel the pain of the accident but in fact experienced an inward feeling of extreme bliss and well-being. Imagine what it would mean for the mother to be convinced that despite appearances, her child had at death a feeling of being entirely *whole* and was engulfed in an ocean of perfect and total love. (This is not, by the way, merely a hypothetical example. I have met and talked with mothers who have lost a child in exactly this fashion and who have expressed the greatest joy on learning about near-death experiences precisely because of these implications. Other researchers report the same.) Or consider the situation of the widow of a combat veteran killed in Vietnam. Perhaps years later she learns from reading accounts of veterans who had NDEs in combat that her husband probably did not suffer when he died. Although nothing can return her husband to her, it may still be a considerable source of comfort to her that the gruesome external circumstances of his death were likely not mirrored in his inner experience. Or, finally, consider an elderly man of no particular religious convictions who is facing imminent death. One day, he idly switches on his TV and catches a portion of an interview with a near-death experiencer, also with no pronounced religious leanings, we'll say, who relates his own NDE and utters his strong conviction that death not only is not to be feared but is instead an experience that ranges beyond joy. How might this affect the old man's life *before* he dies?

Again, it is not necessary to multiply examples further to see how this *interior* view of death that stems from near-death studies may prove to be a potent anodyne to many people who are either facing death themselves or who have to cope with the death of a loved one. To know that there is indeed more to death than meets the eye and that what cannot be seen is a kind of perfection that must be experienced to be understood is to have great peace of mind in the presence of death.

In outlining this new view of death, however, it is very important to be clear about what happens to the traditional understanding of death with which we began—that based on the stance of the witness. That view remains. Near-death experiences and their implications obviously do not banish the pain of death, nor do they appreciably soften the sense of loss we feel when someone we deeply love dies. The interior view of death supplements—it does not supplant—the external perspective. The advantage of having both perspectives to draw on is that one does not have to get caught up solely in the traditional view with all its negativities. The grim reaper is always accompanied by the being of light,[5] as it were, and near-death research has simply enabled us to see the latter.

In the same way, the interior view of death does not deny nor seek to romanticize the process of dying. That, of course, is often painful, both for the dying person and those near. And near-death experiencers rarely say they lose their fear of dying; it is only of death itself that fear is dissolved. Here it is critical to remember that the implications of near-death research apply not to the trajectory toward death but directly to the moment of (apparent) imminent death. It is in that moment—from the standpoint of inner experience—that, metaphorically, the grim reaper is transmuted into the being of light, and pain gives way to inner peace.

In brief, the traditional perspective is appropriate to the situation of the dying person; the interior perspective enters the picture with that person's death. Both are indispensable for a comprehensive understanding of what death is. Thus, by providing an appreciation of death "from the inside," near-death studies have contributed significantly to a more holistic conception of the dying process.

Life at the "Near-Death Hotel"

While this new view of death deriving from near-death research was being fashioned and conveyed to the American public, I was busy with my own research and writing. In 1980 I published *Life at Death*, the first scientifically grounded investigation of near-death experiences. That study, based on my first hundred interviews with near-death survivors,[6] largely confirmed the earlier anecdotal research reported by Raymond Moody and Elisabeth Kübler-Ross and provided new data concerning various features of the NDE. In brief, the findings of *Life at Death* revealed that the NDE was indeed a commonly reported event in near-death incidents, that it tended to unfold in a series of discrete stages, and that its form and content were highly consistent in different individuals regardless of the circumstances that had brought them close to death. When I finished the manuscript, I felt it would be the only book on NDEs I would ever write; indeed, I remember feeling at the time that it would probably be the last book I would write. In doing the research for the book, many of my own personal questions about NDEs were answered. My personal contact with NDErs, furthermore, had such a powerful impact on my thinking about escatological matters that it seemed to me necessary only to try to live my life in accordance with what I had learned; it did not feel appropriate to do any more research on the topic of NDEs. So I published my book feeling grateful for what I had been privileged to learn and, although I recognized the methodological deficiencies of *Life at Death*, especially in its lack of a randomly selected sample of cases, I nevertheless believed it was my last word on the subject.

I was wrong.

Since *Life at Death* was published by a commercial rather than an academic firm, I was asked to appear on some radio and television programs to help publicize the book. That was the beginning. Although the book hardly set any sales records, the subject seemed to arouse keen interest in many people. Some people who had heard or seen me, or who had already read *Life at Death*, began to write me; in many cases, their letters described their own NDEs. One thing led to another. More programs followed, and I was asked to give many talks and seminars on near-death experiences. I'm not a bad speaker (anyone who has been a professor for twenty years has had plenty of opportunity to practice), but I often would joke that even an idiot could not miss with this material—it was just so intrinsically interesting to most people that the response was almost always gratifying.

Invariably, after such programs, I would meet persons who had had NDEs and who would be waiting for the opportunity to share their own experiences with me. Typically, this was done on the spot or over a drink afterward, and I usually found myself absorbed in these narratives. You might think that after having heard hundreds of similar accounts of NDEs, one's attentiveness would begin to waver. I did not find this happening, however, and in comparing notes with other researchers, I found that this is the usual response: There is no habituation. Why not?

On reflection, there seem to be two principal reasons. One is that normally the NDEr is describing the experience for the first time (and in some cases, it is the first time *ever*) to a person who is perceived to care genuinely about hearing it and who is presumed to know something about NDEs in general. Since NDErs are apt to say or imply that their experience is "the most important thing that ever happened to me," there is often an intensity to the interaction that is all the more remarkable in view of the brevity of the contact. Under such circumstances, it is almost impossible *not* to be completely taken up with an NDEr's story. The second reason is that one would have to be a stone not to be moved and impressed by these experiences. And this is as true for written narratives as spoken ones; more than once my eyes have welled with tears on reading an account of an NDE from a correspondent.

You can see that under these conditions, it would be difficult simply to thank such people politely and then run off and catch one's plane. Instead, I'd find myself saying something like, "Listen, if you're ever up in Connecticut . . ."

My companion, Norma, and I live in a converted inn situated

on the banks of an appealing river in a small town in rural Connecticut, not far from the state university where I teach. It is a very pleasant old house that still retains the rustic ambience of a country inn. And, soon, we found that the people to whom I had issued those spontaneous invitations to visit were actually calling up to arrange to do exactly that. Most of those NDErs were from the Northeast, but some came from considerable distances to our home. One man even hitchhiked from California to visit! It took him a week to arrive and he stayed for two.

It wasn't until early 1981, however, that the near-death traffic through our house began to tax our floors. In December 1980, I had reluctantly agreed to take over the administration of a small, fledgling organization for the scientific study of NDEs that several of us near-death researchers had founded a couple of years earlier. We renamed the organization, somewhat grandly, "The International Association for Near-Death Studies" (IANDS) and found office space for it at the university (the work of IANDS is described in detail in Appendix IV). Since IANDS was to publish various periodicals including a professional journal, arrange conferences and other programs on NDEs, and serve generally as a resource center for persons and organizations wanting information about NDEs, I suppose it was inevitable that I should soon find my life almost completely dominated by "near-death events" of every kind. In addition to what we soon came to accept as routine—more correspondence than we could handle, manuscripts needing editing, requests from the media, and so on—we continued to receive visitors. Sometimes people would literally walk in off the street seeking to relate their NDEs (which they did). Researchers from foreign countries—as well as from America—would write asking if they could come to IANDS to make use of our archives and contacts with NDErs (and they did; you can guess where they stayed). In the case of professional conferences or IANDS' board of directors' meetings, it seemed only appropriate to hold these at the university or our home as well. Indeed, sometimes the only difference between home and the office seemed to be a five-mile ride; in both places, the same people would meet and the same matters would be discussed. It was a rare evening meal when death was *not* mentioned! And all the while, new NDErs whom I would meet in the course of my travels would be making their way to Connecticut for weekend visits.

Since our house was now fairly teeming with IANDS staffers, near-death researchers, and scholars as well as a great number of near-death experiencers, Norma and I could scarcely do otherwise than to dub our home, "the Near-Death Hotel," for that indeed was what it had turned into. At that time we had a single guest room (it now seems to be permanently occupied by a nurse from Spain who, it goes without saying, has come to America to study NDEs). Naturally, we turned it into "the Near-Death Room." And I'm sure that its bed has slept more near-death survivors than any bed in history! And certainly at the Near-Death Hotel, more NDEs have been recounted after dinner than at any other single location in the world.

I am writing lightly about all this because, despite our occasionally feeling overwhelmed by all our visitors, there was a great deal of humor expressed during such times and we all took very considerable pleasure in one another's company. There were also strong feelings of love exchanged among us, and usually by the time our guests were to leave it was evident that a kind of bonding had taken place that would leave us friends for life. Thus, these visits were also special occasions for us and transformed the initial feelings of rapport into the more solid ties of lasting friendship.

Something else was becoming evident to me during these visits as well. I began to realize that through my friendship with these NDErs—as well as with quite a few of the persons I had met while researching *Life at Death*—I had been in a position to observe something that most near-death researchers were unlikely to see, at least not on such a scale. This was possible simply as a result of being with such persons in a natural setting and becoming friends with them. This was very different than arranging to interview a near-death survivor in a neutral setting on a single occasion. I was now seeing aspects of a person's character and appreciating certain nuances in conduct that I had just not been cognizant of in my earlier work—and couldn't have been, given the conditions under which that research was carried out. But, more than that, I felt that through these informal interactions I was becoming aware of certain *patterns* I knew had never been discussed in the literature in near-death studies. When all this had occurred to me, I found that I'd been hooked again. My researcher's mind was beginning to re-awaken. I just couldn't help myself. I had to pursue more carefully what our casual days at the Near-Death Hotel had suggested to my researcher's mind.

I felt I was beginning to glean the real, hidden meaning of these NDEs. The larger context for a complete understanding of NDEs was forming itself in my mind. I came to see that while *Life at Death* was in the main accurate in what it had said about NDEs, it did not go nearly far enough in probing the deep-lying significance of these phenomena. I also saw that my earlier work was bound to be limited in this way because I had focused my attention, naturally, on the NDE itself. But one must look *beyond* the typical experience to begin to comprehend its essence.

This book, then, is the story of that search for meaning and of the people I met who have given me the eyes to discern it.

The Search for Meaning

If it weren't that it so clearly smacks of spiritual sleaze, the title of this book might well be *Beyond Life at Death*. I say this because there are at least two ways in which the research reported in this book takes us beyond the material presented in my initial volume.

In the first place, I have made a special effort to locate and to interview persons who have had unusually deep NDEs. In *Life at Death* I confined myself exclusively to NDErs whose experiences were limited to what I there called the five stages of the core experience:[7] peace, body separation, entering the darkness, seeing the light, and entering the light. This was not by conscious design but rather the result of the vicissitudes of my sampling procedure. Shortly after completing the collection of cases for that book in May 1978, however, I began to encounter instances of NDEs that went deeper than any I had come across in my previous work. These people were seeing more in their near-death visions than had previously been reported. Aware of the implications of these deeper experiences, I then began to search specifically for others. My assumption was that if one truly wanted to understand the full significance of NDEs, it would pay dividends to seek out those persons who had traveled farther along the NDE pathway. It would be those persons, I reasoned, who could give me the most informed understanding of the meaning and implications of NDEs. I will refer to these cases at various points throughout this book but will concentrate on them in detail in Chapters 3 and 8.

The second way in which this book goes beyond *Life at Death* relates not to the NDE itself but to its effects on the lives of near-death experiencers. In our conversations at the Near-Death Hotel and in other informal settings, I was able to come to an intuitive understanding of the thesis that underlies this book: *The key to the meaning of NDEs lies in the study of their aftereffects.* By being in a position to observe NDErs repeatedly over a period of several years in a variety of social situations, I was beginning to see the subtle yet powerful transformations that their NDEs were triggering in their lives. Furthermore, our informal but far-ranging conversations helped me to see better which circumstances hindered the transformative process and which facilitated it. Finally, by having access, even indirectly through our IANDS archives, to a large sample of NDErs, I could appreciate how pervasive these transformations were—and how charged with meaning they were.

Perhaps I can best express this dawning insight by a simile. Imagine a garden in which are sown similar seeds of unknown origin. It is a large garden and some seeds are tended better than others. The result is that some never germinate, while those that do, grow at different rates. Each day the gardener comes out wondering what kind of plants the seeds will produce. After a while, enough of them have assumed a form that is clear enough to suggest their eventual configuration. The weaker ones, of course, conform to this configuration more uncertainly, but the hardiest specimens leave no doubt. The seed has disclosed its nature only through its maturation.

The NDE is like a seed. It is, more precisely, a *seed experience*. As an experience, it is very beautiful and may seem complete within itself. In one sense it is, but it is a seed's nature to grow. It has the potential to grow, at least, but whether it does and at what rate depends on many factors. If it grows, you can see what kind of plant fulfills the promise of the seed—"by their fruits ye shall know them." As NDErs "mature" following their experience, the nature of that seed experience—its meaning, if you like—becomes increasingly manifest. And as more and more of these NDErs begin to mature, there seems to be a significance also in their sheer numbers and not merely in their form.

This is why all of us early researchers necessarily missed the full meaning of the phenomenon with which we were dealing. We were observing the garden, as it were, just after seeding. But now enough time has elapsed and we can see more clearly just what has been sown. We begin to understand that we have seen only a small fraction of the beauty before us.

The task I have set for myself in this book is to describe something of that greater beauty now becoming visible to all of us and revealed by examining the lives of those who have had the seed experience of an NDE.

The Omega Study

In *Life at Death,* all my data were collected through detailed, structured interviews with about one hundred near-death survivors. In this work, I have increased both the diversity of my methods and the size of my sample. In addition to direct interviews, I have designed and used a variety of questionnaires to probe more deeply and specifically into particular aftereffects. Beyond this, I have made extensive use of the many letters and tapes sent to me at IANDS; in some cases I have also been able to interview persons I first heard from through correspondence or telephone conversations. The nature of the interviews I conducted and the questionnaires I used in this study will be described in the appropriate chapters of this book, but my standard interview schedule as well as all my other instruments are reproduced in full in Appendices I and II for the interested reader.

Hundreds of respondents took part in this research, which was actually comprised of several different studies. The number of participants varied from forty-two persons who were directly interviewed to 174 who filled out one of my questionnaires. From our file of over 150 letters from NDErs, I selected sixty-two for inclusion in this study; that represents all our correspondents who made reference to aftereffects in sufficient detail that their answers could be coded. Again, the particulars will be given in connection with the different studies as they are described in the following chapters.

There is one feature of my sample, however, that deserves to be mentioned here. Among the 111 persons whose data furnish the principal basis for the study of aftereffects—and they include respondents whom I interviewed, others who completed lengthy questionnaires for me and my correspondents—there is a preponderance of women. Altogether, eighty females are represented here, nearly 72 percent of my entire sample. The reason for this disproportion is simply that women write more often to describe their NDEs than do men, and women are also often more amenable to interviews. This was not so serious a problem as it might appear, however, since previous research shows that men and women report similar NDEs. It is unlikely, then, that there are marked differences between the sexes in aftereffects either, especially since, as I have argued in *Life at Death*, NDEs and their aftereffects appear to be all of a piece. In any event, my impressions as well as the data themselves suggest that the similarities between men and women in this respect appear to be much more striking than their differences.

Other methodological matters cannot be so blithely dismissed, however. The professional or simply critical reader will soon become aware of some of the faults of this research. Just to forewarn the reader, I will enumerate the worst of them here.

First, my sample of cases is obviously not randomly selected, nor is it likely to be representative in all particulars of near-death experiencers in general.[8] Obviously, respondents who are willing to complete questionnaires or submit to lengthy interviews are not necessarily typical of most NDErs. How much less so are the people one meets at lectures or those who come to visit at the Near-Death Hotel. Accordingly, I have not presented the usual tests of statistical significance simply because the assumption of random sampling is so plainly violated. Second, it was not always possible to arrange to have the appropriate control or comparison groups to show that certain effects were limited to or found more often among NDErs. Where such groups are missing I will qualify my findings. Finally, some of my interviews were conducted more informally than those done for *Life at Death*. It is hard to interview a friend as strictly as one might a stranger, especially at the Near-Death Hotel.

These are not small points; they are major shortcomings. They can only be rectified by future research directed to the same issues under investigation here and that include the appropriate controls. As a result of these methodological deficiencies, some of the conclusions I will draw will have to be taken tentatively from a scientific point of view. Perhaps they should be regarded as hypotheses to be more rigorously tested in subsequent research. I would encourage and welcome such investigations.

Now that these provisos have been acknowledged, however, I will permit myself a couple of statements in justification of the research reported in this book. First, I am willing to stake my reputation that the broad outlines of my findings and conclusions will be upheld by future and better research. In my judgment—and the reader will have the evidence on which my judgment is based—there are just too many tiles that fit altogether too neatly for the entire mosaic I've built to be in error. In this respect, I feel the same confidence about these data holding up as did Raymond Moody when he delineated the basic NDE pattern in *Life After Life*. Second, in writing *Omega*, unlike *Life at Death*, I am not writing a book dealing mainly with empirical matters to be decided by reference to the canons of scientific inquiry. There are data, to be sure, in this book, but I will be mainly concerned with their *meaning*. *Omega* is not meant to be merely another scientific investigation of NDEs. The reader must be prepared to consider issues that science alone is not equipped to resolve.

Plan of the Book

Just what facets of the lives of near-death experiencers will we be examining?

After summarizing the most recent findings from the field of near-death studies to lay a foundation, we will begin our inquiry by addressing the issue of what the near-death experience is at its core. In Chapter 3 I will provide a full statement of the thesis that will guide the remainder of our inquiry. In Chapter 4 I will present my findings on the personal transformations in the lives of NDErs, while the next chapter will profile their shift in values. Chapter 6 will concern itself with the changes in religious and spiritual beliefs and practices that tend to occur following an NDE as well as with the spiritual knowledge that tends to be disclosed to persons who have deep NDEs. Chapter 7 is devoted to a discussion of the ways in which NDEs tend to promote psychic development. In Chapter 8 I treat a very controversial issue: the prophetic visions that some NDErs claim to have received during deep NDEs. Throughout these chapters I will be quoting extensively from my respondents for illustrative purposes and supplementing these qualitative materials with a few tables of statistical information provided in Appendix III. Chapters 9 and 10 are both concerned with the interpretation of the findings that will have been arrayed in the preceding chapters. In Chapter 9 I will present a biological explanation of NDEs that honors rather than explains away the transcendental features of the experience. In the concluding chapter of the book I will give my own interpretation of the meaning of NDEs and their aftereffects and discuss their significance for our time and for the evolution of planetary consciousness.

A New View of Life

I began this chapter by outlining the new view of death that has come chiefly from the recent study of near-death experiences. From this research we can learn not only to drop much of our fear of death but also to see it in a new light altogether. From the standpoint of near-death experiences, the entrance into death seems to be the encounter with the Beloved and is a moment of such supreme rapture that it can never adequately be expressed. Even Dante, it will be recalled, despaired of rendering the beauties of paradise into the comparative coarseness of human language. As near-death research has already shown—and as we will once more see in this book—no one who has experienced, even vicariously, what NDErs have can ever again regard death with anything other than a sense of infinite gratitude for its existence.

This, I submit, is what follows from a careful perusal of near-death experiences, but what follows from a study of their *aftereffects* is different—and just as profound. It is nothing less than a new view of life. What we will be able to glimpse by the time we are through with our inquiry is at least something of the new life to come. I am not referring here to what people are wont to call "the afterlife." This is not a book about "the afterlife" or about what NDEs may imply about a life after death. It is about our life here on earth, not in the hereafter, and about how we may see human destiny prefigured in the lives of those who have survived death and have matured enough so we can discern what death planted in them.

CHAPTER 2

· · · · · · ·

NDEs: What We Now Know

∴

Since the publication of *Life at Death* in 1980, the field of near-death studies has experienced rapid growth and development.[1] In these few years, we have solidified some of the earlier anecdotal findings and added many new ones. Both because some readers may not be familiar with this body of literature and because these previous research findings provide the foundation for the work reported in this volume, it seems mandatory that I give here a brief overview of the present state of our knowledge concerning NDEs in general. With this information we will be better prepared to appreciate the particular significance of the deeper NDEs we will encounter in this book as well as the aftereffects described later.

Before doing so, however, a word of reassurance for the nonprofessional reader may be helpful. I do not intend to present here an academic "review of the literature" of the sort found in scholarly journals in which there is an attempt made to cite every pertinent study and to examine each contribution critically. For readers interested in that kind of detailed evaluation of the literature in the field, I recommend the articles by Vicchio[2] and Greyson[3] in particular as well as the various issues of *Anabiosis—The Journal for Near-Death Studies*.[4] Here I will cover in a nontechnical way the major findings of the field, confining myself to the minimum necessary number of references.

To arrange this information in a tidy fashion, it will be convenient to list a series of questions recently addressed by near-death researchers and then to refer to the findings of the studies that have attempted to answer them. Since the bulk of this book will examine

NDE aftereffects at great length, I will limit myself here to the research that treats the NDE per se and the factors that might be supposed to affect its incidence or content.

How Common Is the NDE?

Thousands of persons who claim to have had NDEs have been interviewed by near-death researchers. But even this impressive figure begs an even more fundamental question: How many of those persons who come close to death report NDEs? As I observed in *Life at Death,* none of the previous research addressed this issue. At present, however, we already have enough data on which to base a good estimate.

In *Life at Death* I found that of my *entire* sample of 102 cases, 48 percent related NDEs similar to those that had already been described by Moody and Kübler-Ross. In that same work, however, I cautioned[5] that that figure was probably somewhat inflated and suggested that a more representative estimate might be closer to 40 percent. Not long afterward, Michael Sabom, a cardiologist, published his own study of NDEs, *Recollections of Death,* based on 116 cases, mostly of cardiac arrest victims. His best estimate of the percentage of NDEs—42 percent—obviously is very close to mine. There have, of course, been numerous other studies of NDEs besides Sabom's and my own, but all of those so far published,[6] while finding abundant evidence of NDEs, are comprised of samples of fewer than one hundred cases and thus do not provide a more reliable basis for estimating the incidence of NDEs in the population at large. In addition, all of these studies suffer from a problem common to most of the research in this field: nonrepresentative sampling.

Most of the uncertainty about the incidence—at least in the United States—of NDEs has recently been dissipated by a landmark study carried out by the prestigious Gallup Poll and reported in the book *Adventures in Immortality* by George Gallup, Jr. Gallup's work, of course, is based on rigorous survey research methods *and* a large sample of cases. Thus it suffers from neither of the usual sampling problems still characteristic of near-death research.

On the basis of his findings, it appears that approximately 35 percent of those persons who have come close to death undergo an

NDE. In fact, there are technical reasons to suspect that this figure may be an underestimate, but even so, in view of the methodological deficiencies of our research, it accords remarkably well with the provisional estimates given by Sabom and me in our separate studies.

Taking into account all the relevant research so far published then, and allowing for the possibility that Gallup's own figure may reflect a minimum value for the population, I would propose that somewhere between 35 and 40 percent of those who come close to death could report NDEs.

How many people would that represent?

Again based on Gallup's figures, the answer is: eight million!

Gallup's sample is restricted to adult Americans, and that number, at the time of his survey, was approximately 160 million. Of those Americans, Gallup has determined that one in twenty—or 5 percent of our adult population—has had at least one NDE. If you work out the arithmetic, you will see where the estimate of eight million adult NDErs comes from.

Of course, even Gallup's survey methods are subject to sampling error. His estimate of NDErs could be off by a half million or so. But even if it were in error by *several* million—and this is a virtual impossibility—we would still be dealing with a very significant and pervasive phenomenon. Obviously, the thousands of NDErs who have been interviewed are speaking for millions of their silent brethren.

And not only do we now have good evidence that the NDE phenomenon has occurred to millions (and has indirectly touched the lives of millions of others), but because of the highly developed state of our resuscitation technology, we can safely assume that millions more will have this experience themselves in the years to come. This will be true, naturally, not only in the United States but also wherever the means exist to resuscitate people in significant numbers from the brink of death.

In evaluating all this statistical information on the incidence of NDEs, it is important to remember the distinction between a *report* of an NDE and an *actual experience* of one. Throughout this discussion I have been careful to refer to reports of NDEs because that is all we have to go on. But it is quite conceivable that more people will have had NDEs than those who relate them to an investigator. An appropriate analogy here is that we know almost everyone dreams at night, but certainly not everyone remembers dreams in the morning. In the case of NDEs, however, faulty memory is not the only reason for lower reporting rates. There is also good reason to believe[7] that some NDErs deliberately withhold their NDEs from public or professional scrutiny. Thus it could well be that the actual incidence of NDEs is considerably higher than 35 to 40 percent, but we cannot be certain of this, however reasonable our grounds of suspicion might be.

All we can say with conviction is that NDEs are much more common than even we near-death researchers used to believe. Score one for every score of persons. . . .

What Occurs in the Typical NDE?

As Moody[8] was the first to say, no two NDEs are identical, but most seem to adhere to a common pattern. NDEs differ principally in terms of how much of that pattern is disclosed to an experiencer. In *Life at Death* I presented a composite description of this pattern as it would be reported by a hypothetical NDEr who had a "complete" experience:

The experience begins with a feeling of easeful peace and a sense of well-being, which soon culminates in a sense of overwhelming joy and happiness. This ecstatic tone, although fluctuating in intensity from case to case, tends to persist as a constant emotional ground as other features of the experience begin to unfold. At this point, the person is aware that he feels no pain nor does he have any other bodily sensations. Everything is quiet. These cues may suggest to him that he is either in the process of dying or has already "died."

He may then be aware of a transitory buzzing or windlike sound, but, in any event, he finds himself looking down on his physical body, as though viewing it from some external vantage point. At this time, he finds that he can see and hear perfectly; indeed, his vision and hearing tend to be more acute than usual. He is aware of the actions and conversations taking place in the physical environment, in relation to which he finds himself in the role of a passive, detached spectator. All this seems very real—even quite natural—to him; it does not seem at all like a dream or an hallucination. His mental state is one of clarity and alertness.

At some point, he may find himself in a state of *dual awareness*. While he continues to be able to perceive the physical scene around him, he may also become aware of "another reality" and feel himself being drawn into it. He drifts or is ushered into a dark void or tunnel and feels as though he is floating through it. Although he may feel lonely for a time, the experience here is predominately peaceful and serene. All is extremely quiet and the individual is aware only of his mind and of the feeling of floating.

All at once, he becomes sensitive to, but does not see, a presence. The presence, who may be heard to speak or who may instead "merely" induce thoughts into the individual's mind, stimulates him to review his life and asks him to decide whether he wants to live or die. This stock-taking may be facilitated by a rapid and vivid visual playback of episodes from the person's life. At this stage, he has no awareness of time or space, and the concepts themselves are meaningless. Neither is he any longer identified with his body. Only the mind is present and it is weighing—logically and rationally—the alternatives that confront him at this threshold separating life from death: to go further into this experience or to return to earthly life. Usually the individual decides to return on the basis, not of his own preference, but on the perceived needs of his loved ones, whom his death would necessarily leave behind. Once the decision is made, the experience tends to be abruptly terminated.

Sometimes, however, the decisional crisis occurs later or is altogether absent, and the individual undergoes further experiences. He may, for example, continue to float through the dark void toward a magnetic and brilliant golden light, from which emanates feelings of love, warmth and total acceptance. Or he may enter into a "world of light" and preternatural beauty, to be (temporarily) reunited with deceased loved ones before being told, in effect, that it is not yet his time and that he has to return to life.

In any event whether the individual chooses or is commanded to return to his earthly body and worldly commitments, he does return. Typically, however, he has no recollection *how* he has effected his "re-entry," for at this point he tends to lose all awareness. Very occasionally, however, the individual may remember "returning to his body" with a jolt or an agonizing wrenching sensation. He may even suspect that he reenters "through the head."

Afterward, when he is able to recount his experience, he finds that there are simply no words adequate to convey the feelings and quality of awareness he remembers. He may also be or become reticent to discuss it with others, either because he feels no one will really be able to understand it or because he fears he will be disbelieved or ridiculed.[9]

In retrospect, I might be tempted to alter a line or two of this account or add a qualification here or there, but on the whole in the light of subsequent research, this narration holds up very well. There is nothing in it that hasn't been independently confirmed by more recent investigations into the NDE phenomenon. For that matter, it contains nothing that wasn't already stated or implied on Moody's earlier version of the prototypic NDE.[10] One of the firmest conclusions to be drawn from the body of near-death research is that the NDE itself is an authentic and much replicated phenomenon—there is simply no doubt that it occurs. (This is not to imply, of course, that there is any unanimity among investigators concerning its *interpretation;* that is another story, but it is not germane here.)

Perhaps for those not familiar with any of the literature on NDEs, or to refresh the memory of those who are, it might be useful to cite an illustrative case if only to provide a specific example of how the various elements in the NDE pattern tend to cohere in an actual experience. For this purpose I'll select that of one of our visitors at the Near-Death Hotel who one evening during his stay was induced to recount his experience for the benefit of a few friends Norma and I had over for dinner. As long as he was agreeable, I asked him (my researcher's mind dominating) if he would mind if I tape-recorded his account. He cheerfully gave his consent.

Before presenting some excerpts from his NDE, you should know that this man, who was fifty-one years old at the time of his visit and had had his experience five years earlier, had been an agnostic. At that time of his NDE he had spent many years as an anthropologist and professor and had achieved some prominence in his field.

His NDE resulted from an automobile accident—ironically enough, it took place in Death Valley!—in which he was thrown from his car a distance, he was later told, of approximately fifty feet. Providentially, an ambulance happened to be traveling in the opposite direction along the same road not long after the accident took place. Our visitor, whose name is Patrick Gallagher, was soon airlifted to a hospital near Los Angeles, where he arrived comatose and close to death. His skull had been fractured on the left side, and as a consequence the right side of his body was paralyzed. Both because of his paralysis and the broken ribs he had sustained, he had great difficulty breathing. He had suffered other internal injuries as well and had received numerous lacerations. As a consequence of all the damage inflicted on his body by this accident, he remained unconscious for weeks while hospitalized. Sometime during that period—he is not sure exactly when—he had his NDE.

. . . [It] seemed to be in a sequential nature, more or less, I say more or less because time itself seems to have disappeared during this period. But the first thing that I noticed was that I was dead and . . . I sort of had the perspective that I was dead in the same way that you see in television movies where the sheriff will say, "Yup, he's gone." [Could you see your body?] Oh, yes, quite clearly. I was floating in the air above the body . . . and viewing it down sort of a diagonal angle. This didn't seem to cause any consternation to me at all. I really was completely dead but that didn't cause emotional difficulties [for me].

Then, after that, I realized that I was able to float quite easily, even though I had no intention of doing that. . . . Then I very quickly discovered also that not only was I floating and hence free from gravity but free also from any of the other constrictions that inhibit flight. . . . I could also fly at a terrific rate of speed with a kind of freedom that one normally doesn't experience in normal flight, in airplanes, but perhaps experiences a little more in hang-gliding and things like that. . . . But I noticed that I could fly at a phenomenal rate of speed and it seemed to produce a feeling of great joy and sense of actually flying in this total fashion.

. . . Then I noticed that there was a dark area ahead of me and as I approached it, I thought that it was some sort of a tunnel and immediately, without further thought, I entered into it and then flew with an even greater sensation of the joy of flight. . . .

[After] what now I would imagine to be a relatively short period of time—although again time was dispensed with—I noticed a sort of circular light at a great distance which I assumed to be the end of the tunnel as I was roaring through it . . . and the light—the nearest thing I can barely approximate its description to is the setting of the sun at a time under ideal circumstances when one can look at this object without any of the usual problems that staring at the sun causes. . . .

The fact is, this seemed like an incredibly illuminating sort of a place, in every sense of that word, so that not only was it an awesome brightness . . . with a tremendous beauty, this kind of yellowish-orange color, but it also seemed a marvelous place to be. And so, this even increased the sense of joy I had about this flight. And then I went through the tunnel and seemed to be in a different state. I was in different surroundings where everything seemed to be similarly illuminated by that same light and, uh, I saw other things in it, too . . . [a] number of people. . . . I saw my father there, who had been dead for some twenty-five years. . . .

I also felt and saw of course that everyone was in a state of absolute compassion to everything else. . . . It seemed, too, that love was the major axiom that everyone automatically followed. This produced a phenomenal feeling of emotion to me, again, in the free sense that the flight did earlier, because it made me feel that . . . there was nothing *but* love . . . it just seemed like the real thing, just to feel this sense of total love in every direction.

[Later] I did feel, because of my children and the woman I was married to then, the urge to return . . . but I don't recall the trip back. . . .

[Did it seem like a dream?] No, it seemed nothing like a dream. . . . It really is a strange sensation to be in, but it does give you a feeling that you are in a kind of eternity.

There is much of Patrick's nearly two-hour conversation that I have omitted, of course (though I did retain his sequence of statements in editing his remarks), but I think I have reproduced enough of this account for you to see how many of the prototypical features of the NDE it includes. It is representative of full NDEs—though full NDEs are not themselves typical of NDEs in general. Most accounts include fewer features than does Patrick's, but in this book it is precisely these richer NDEs in which we will be especially interested. Indeed, later in this book we will return to Patrick's narrative to consider additional elements that are usually *only* found in deeper NDEs and are just hinted at in composite descriptions of the kind that began this section. For now, however, we will just let it serve its designated illustrative function.

Perhaps the only specific feature of the NDE that deserves special comment here is the out-of-body experience (usually abbreviated OBE) in which a person will report, as Patrick did, a sense of being separate from and above the physical body, which itself is viewed from an external vantage point as though one is a spectator to it. All near-death researchers have found such cases in profusion, but attention has recently been drawn once again to this phenomenon by the work of Michael Sabom, which is described in full in *Recollections of Death*.[11] Sabom has made a diligent search for detailed OBE accounts from NDErs on the grounds that such reports provide one of the few avenues through which to secure data about NDEs that can be independently corroborated. That is, in general NDEs constitute self-reports of internal perceptions and feelings: If an NDEr describes seeing a brilliant golden light, for example, all a researcher can do is to note that statement; there is obviously no way the researcher can directly confirm it. If, on the other hand, a patient—whose eyes, let's say, are taped shut—suffers cardiac arrest during surgery and has an OBE during which he later claims to have seen two physicians, one of them black, whom he had never met before, hurriedly enter the operating room to assist in the defibrillation procedure whose details he then describes in correct sequence, this is obviously an account that does not depend for its veracity only on the patient's say-so. The alleged facts can be checked directly and independently to determine their correspondence with reality.

This is precisely what Sabom has done in a half dozen instances where his respondents had given him highly specific and sequential accounts of their OBEs while near death. By interviewing members of the original medical team involved in these cases, talking to family members who had pertinent information, and checking the medical records directly, Sabom was able to produce impressive if not conclusive evidence of apparently accurate perceptions during OBEs. In short, according to Sabom, patients were describing events they could not have seen given the position of their body and could not have known given their physical condition.

In my own work also I have encountered similar provocative cases, and though I was not able to secure the kind of documentation that Sabom furnishes for his examples, I can at least offer an illustrative instance of the kind of OBE that suggests the distinct possibility that NDErs can have extraordinarily precise visual perceptions that appear to defy conventional explanations. Consider, for example, this account from a forty-eight-year-old woman who described in an interview with me her OBE following postsurgical complications in 1974.

Her anesthesiologist, she told me, was a physician who often worked with children. Because he found that children often expressed great fears about not being able to distinguish one green-garmented physician from another, he took to wearing a yellow surgical hat with magenta butterflies on it so his young patients could know it was he. The relevance of all this will be apparent in this woman's rendering of her experience. She had gone into shock and heard her physician say "This woman's dying" when

Bang, I left! The next thing I was aware of was floating on the ceiling. And seeing down there, with his hat on his head, I knew who he was because of the hat on his head . . . it was so vivid. I'm very nearsighted, too, by the way, which was another one of the startling things that happened when I left my body. I see at fifteen feet what most people see at four hundred. . . . They were hooking me up to a machine that was behind my head. And my very first thought was, "Jesus, I can see! I can't believe it, I can see!" I could read the numbers on the machine behind my head and I was just so thrilled. And I thought, "They gave me back my glasses." . . . I was kind of bewildered because I wasn't sure where I was looking at first. In those days, I had hair almost to my waist and that was the first thing I recognized—my hair hanging over the side of the bed. And these people were working on me. And somebody was shaving my belly and I couldn't see my head right away because of all these heads over me. . . . They were hooking me up. They put a tube in my arm to my heart and were flooding my system with antibiotics, I found out later, and they had a tube in my nose to keep my stomach clear. I don't remember now whatever else they were doing. They weren't breathing for me until later. [You could see all of this clearly, then, judging from how well you could see the numbers?] Yes, at that time I could still remember them. . . .

Things were enormously clear and bright. . . . From where I was looking, I could look down on this enormous fluorescent light . . . and it was so dirty on top of the light. [Could you see the top of the light fixture, then?] I was floating *above* the light fixture. [Could you see the top of the light fixture?] *Yes* [sounding a little impatient with my question], and it was filthy. And I remember thinking, "Got to tell the nurses about that." . . . I don't know how long I was there [but] I could see what was going on in the cubicle next to mine. We were in a series of cubicles with curtains in between and I could see the woman in the cubicle next to me and she was asleep, but I didn't go anywhere else. I just stayed right above my body.

This woman later told me that after she recovered she asked permission to return to the operating room to determine whether the numbers she had seen on the machine were correct. She claims that this was indeed so and that she told her anesthesiologist at the time, but since he is no longer practicing in Connecticut and she has lost track of him, it was not possible for me independently to corroborate her testimony. Nevertheless, her case well serves to indicate how *in principle* these accounts do lend themselves to external verification.

Another potentially verifiable feature of OBEs is suggested by the foregoing experience. My respondent, you will recall, implied that it would have been possible for her to "travel" to other locations in the hospital. Just this kind of movement is sometimes reported by NDErs, and these claims, too, can be independently investigated. I will give just one example here from the account of Barbara Harris, a thirty-nine-year-old woman who underwent a spinal fusion operation in 1975.

[During her OBE] I went into the laundry room—is the only way I can explain it because I remember they had windows and I could see the pillows that I had urinated on in the dryer. I don't know how I knew—the only thing I remember is *seeing.* I saw those dryers. . . . It really bothered me that they had put the pillows in the dryer. [In other words, they hadn't put them first in the washer?] No. . . . When they came in to see me after and I was back in bed . . . I told them that they shouldn't have put the pillows in the *dryer,* that they should have washed them first because I had urinated on them. And I didn't care about them for myself, but what about the next patient? And they just hushed me up! They looked at me, really, like, "how did she know?" And covered it up and brought me a shot of Valium and a shot of Demerol. And then I was gone again.

Before concluding this section on the form and content of the typical NDE, perhaps I should add a word or two about so-called negative NDEs. Occasionally one hears reports of NDEs that not only fail to conform to the general pattern given at the beginning of this section but also are alleged to be very unpleasant, even hellish. It is true that a few such experiences have been described in the literature, but they are very far from being typical. Most authorities seem agreed that they may represent perhaps 1 percent of all reported cases, perhaps less. In my own experience, having talked to or heard the accounts of many hundreds of NDErs, I have never personally encountered a full-blown, predominantly negative NDE, though I have certainly found some NDEs to have had moments of uncertainty, confusion, or transitory fear. At this point we simply don't have enough information about negative NDEs to make any definite statement about them other than that they turn up exceedingly rarely.[12]

Does the Way One Nearly Dies Affect the NDE?

In *Life at Death* I compared the NDEs of three categories of people who differed chiefly in the circumstances that had brought them close to death: illness victims, accident victims, and suicide attempters. On the basis of my own findings, I then proposed what I called the invariance hypothesis to indicate how situations such as how one nearly dies affect the NDE. What the invariance hypothesis states is that there is *no* relationship: However one nearly dies, the NDE, if it occurs, is much the same.

Research published since *Life at Death* has tended to lend strong support to the invariance hypothesis. We now have cases on file of almost every mode of near-death circumstance that you can imagine: combat situations, attempted rape and murder, electrocution, near-drownings, hangings, etc., as well as a great range of strictly medical conditions—and none of these seems to influence the form and content of the NDE itself. Rather it appears that whatever the condition that brings a person close to death may be, once the NDE begins to unfold it is essentially invariant and has the form I have earlier indicated.

Subsequent research on suicide-related NDEs by Stephen Franklin and myself and by Bruce Greyson [13] has also confirmed my earlier tentative findings that NDEs following suicide attempts, however induced, conform to the classic prototype.

In summary, so far at least, situations covering a wide range of near-death conditions appear to have a negligible effect on the experience.

Are Some People More Likely Than Others to Report NDEs?

If situational variables do not significantly influence NDE, what about personal characteristics of individuals who have had NDEs? Are certain people especially likely to have NDEs depending on their social background, personality, prior beliefs, or even prior knowledge concerning NDEs?

Demographic characteristics such as age, sex, race, social class, educational level, occupation, and the like seem to have no particular relationship to NDE incidence. Here Gallup's findings on adult Americans are the most reliable because of the size and representativeness of his sample. His data show little or no relationship between NDEs and a person's age, sex, race, educational level, income, occupation, religious affiliation, size of city or town, or region of residence. [14] Sabom reports the same lack of relationship for such variables as age, area of residence, size of home community, educational level, religious background, or frequency of church attendance.[15] Similarly, in *Life at Death*, I found no relationship for such demographic variables as social class, race, marital status, or religious affiliation.[16] Altogether there is no support in the literature for the view that such demographic factors significantly influence the incidence or content of NDEs.

We know less about the relationship between personality or individual characteristics and NDEs for reasons that will become obvious. Unlike most demographic attributes that are relatively stable, our individual characteristics change considerably over time. And one of the findings of near-death research that now seems most secure—as the data in this book will substantiate—is that NDEs can change, often drastically, an individual's personality. Since we discover our NDErs only *after* the fact, it is often impossible to state with certainty just how, if at all, they were different from others at the time of their NDEs.

Such considerations make this kind of research difficult though not impossible, but we can at least say that the meager information we have on this matter does not give any strong indication that there is any one type of person especially likely to report an NDE. Consistent with this comment are some recent findings from the research by Gabbard and his colleagues.[17] In their major study of 339 OBErs, they failed to discover any distinctive personality profile for those subjects that differentiated them from other individuals. It does not seem unreasonable, then, to postulate that what appears to be true for OBErs might hold for NDErs as well.

When we come to the area of personal beliefs, however, we might expect to find some definite correlations with NDEs. Persons who have a strong religious orientation (quite apart from church attendance) or a deep conviction in an afterlife might well be thought to be more likely than, say, agnostics or atheists to undergo NDEs.

Despite the reasonableness of this supposition, the findings of several different research studies demonstrate that it is simply not so. There is, in fact, no difference in either the type or incidence of NDEs as a function of one's religious orientation—or lack of it. To be sure, an agnostic or an atheist might—and actually appear to— have a more difficult time coming to terms with the experience and may be less likely to interpret it in conventional terms than a believer, but the form and content of the NDE will not be distinctive. An NDE is an NDE to whatever sort of person it comes.

Finally, we may wonder whether having read or heard about NDEs before one's own near-death incident might make one more likely to relate it. Again this hypothesis seems quite reasonable, but once more the available data show it to be wrong.

Both Sabom and I in our separate studies specifically examined our data for such a relationship and we each found that, contrary to our fears, persons who had prior knowledge of NDEs were actually less likely to report one. In a major, methodologically sophisticated forthcoming study of NDEs conducted by Audette and Gulley, there was simply no relationship whatever between these two variables.[18] Thus, prior knowledge of NDEs definitely does not seem to induce them or cause them more often to be related to researchers.

In short, there is no persuasive evidence thus far to suggest that personal or social factors have any decided effect on NDEs.

How Universal Is the NDE?

Since most of the research published on NDEs has been carried out in the United States, it is natural to wonder whether NDEs take the same form in other countries, particularly in cultures very different from our own. What do we know, then, concerning the universality of this phenomenon or—to put it another way—the extent to which it is culture-bound?

Unfortunately, not nearly enough. We have an international NDE file at IANDS, but its contents are very slender. On this front most of our work remains to be done, but I will summarize here what we do know.

We already have enough information to assert that in England and in continental Europe, NDEs take the same form as in the United States.[19] This, of course, is scarcely surprising, since we share a Judeo-Christian heritage. At IANDS we have a handful of cases from South America, India, and Japan and some from the anthropological literature referring to apparent NDEs in preliterate societies. In general, these few cases show obvious parallels to the classic pattern, but there is at least a suggestion that they may in some ways deviate from that pattern, especially in the deeper stages of the NDE, where more archetypal imagery comes into play. Furthermore, I have heard informal and in some cases secondhand references to preliminary findings of NDE research projects in India and the Far East that again suggest overall conformity to the basic model with the possibility of some distinctive culturally determined features. At this point the prudent conclusion would have to be that, excepting NDEs in Western cultures, our data are simply too fragmentary to permit any firm judgment concerning the universality of the NDE model given at the beginning of this chapter.

There are enough relevant data, however, for me to hazard a guess about the limits of that model. If we draw on the well-known cross-cultural research of Osis and Haraldsson[20] on deathbed visions, which are certainly related to and partially overlap NDEs, we have a solid basis for extrapolating to NDEs proper. In their work, Osis and Haraldsson compared visions of dying persons in India and the United States. From their nearly nine hundred cases, Osis and Haraldsson concluded that on the whole there were substantial similarities in deathbed visions between Indians and Americans. Yet there were clearly some culturally determined effects, such as the particular religious personages who were perceived when their subjects were close to death. It was as though the form of the visions was the same but the content varied between cultures.

My suspicion is that something similar may well be found for NDEs. The feelings, the OBE, the passage through an area of darkness toward a brilliant light and the entry into a paradisiacal realm are likely, in my judgment, to be among the universal constants of the NDE. The beings who appear to the NDEr as well as the particular environments perceived can be expected to be more variable—but beings and environments of some kind should be reported.

This, as I say, is guesswork. As matters now stand, the hypothesis of NDE universality remains untested—but tempting.

Conclusion

The survey of basic NDE findings that we have conducted in this chapter upholds three conclusions very amply: (1) the NDE is a pervasive phenomenon in Western cultures; (2) it tends to adhere to a basic pattern characterized by extremely positive feelings and transcendental imagery; and (3) it is a very robust experience—i.e., it plays no favorites and occurs under a wide variety of conditions.

From all the work in near-death studies, we now can say with assurance that the NDE has been established as a certifiable phenomenon that occurs in many people who come close to or experience clinical death. This we know beyond doubt.

But knowing the basic parameters of the NDE only allows us to commence our inquiry into its meaning; it scarcely answers it. Knowing all we do, we still need to ask: Why is this so significant a phenomenon that we should examine it so penetratingly?

For the beginnings of an answer to this query, we need to probe to the core of the deepest NDEs. And there we shall see the source of the secret that all NDErs share and that they try, often in vain, to make known to others.

CHAPTER 3

· · · · · · ·

Core NDEs and Spiritual Awakening

÷

When we come to examine the core of full NDEs we find an absolute and undeniable spiritual radiance. This spiritual core of the NDE is so awesome and overwhelming that the person who experiences it is at once and forever thrust into an entirely new mode of being. As we will see, it may take years before the effects of this transformation manifest themselves fully, but they plainly have their origin in the core NDE itself. After that experience, the person can never again return to the former way of being—though some would like to. No longer can a person take refuge in the comfort of the conventional views and values of society. What he has experienced in and retained from his NDE has for him a higher and timeless validity. It comes to take precedence over whatever he had been taught or had previously believed. When one experiences a core NDE, beliefs as such become irrelevant because beliefs are always mere ideas that substitute for direct knowledge. When you can feel your heart beating, you don't have to believe it is—you know.

Core NDErs are people who know, but they do not merely have a certain knowledge of matters we will be discussing shortly. In some sense, they have become what they know; their knowledge lives and grows within them. It is as if the core of the NDE becomes their core. The NDE is, then, not merely an experience that becomes a cherished memory that people may later take comfort in. It is not even just an experience that "changes one's life." It *is* one's life. And it becomes the source of one's true being in the world.

Unless this is understood about NDErs in general and core NDErs—that is, those that have experienced this spiritual radiance most deeply—in particular, what is most essential about them will not be grasped. And what they are capable of teaching the rest of us will then be lost.

The NDE as a Catalyst for Spiritual Awakening: A Hypothesis

The spiritual dimensions of NDEs are, then, fundamental to any thorough understanding of their ultimate significance. In this book, of course, to achieve at least something of that understanding is our chief aim. In an effort to reach that objective, I believe it will prove helpful to frame here a hypothesis that will serve to direct our inquiry from this point on. We can call it, I suppose, "the spiritual catalyst" hypothesis for NDEs. In its simplest terms, it says the following:

The NDE is essentially a spiritual experience that serves as a catalyst for spiritual awakening and development. Moreover, the spiritual development that unfolds following an NDE tends to take a particular form. Finally, as a by-product of this spiritual development, NDErs tend to manifest a variety of psychic abilities afterward that are an inherent part of their transformation.

The next five chapters will be devoted to presenting some of the empirical data that tend to support, or are at least consistent with, this hypothesis. Thus, by the time we are finished with our examination of this material, we should have abundant evidence to arrive at an informed judgment concerning the guiding thesis of this book—and the implications that derive from it.

Spiritual Dimensions of the Core NDE

My object for the remainder of this chapter, however, is to be more specific concerning just what is experienced during a core NDE. Obviously, to have any meaningful basis for assessing the significance of NDEs and their effects, we must first grasp firmly the essence of the core NDE. This means, of course, that we need to ask such questions as: (1) What are the features of the core NDE that apparently make it an overwhelming, if numinous, spiritual experience? (2) What is the kind and the form of the knowledge conveyed to the core NDEr? and (3) What is the basis for the transformative effects said to be inherent in core NDEs?

Before turning to the materials that will answer these questions, a few words of caution and advice are in order.

First, you must be aware—and some of the respondents I will be quoting make this point explicitly—that there is absolutely no way in which ordinary human language can communicate the essence of these deep NDEs. No verbal or written account can possibly do more than hint at the experience; never can one describe it adequately. So in reading the narratives that will make up the bulk of this chapter, I recommend that you do not merely read them as one usually reads textual material; instead allow yourself to feel the words as much as possible and try to imagine that you are undergoing the experience. I have found that when listeners allow themselves empathetically to identify with accounts of NDEs they seem to appreciate them at a deeper level of understanding. That kind of understanding, at any rate, will be useful to cultivate for a more profound insight into the meaning of the experiences we will be considering throughout this book.

Second, some of the following accounts are those of plain, spontaneous speech; others are more literary renderings of core experiences. Do not let yourself be distracted by these stylistic variations—they are irrelevant. It certainly isn't the case that the more articulate narratives are as such more valuable for our purposes. Our task here is simply to allow the words, whether humble or polished, to lead us to something that lies beyond the power of words to convey.

Third, some of the material about to be presented may not be entirely new to readers already familiar with some of the basic literature in near-death studies. Yet the context of these experiences is new, and this context should be borne in mind in perusing these cases. I am not merely presenting more examples of NDEs, but fresh material illustrative of core NDEs. By the end of this chapter, the differences here should be evident and its implications clear.

Finally, I have selected a fair number of cases—fourteen in all—to exemplify core NDEs, and some of the extracts I've chosen are quite lengthy. Actually, because of a wealth of new data here, I could easily have quoted more cases and more extensively, but only a specialist would have the interest to read more than I've included in this chapter. My advice to the general reader, to avoid a sense of repetition, is to read each case slowly, in the way I suggested earlier, and then linger over it a moment before turning to the next account. There is no reason to rush through this material—you're not in a hurry, are you? There is every reason to take your time with it. If you do, I can virtually guarantee that the case histories you will encounter will have a cumulative emotional impact on you that will in no way be boring.

Core NDEs: Some Illustrative Cases

Let's begin with a brief account from a forty-one-year-old man from Connecticut I know well. Joe Geraci, too, has been a visitor at the Near-Death Hotel, but I've been with him many times in various settings, often in conjunction with programs on near-death experiences or at some of my classes at the university where I have invited Joe to share his NDE with my students. Although I did interview Joe at the university where we arranged to meet for the first time in March 1981, I have chosen to reproduce some of his remarks from a documentary television program on NDEs Joe and I participated in not long afterward.[1]

Joe had his NDE in the spring of 1977 after having returned home from a hospital following surgery. Suddenly one evening he began to hemorrhage profusely and was rushed back to the hospital where, he was told later, he had been clinically dead for two to three minutes. It was during this interval that Joe believes he had his NDE. As he relates it:

It was then that I experienced—experienced what we call a near-death experience. For me, there was nothing "near" about it—it was there.

It was a total immersion in light, brightness, warmth, peace, security. I did not have an out-of-body experience. I did not see my body or anyone about me. I just immediately went into this beautiful bright light. It's difficult to describe; as a matter of fact, it's impossible to describe. Verbally, it cannot be expressed. It's something which becomes you and you become it. I could say, "I was peace, I was love." I was the brightness, it was part of me. . . . You just know. You're all-knowing—and everything is a part of you—it's—it's just so beautiful. It was eternity. It's like I was always there and I will always be there, and that my existence on earth was just a brief instant.

As we will see by examining other core NDEs, many of the points Joe makes so succinctly will be eloquently enlarged upon by others, yet the essence of the experience itself is all here in a few words, just as a small portion of a holographic plate contains the image of the whole.

Consider next the account of a near-drowning incident that took place in 1956 when the man who sent it to me, who is now forty and the father of two small sons, was only fourteen. This man, whom I know only through the correspondence we've exchanged, was at that time on a family trip from Texas to Mississippi when the automobile in which he was riding was trapped and submerged in a flash flood. At one point, as he writes,

I knew I was either dead or going to die. But then something happened. It was so immense, so powerful that I gave up on my life to see what it was. I wanted to venture into this experience, which started as a drifting into what I could only describe as a long tunnel of light. But it wasn't just a light, it was a protective passage of energy with an intense brightness at the end which I wanted to look into, to touch. There were no sounds of any earthly thing. Only the sounds of serenity, of a strange music like I had never heard. A soothing symphony of indescribable beauty blended with the light I was approaching.

I gave up on life. I left it behind for this new wonderful thing. I did not want to go back to life. For what I knew was that what lay ahead was to be so wondrous and beautiful that nothing should stop me from reaching it.

As I reached the source of the light I could see in. I cannot begin to describe in human terms the feeling I had at what I saw. It was a giant infinite world of calm, and love, and energy and beauty. It was as though human life was unimportant compared to this. And yet it urged the importance of life at the same time it solicited death as a means to a better, different life. It was all being, all beauty, all meaning for existence. It was all the energy of the universe forever in one immensurable place.

This man's narration of his core experience is by no means unrepresentative of such accounts in my files. Though it is, to be sure, better written than many, it shares with the others the same use of seemingly extravagant language to describe the ineffable. In my judgment, the wording here and the resort to superlatives common to these descriptions is not at all extravagant—it is simply fitting. Still, it is important to remember, as I have already said and as the following testimony will again claim, that truly no words exist to relate the things seen and felt in core NDEs.

The next case is based on the NDE of a sixty-four-year-old woman from Seattle with whom I often corresponded over the past several years before spending five days with her and her family in September 1982, when I was in Seattle to give a workshop on NDEs. Although a very loving relationship had already existed between us through our previous correspondence, it proved to be even more so as a result of my visit, when we finally had a chance to express in person all the love we had felt for each other at a distance of three thousand miles. At any rate, by the time I left, I felt I was part of her family and she had become part of mine.

Before I met her, she had sent me a tape of her experience, but I prefer to quote briefly here from a pamphlet she wrote entitled "Fear Not," in which she describes her NDE. Her experience came about because of open-heart surgery performed in 1975. She writes, in part:

I was aware . . . of my past life. It was like it was being recorded. . . . There was the warmest, most wonderful love. Love all around me . . . I felt light-good-happy-joy-at ease. Forever—eternal love. Time meant nothing. Just being. Love. Pure love. Love. The Light was Yellow. It was in, around, and through everything. . . . It is God made visible. In, around, and through everything. One who has not experienced it cannot know its feeling. One who has experienced it can never forget it, yearns for its perfection, and longs for the embodiment of It.

Let us now look at some longer accounts to bring out more fully certain features we've already encountered as well as some new elements of core NDEs. We'll begin here with one of my good friends and a family favorite at the Near-Death Hotel—Tom Sawyer.

You may think I'm using a humorous pseudonym for Tom to protect his anonymity, but—so help me—his real given name is Tom Sawyer (and not Thomas, either—just plain Tom). How he came apparently to be named after one of Mark Twain's best known fictional characters is itself an amusing story. It turns out that Tom's mother, whom I've also met and who confirmed this story, had always intended that her firstborn son should be named Tom. Well, you can guess what was the last name of the man she later married! Mom contributed the first name and Dad the last—and Tom Sawyer, bless him, was the result.

Tom first came into my life shortly after *Life at Death* was published in 1980. At that time he wrote me offering to send a recently recorded tape concerning his NDE. When I wrote to assure him that of course I'd be most interested to listen to it, our friendship began. Since then, Tom has visited us several times for extended stays (once with his wife and two boys), and Norma and I have also visited the Sawyers at their home in upstate New York. Tom has also sent me several additional tapes that describe more of the aftereffects of his NDE. As a consequence of all this, I guess I could safely say that I know Tom just about as well as any NDEr of my acquaintance.

My interest in Tom, however, is based on more than the fact that he is an extremely lovable guy, nor is it simply because he had a deep NDE. That interest rests in part on the extraordinary—at this point I would have to say unique—aftereffects Tom has experienced in his life following his NDE. That part of Tom's story will, however, have to wait until the next chapter, where I will discuss his background more fully. Here we must content ourselves with his core NDE itself.

That experience came about in May 1978, when Tom was

thirty-three years old. He had spent the day working underneath his truck (I have a photograph of it in my files along with his medical records) when its supports gave way and it fell on him, crushing his chest. Tom was suffocating when he was rescued by a team of paramedics who were summoned by his quick-thinking son, Todd, then nine years old. In quoting from Tom here, I am relying on that original tape he made for me in which he rendered his experience not only carefully but evidently with barely controlled emotion. He begins here by referring to his experience while still in the "tunnel":

Then all this time, the speed is increasing. . . . Gradually, you realize . . you're going [at] at least the speed of light. It might possibly be the speed of light or possibly even faster than the speed of light. You do realize that you're going just so fast and you're covering vast, vast distances in just hundredths of a second. . . .

And then gradually you realize that *way,* way off in the distance—again, unmeasurable distance—it appears that it might be the end of the tunnel. And all you can see is a white light. . . . And again, remember that you are traveling at *extreme* speed. [But] this whole process only takes . . . [say] one minute and again emphasizing that you might have traveled to infinity, just an unlimited number of miles.

You then realize that you are coming to the end of this tunnel and that this light is not just a brilliance from whatever is at the end of the tunnel—it's an *extremely* brilliant light. It's pure white. It's just so brilliant. . . .

And then, before you is this—excuse me [he pauses here]—is this most magnificent, just gorgeous, beautiful, bright, white or blue-white light [another pause]. It is *so* bright, it is *brighter* than a light that would immediately blind you, but this *absolutely* does not hurt your eyes at all. . . . It is so bright, so brilliant, and so beautiful, but it doesn't hurt your eyes. And the next series of events take place—oh, within a millisecond, they take place—more or less all at once, but of course in describing them I'll have to take them one at a time.

The next sensation is this wonderful, wonderful feeling of this light. . . . It's almost like a person. It is *not* a person, but it is a being of some kind. It is a mass of energy. It doesn't have a character like you would describe another person, but it has a character in that it is more than just a thing. It is something to communicate to and acknowledge. And also in size, it just covers the entire vista before you. And it totally engulfs whatever the horizon might be. . . .

Then the light immediately communicates to you. . . . This communication is what you might call telepathic. It's absolutely instant, absolutely clear. It wouldn't even matter if a different language was being spoken . . . whatever you thought and attempted to speak, it would be instant and absolutely clear. There would never be a doubtful statement made.

The first thing you're told is, "Relax, everything is beautiful, everything is OK." . . . You're immediately put at absolute ease. It's the most comfortable feeling that you could ever imagine. You have a feeling of absolute, pure love. It's the warmest feeling. [But] make sure you don't confuse it with warm in temperature, because there's no temperature involved. Whatever your senses would feel absolute perfect—if it's temperature, it's a perfect temperature. If it's either an exciting emotion or a placid emotion, it's just perfect and you feel this and you sense this. And it's so *absolutely* vivid and clear.

Then the thing is, the light communicates to you and for the first time in your life . . . is a feeling of true, pure love. It can't be compared to the love of your wife, the love of your children, or some people consider a very intense sexual experience as love and they consider [it] possibly the most beautiful moment in their life— and it couldn't even begin to compare. All of these wonderful, wonderful feelings combined could not possibly compare to the *feeling,* the true love. If you can imagine what pure love would be, this would be the feeling that you'd get from this brilliant white light.

Tom then goes on to describe another key aspect of the core NDE that our previous excerpts only hinted at but that will become increasingly prominent in many of the accounts to follow.

The second most magnificent experience . . . is you realize that you are suddenly in communications with absolute, total knowledge. It's hard to describe. . . . You can think of a question . . . and *immediately* know the answer to it. As simple as that. And it can be any question whatsoever. It can be on any subject. It can be on a subject that you don't know anything about, that you are not in the proper position even to understand and the light will give you the instantaneous correct answer and make you understand it. . . .

Needless to say, I had many questions answered, many pieces of information given to me, some of which is very personal, some of which is religiously orientated . . . one of the religious-orientated questions was in regards to an afterlife and this was definitely answered through the experience itself. . . . There's absolutely no question in my mind that the light is the answer. Upon entering that light . . . the atmosphere, the energy, it's total pure energy, it's total knowledge, it's total love, pure love—everything about it is definitely the afterlife, if you will.

Tom concludes this account with a statement clearly implied by what he had already described; it is a recurrent motif in all these narratives:

As a result of that [experience], I have very little apprehension about dying my natural death . . . because if death is anything, anything at all like what I experienced, it's gotta be the most wonderful thing to look forward to, absolutely the most wonderful thing.

Tom's story leads naturally to a consideration of the core NDE of another good friend of mine, a forty-year-old woman I'll call Janis. I first met Janis in Detroit early in 1981 where we were both to appear on a television program. While we sat, before going on, in the greenroom at the station, she informally described her NDE to me. Afterward, she and a friend took me to the airport, and Janis and I exchanged hugs and promised to write. She did—long and extraordinarily beautiful letters—and as she traveled around the country, we often expressed a desire to meet again and talk for a longer time.

Finally, in October 1982, some of us from IANDS were driving back through Pennsylvania, where Janis was then living, following a conference in Virginia, and we stopped to visit one evening. After the social amenities were over and my traveling companions had retired, Janis and I stayed up until 3:00 A.M. as she gave me for the first time a full account of her NDE. The edited transcript of that interview runs ten single-spaced pages, and from that transcript I can quote just a few paragraphs here. As with Tom, we will return to Janis later in the book, but it will be instructive to compare Janis's NDE *with* Tom's; the similarities will prove evident.

Janis nearly died as a result of an automobile accident in California in June 1973. Among other injuries, she sustained a subdural hematoma and "was comatose for a long time." Because of her injuries, she now suffers from progressive epilepsy. As with Tom also, she made a "journey to the light," but in her case, we will pick up her story with her "arrival" there:

There was just me before this huge—it was like a golden sun. [Did it hurt your eyes to look at it?] No! It was brilliant. It was so bright and so powerful that had it been the sun and had I looked upon it, like I would the sun, I would have burnt my retinas. I'd have been blind. But no. It didn't hurt me at all. [What was your feeling in the presence of this light?] Peace. Homecoming. It's strange, because I never really verbalized that before. It was really like a homecoming. It was beautiful, it was magnificent. And it was so warm. [In what way?] In all ways. There was that sense of tactile warmth that I had experienced [earlier]. . . . But it was even more intense. I mean, it wasn't hot; it was just a greater warmth. There was that warmth, but there was another warmth. An acceptance, a real acceptance.

I was asked if I was ready to stay. [Who asked you?] This light. [Was there a sense of a presence associated with this light?] Oh, yes. Oh, yes. In fact, I should say that when I communicated . . . with the light, there wasn't a transfer of words. I mean, no words were spoken. It's like thinking a thought and having them know it and answer it immediately. I mean, it's transference of thought. It was instantaneous.

And I was asked if I was ready to stay. And I didn't know. I really didn't know. And I was told that I would have to go and make up my mind. I'd have to go make a decision. . . .

[Later] before making that decision . . . I had the life review. [Tell me about that.] This review of my life passed by. A "psssssh" [she makes a fast, hissing sound]—just like [that]. Yeah, a 35-milli-meter film went "click, click" in a split second. It was all black and

white and I saw everything. I saw my whole life pass right by me.
[In any order particularly?] Oh, yeah. All chronological. All precise.
It all just went right by. My whole life. [Were you reliving these
events or just watching like a spectator?] I was, yeah, more of a
spectator . . . there were no emotions. I was just watching this and I
saw my whole life pass in review. And after my whole life went
by—in black and white—zoooom!—and the black and white
ended and it got into color and it got into things that hadn't happened yet. Things that I didn't realize but things that have happened
since then![2]

In reading the first portion of Janis's account of her core experience, you'd be forgiven for thinking she had already been familiar
with Tom's NDE and had unconsciously mimicked it. I can assure
you this is not so, however; neither one even knows of, much less
knows, the other.

And here is a third, very similar independent description of a
core NDE. Jayne Smith is a woman in her early fifties whom I met
in April 1982 at a conference on NDEs held in Philadelphia and who
has since become a good friend also. A friend of hers had told me
that Jayne had had an NDE some years ago. When I had a chance, I
asked Jayne if she would feel comfortable sharing it with the group.
Although she had never done this before, she graciously agreed to
do so. I am not only very glad she did—for it was a very deep NDE,
it turned out—but also particularly grateful to a man who happened
to be tape-recording the proceedings that day. He was kind enough
to send me a copy of the tape I needed to make a transcript of
Jayne's story. I have taken the following excerpts from that spontaneous recitation.

Jayne's experience occurred in 1952 in conjunction with the
birth of her second child. She felt herself going (and her physician
later implied to her that she had indeed been in danger of dying)
when all at once:

. . . the next thing I knew, I was in—I was standing in a mist and I
knew *immediately* that I had died and I was *so* happy that I had
died but I was still alive. And I cannot tell you how I *felt*. It was,
"Oh, God, I'm dead, but I'm here! I'm me!" And I started pouring

out these enormous feelings of gratitude. . . . My consciousness was filled with nothing but these feelings of gratitude because I still existed and yet I knew perfectly well that I had died. . . .

While I was pouring out these feelings . . . the mist started being infiltrated with enormous light and the light just got brighter and brighter and brighter and, it is so bright but it doesn't hurt your eyes, but it's brighter than anything you've ever encountered in your whole life. At that point, I had no consciousness anymore of having a body. It was just pure consciousness. And this enormously bright light seemed almost to cradle me. I just seemed to exist in it and be part of it and be nurtured by it and the feeling just became more and more and more ecstatic and glorious and perfect. And everything about it was—if you took the one thousand best things that ever happened to you in your life and multiplied by a million, maybe you could get close to this feeling, I don't know. But you're just engulfed by it and you begin to know a lot of things.

I remember I knew that everything, everywhere in the universe was OK, that the plan was perfect. That whatever was happening—the wars, famine, whatever—was OK. Everything was perfect. Somehow it was all a part of the perfection, that we didn't have to be concerned about it at all. And the whole time I was in this state, it seemed infinite. It was timeless. I was just an infinite being in perfection. And love and safety and security and knowing that nothing could happen to you and you're home forever. That you're safe forever. And that everybody else was.

Later in her experience, Jayne described an encounter and "telecommunication" with one of the "beings" who approached her. It was not, she related, anyone she knew. She told him:

"I know what's happened, I know that I've died." And he said, "Yes, but you aren't going to be staying because it isn't time for you yet." And I said to him, "This is all so beautiful, this is all so perfect, what about my sins?"

And he said to me, "There are no sins. Not in the way you think about them on earth. The only thing that matters here is how you think."

"What is in your heart?" he asked me.

And then I asked him, "Since I can't stay, since I'm going to be going back, I've another question to ask. Can you tell me—what it's all about?" [Laughter from the audience. In other words, she was asking, she said, how does "the whole thing" work?]
I'd forgotten it until he'd reminded me of it. "Of course!"

And then I asked him, "Since I can't stay, since I'm going to be going back, I've another question to ask. Can you tell me—what it's all about? [Laughter from the audience. In other words, she was asking, she said, how does "the whole thing" work?]

And he *did* tell me. And *it* only took two or three sentences. It was a very short explanation and I understood it perfectly. And I said again, "Of course!" And again, I knew it was something I had always known and managed to forget.

And so I asked him, "Can I take all this back with me? There's so many people I want to tell all this to."

And he said, "You can take the answer to your first question—which was the one about sin—but," he said, "the answer to the second question you won't be able to remember." [And she found in fact that when she returned to physical life, she could not.]

And that was the last thing I heard . . . [before coming back].

We will consider another aspect of Jayne's NDE later in this chapter, but to continue our progression through this case material on core NDEs, we need next to present a lengthy extract from a man who differs in several respects from the individuals whose experiences we have reviewed thus far.

Joseph F. Dippong is a forty-six-year-old author, publisher, and businessman who heads the Kundalini Research Institute of Canada.[3] Unlike almost all the other persons I have cited to this point who have completed various questionnaires for me and became my personal friends as well, I know Mr. Dippong mainly through some professional, if lengthy, correspondence we have exchanged. Even before corresponding with him, however, I had read some time before a published account of his own NDE, which had impressed me very much and which I placed in my file of such cases. I have since seen it reprinted elsewhere and, because I have had some congenial professional contact with him in the meantime, I felt I would like to quote a portion of his NDE here. The form and style of Mr. Dippong's account, then, will contrast with the previous cases since it is given formal literary expression. Nevertheless, as you will see, it speaks most eloquently of the same transcendental features we have already encountered and in such a way as to make us appreciate anew the awesome and numinous quality of the core experience. In this sense it may serve as a capstone to the foregoing examples—and as a preface to what is to come.

Mr. Dippong's experience took place in November 1970 and occurred when he was set upon by some angry companions at a business meeting and nearly suffocated to death. According to Mr. Dippong's account of this episode, the meeting had been characterized by mounting verbal hostility over his intransigence and refusal to yield to group consensus. Eventually, one of the participants cried, "Let's kill him." This was intended, Mr. Dippong says, as a joke, but it became a joke that got out of hand as was soon evident to those present. As he describes it:

I was not aware of any of the activity going on in the room because where I was and what I was experiencing was not of this world. The last thing I remembered was that I prayed to God.[4] Then another consciousness slowly began to unfold. It could have happened in seconds, in minutes, in years, or even in an eternity.

At first I became aware of beautiful colors which were all the colors of the rainbow. They were magnified in crystallized light and beamed with a brilliance in every direction. It was as if all this light was coming at me through a prism made by a most beautiful and purified diamond, and yet at the same time it was as if I were in its center. I was in a heavenly pasture with flowers. It was another place, another time, and perhaps it was even another universe. But it was definitely another consciousness—vibrant and more alive than the one I had known in my earthly life. My ears were filled with a music so beautiful no composer could ever duplicate it. It too was not of this world. It was soothing, gentle, and warm and seemed to come from a source deep within me.

Everything that occurred to me while I was in this state of conscious[ness] was vastly beyond anything I had ever experienced and yet at the same time it was familiar—as if I had always known of its existence. Even now when I try to describe something so beautiful I am mute with awe. There are no words in any language to describe such grandeur. Even the great literary works by men and women fortunate enough to have experienced this blissful state only paint a shadow of its glory. I don't know to this day where I was, I was no longer aware of my physical existence on earth, of my friends, my family, or my relatives. I was in a state that existed of nothing more than consciousness, but what a sublime consciousness it was! It was like a rebirth into another, higher kind of life.

As my senses expanded I became aware of colors that were far beyond the spectrum of the rainbow known to the human eye. My awareness stretched out in all three hundred sixty degrees. It was as if I was in the center of a lotus flower which was unfolding its beauty around me in every direction. I became aware of being in the middle of a tunnel. I was speeding closer and closer to a light at the other end. In the far distance I saw what I can only describe in the limited language available to me now, as two circles.

In the middle of one circle was a most beautiful being. It was neither a man nor a woman, but it was both. I have never, before or since, seen anything as beautiful, loving, and perfectly pleasant as this being. An immense, radiant love poured from it. An incredible light shone through every single pore of its face. The colors of the light were magnificent, vibrant and alive. The light radiated outward. It was a brilliant white superimposed with what I can only describe as a golden hue. I was filled with an intense feeling of joy and awe. I was consumed with an absolutely inexpressible amount of love. I had the overpowering feeling that I was in the presence of the source of my life and perhaps even my creator. In spite of the tremendous awe it inspired, I felt I knew this being extremely well. With all my heart I wanted to embrace and melt into it as if we were one—for although it was neither my mother nor my father, it was both.

The second circle surrounded the first. In it I became aware of six shimmering mother-of-pearl-like impressions which unfolded and opened up in the way the petals of a freshly created flower open up to the sun. They were living beings. Their beauty, charm, splendid emanating colors, and the closeness I felt to them were breathtaking. From beyond this impression, I became aware of the most powerful, radiant, brilliant white light. It totally absorbed my consciousness. It shone through this glorious scene like the sun rising on the horizon through a veil which had suddenly opened. This magnificent light seemed to be pouring through a brilliant crystal. It seemed to radiate from the very center of the consciousness I was in and to shine out in every direction through the infinite expanses of the universe. I became aware that it was part of all living things and that at the same time all living things were part of it. I knew it was omnipotent, that it represented infinite divine love. It was as if my heart wanted to leap out of my body towards it. It was almost as though I had met my Maker. Even though the light seemed thousands and thousands of times stronger than the brightest sunlight, it did not bother my eyes. My only desire was to have more and more of it and to bathe in it forever.

At this point, I suggest that you stop here for a moment and return to the brief description of Joe Geraci's NDE that began this section. Simply reread the second paragraph. In the light of all you have read since, ending with Mr. Dippong's account, can you now see why I said of Joe Geraci's brief narrative that the essence of the core experience is contained in those few words? And why Joe—agreeing with Mr. Dippong—despaired of ever being able to relate verbally what he had experienced? Yet, somehow, through these multiple perspectives on a common experience, we can at least begin to sense what no one single voice could ever tell us. That, of course, is one of the main reasons for presenting so many descriptions of the core NDE in this chapter.

We may now move on to some further cases that will provide ample evidence of certain features of the core experience that have so far only been alluded to in passing or have been neglected altogether.

We begin these new cases with the account of a sixty-four-year-old man whom I'll call Harold. Since Harold is retired and has a mobile home, he travels quite a bit and once, when he was in the Northeast, he was kind enough to drive to the university so that I could interview him. I'll quote, however, from a written version of his NDE that he later sent to me.

In April 1977, while raking leaves in front of his house, Harold suffered a heart attack. He describes the unfolding of his core experience as follows:

A brilliant white-yellow warm pillar of light confronted me. I was now in a light golden cellular embodiment and the greatest feeling of warmth and love and tenderness became part of me. My consciousness or soul was at the foot or base. When I tried to look up (not exactly so, but the closest words I can use) I saw the sweet smile and love of my father at the time when I was a young child and he held me and loved me. I felt this love permeating my being. (I had never any conscious remembrance of this nor thought of my father for years.)
   Instantly my entire life was laid bare and open to this wonderful presence, "GOD." I felt inside my being his forgiveness for the things in my life I was ashamed of, as though they were not of great importance. I was asked—but there were no words; it was a straight mental instantaneous communication—"What had I done to benefit or advance the human race?" At the same time all my life was presented instantly in front of me and I was shown or made to understand what counted. I am not going into this any further but, believe me, what I had counted in life as unimportant was my salvation and what I thought was important was nil.

We see here many of the now familiar elements of the core experience—the light, the love, the sense of total acceptance and forgiveness, and so on—but the life-review phenomenon is of especial interest to us here. In this case, that review was presented in the context of the question, in effect, "What have you done with your life?" And as Harold himself observes, what he thought mattered, didn't, and what he held to be important turned out to be insignificant. We will see in some of the cases to follow that Harold's experience in this respect was not unique.

Next I present the case of another good friend, whom I'll call Hank. Another researcher, John Audette, who had first interviewed Hank, introduced me to him. Hank and I first met in August 1979 at the American Psychological Association convention in New York. Norma was with me on that trip and we both took an instant shine to

Hank. Since that time we've visited one another's home on several occasions (Hank lives in Virginia) and have had many conversations centering on his NDE and the aftereffects. On one occasion I met Hank late one evening at a Baltimore hotel prior to a television engagement we both had the next day, and I taped his experience in full. The following excerpt is taken from that conversation.

In November 1975, when he was just nineteen years old, Hank was badly injured in an automobile accident. He suffered numerous physical injuries and it was thought for some time that he would not survive them.

In the first part of his NDE, he found himself in something like a "very large room" in which he became aware of other "beings." At one point,

. . . from the forward left-hand corner of the room, another being entered. This being was of an even brighter aura—glow—than we were. His glow was almost like reaching out, so to speak; it just came out and engulfed you. It filled every corner of the room. . . . Even though the brightness was intense you could still make out something of the features, that kind of thing. The brightness did not hurt your eyes. . . . It had a kind of golden-type white—mostly white, I would say—and I could make out a form of him. . . . The feeling was so intense, it was almost as if I could have been completely engulfed by it, and the light also provided a warmth and love. I had the warmth and love toward this person so intense, total trust, not like a love I've had for anything or anybody. It is so hard to describe 'cause it's hard to realize a total surrendering-type love, a total love that kind of immerses you. The kind that no matter what he would have told me, I'd have done . . .

This part of the core experience we now know well, but it is what Hank reported afterward that makes his words of special value here. Hank's conversation rambles a bit in what follows, but his meaning is clear and instructive.

. . . He [then] asked me, "Do you know where you are?" . . . I said, "Yes." . . . And he said, "What is your decision?" When he said that . . . it was like I knew everything that was stored in my brain. Everything I'd ever known from the beginning of my life I immediately knew about. And also what was kind of scary was that I knew everybody else in the room knew I knew and that there was no hiding anything—the good times, the bad times, everything. . . . I had a total complete clear knowledge of everything that had ever happened in my life—even little minute things that I had forgotten . . . just everything, which gave me a better understanding of everything at that moment. Everything was so clear.

. . . I realized that there are things that every person is sent to earth to realize and to learn. For instance, to share more love, to be more loving toward one another. To discover that the most important thing is human relationships and love and not materialistic things. And to realize that every single thing that you do in your life is recorded and that even though you pass it by not thinking at the time, it always comes up later. For instance, you may be . . . at a stoplight and you're in a hurry and the lady in front of you, when the light turns green, doesn't take right off, [she] doesn't notice the light, and you get upset and start honking your horn and telling them to hurry up. Those are the little kind of things that are recorded that you don't realize at the time are really important. One of the things that I discovered that is very important is patience toward other human beings and realizing that you yourself may be in that situation sometime.

If you return to another early account—that of the sixty-four-year-old woman from Seattle on pages 55–56—you'll again find a brief allusion in the beginning of her narrative to the process that Hank describes in detail. Recall that she said simply, "I was aware . . . of my past life. It was like it was being recorded. . . ." And certainly what Hank experienced not only provides more information on that aspect of the core NDE but obviously jibes quite closely with Harold's statement that we've just considered.

The next case will reinforce the pattern we see emerging.

Belle is the pseudonym of a woman now in her mid-fifties whom I met on a trip to Georgia in the spring of 1981. I flew to that part of the South specifically to interview Belle and a couple of other people who had originally been interviewed by Raymond Moody. This was for another research project of mine that will be described later.[5] I was able to spend two full days with Belle and her family during which time we were able to talk at length. The excerpts given below come from one of our conversations, which I tape-recorded.

In 1971, Belle underwent surgery for a persisting back condition. During it she experienced heart failure. Although her medical records were not available to me, she told me she had been informed later by her family physician that she had been "clinically dead" for 20 minutes!

The first part of her core experience, of which I'll quote only a few brief sentences here, is again what we have seen before:

I met this beautiful being of light. It is the most beautiful person and it is not at all effeminate. Masculine, filled with love, pulsating love, you're just surrounded with love. It's not a physical or a sexual love. It is God's love of man and man's love of God. It's an all-consuming feeling.

Her next comments, however, speak again to the phenomenon of the life review and echo Harold's and Hank's observations:

You are shown your life—and you do the judging. Had you done what you should do? You think, "Oh, I gave six dollars to someone that didn't have much and that was great of me." That didn't mean a thing. It's the little things—maybe a hurt child that you helped or just to stop to say hello to a shut-in. Those are the things that are most important. . . . You are judging yourself. You have been forgiven all your sins, but are you able to forgive yourself for not doing the things you should have done and some little cheaty things that maybe you've done in life? Can you forgive yourself? This is the judgment.

Another of the persons I met on that trip South was a thirty-two-year-old man I call Darryl. He proved to be one of the most fascinating NDErs I have ever met. I only wish Darryl had permitted me to record more of the conversations we held during the three days we were together, for he related some personal experiences I found most astonishing at the time but can recall now only in their general outlines. But he did consent to my taping his NDE, and I will present some excerpts from this account shortly.

Darryl's experience occurred in September 1971. He was talking to a friend over the phone one evening during an electrical storm. When lightning struck his house, he was electrocuted. He told me that he learned afterward that he was for at least nine minutes without pulse or respiration. He suffers from permanent neurological damage and muscle degeneration as a result of his injuries.

As we will see, Darryl's experience includes some of the elements of the core NDE that have occupied our attention recently—and it also introduces some new ones. As his experience developed, he too became aware of a light:

. . . as the light came toward me, it came to be a person—yet it wasn't a person. It was a being that radiated. And inside this radiant luminous light which had a silver tint to it—white, with a silver tint to it—[was] what looked to be a man. . . . Now, I didn't know exactly who this was, you know, but it was the first person that showed up and I had this feeling that the closer this light got to me, the more awesome and the more pure this love—this feeling that I would call love . . . And this person said, "Do you know where you are?" I never got a chance to answer that question, for all of a sudden—quote, unquote—"my life passed before me." But it was not my life that passed before me nor was it a three-dimensional caricature of the events in my life. What occurred was every emotion I have ever felt in my life, I felt. And my eyes were showing me the basis of how that emotion affected my life. What my life had done so far to affect other people's lives using the feeling of pure love that was surrounding me as the point of comparison. And I had done a terrible job. God! I mean it. You know, I'd done a horrible job, using love as the point of comparison. . . . Lookin' at yourself from the point of how much love you have spread to other people is devastatin'. You will never get over it. I am six years away from that day [of his NDE] and I am not over it yet.

Later, Darryl found himself moving toward something that other core NDErs have also described—a city of lights.

I moved closer to the lights and realized they were cities—the cities were built of light. At the moment I realized what it was . . . we were there. There was no more traveling or floating along this path.

I stood in the square of a brilliant, beautiful city and I will describe the city. The building I went in was a cathedral. It was built like St. Mark's or the Sistine Chapel, but the bricks or blocks appeared to be made of Plexiglas. They were square, they had dimension to 'em, except you could see through 'em and in the center of each one of these was this gold and silver light. And you could see the building—and yet could not for the radiance. . . . Now, this cathedral was literally *built* of knowledge. This was a place of learning I had come to. I could sense it. 'Cause literally all information—I begun to be bombarded with data. Information was coming at me from every direction. It was almost as if I was stickin' my head in a stream and each drop of water was a piece of information and it was flowing past me as if my head was under it.

Other core experiencers have described such cities in even more detail. For example, there is the following word picture painted by a forty-one-year-old woman I met at still another conference on near-death experiences in March 1981. At the workshop I was conducting—this one was in North Carolina, by the way—Stella (a pseudonym) had been asked by the conference organizers to share her NDE with my audience. As usually happens on these occasions, we went out afterward to talk further and eventually Stella, too, came North to the Near-Death Hotel for a couple of extended visits. During one of them, we tape-recorded her narration of her NDE in which she spoke of her experience in a city of light.

Her NDE itself occurred as a result of massive hemorrhaging following surgery in June 1977.

. . . suddenly there was this tremendous burst of light and, uh, I was turned . . . to the light. I saw at a great distance a city. . . . It's not like you'd look out of an airplane and see the layout of a city. . . . Even at tremendous distance, I realized that it was *immense!* It all seemed to have the same dimensions and there seemed to be nothing supporting it and no *need* for anything to support it.

And then I began to realize that the light was coming from within this city and there just seemed to be a laser beam of light and in the midst of that, that was directed to me. And I just rode that laser beam of light through a vastness, being aware that there were other life forms going by [this aspect was also independently mentioned by Belle and Darryl], but this was only a minor part of this experience. The main thrust of my attention was where I was headed. [Did you have a sense of your speed?] Oh, tremendous speed, tremendous speed. [Any change in speed?] I think that as I got closer to it, there was an acceleration to a point. It was almost as though this light was not an arc, but it had that feeling to it; that I was going to the top of what I saw. It's hard to conceive that so much could happen so quickly. And yet, the intensity of it had more depth than anything I've known before or since. Then I got to a point where I was almost looking down. I suddenly thought, "I guess I blew it!" [laughs] Because I was going so fast, I thought I was going on by. And almost at the same instant—it must have been the perfect point—I just went right down into it. I don't know how to explain that. It wasn't as though it was lowering, but I just went from the perfect point above it into this city.

The first thing that I saw was this street. And it had such a clarity. The only thing I can relate it to in this life was a look of gold, but it was clear, it was transparent. . . . Everything there had a purity and clarity. . . . The difference (between things here and there) was also—you think of gold as something hard and brittle; this had a smoothness and softness. Not a giving softness, but almost a blending . . . Everything was very defined, on the one hand, but it also had a blending with everything else. The flowers and the flower buds by that street—the intensity, the vibrant colors, like pebbles that have been polished in a running stream, but they were all like precious stones, rubies and diamonds and sapphires. One that I remember in particular had a yellow color to it and yet I would relate it to a diamond . . . all these things were just around flowers. [What did the flowers look like?] They looked like . . . tulips . . . and yet they had the fragrance of roses. Strong fragrance of roses.[6] And I started to walk further on this street and . . . then I saw, as I was looking down, walking, I saw the feet, just the toes, of this man's feet and the bottom of his garment in my path. And I wasn't allowed to go any further. And I could hear *languages*. All languages. Languages that I had never heard before and I could understand them. I wanted to be allowed to go on. I knew there was so much more there and I wanted to be able to experience it, to see it. . . . There was the knowledge that was beyond anything that I could possibly try to describe to you. I began to realize that I was going to have to leave and I didn't want to leave [begins to cry].

Jayne—whose core NDE I've already given (see pages 61–63)—also reports perceptions very much like Stella's, although Jayne did not describe the city as one of lights. Nevertheless, the parallels are evident. In this portion of her experience, just following, it seems, her sense that she was "an infinite being in perfection" and that, indeed, *all* was perfect, she relates:

. . . after I had been in that for whatever infinite time this was, I suddenly found myself on a green plain. And I had a body again. I was aware of a body. And this was a beautiful green meadow, with beautiful flowers, beautiful flowers, lit again with this glorious radiant light, like no light we've ever seen, but there was sky, grass, flowers that had colors that I'd never seen before. And I remember so well looking at them and thinking, "I have never seen some of these colors!" Just utter glory in color. And I walked along and I saw that there were people up on a little rise in front of me. So I started walking toward that rise to talk with these people and when I had just about gotten up there, I could see a city.

Just as I attempted to sum up our first set of core NDEs by reference to a literary account, I intend to do likewise here by drawing on a narrative that comes from the pen of Rev. Carol Parrish-Harra. This woman, who is both a minister and a healer, and I started corresponding in 1980 and finally had a chance to meet briefly in April 1982. During that time Carol was writing a book[7] on death and dying, which included an account of her own NDE. This took place in 1958, when she had an allergic reaction to a drug while giving birth. I will quote below from the prepublication draft of the chapter in which she describes her experience. I cite it here not only because Carol expresses her encounter with a "being of light" so well, but especially because of her ability to state in general terms the way in which transcendental knowledge is transmitted during these experiences and the form it takes. In addition, Carol's comments—as did Mr. Dippong's earlier—will serve as a bridge to what is to follow later in this chapter. She writes:

By my side there was a Being with a magnificent presence. I could not see an exact form, but instead, a radiation of light that lit up everything about me and spoke with a voice that held the deepest tenderness one can ever imagine . . . as this loving yet powerful Being spoke to me, I understood vast meanings, much beyond my ability to explain. I understood life and death, and instantly, any fear I had, ended. There was a totality, a completeness in the realization that I could continue to experience and that there was absolutely no reason to continue my frantic struggle to exist.

For what seemed to be endless time, I experienced this Presence. The Light Being, pure, powerful, all-expansive, was without a form and it could be said that great waves of awareness flowed to me and into my mind.

As I responded to these revelations, I knew them to be so. Of course, it didn't matter if one lived or died, it was all so clear. There was a complete trust and greater understanding of what these words meant.

It seemed whole *Truths* revealed themselves to me. Waves of thought—ideas greater and purer than I had ever tried to figure out came to me. Thoughts, clear without effort revealed themselves in total wholeness, although not in logical sequence. I, of course, being in that magnificent Presence, understood it all. I realized that consciousness is life. We will live in and through much, but this consciousness we know that is behind our personality will continue. I knew now that the purpose of life does not depend on me; it has its own purpose. I realized that the flow of it will continue even as I will continue. New serenity entered my being.

As this occurred, an intensity of feeling rushed through me, as if the light that surrounded that Being was bathing me, penetrating every part of me. As I absorbed the energy, I sensed what I can only describe as bliss. That is such a little word, but the feeling was dynamic, rolling, magnificent, expanding, ecstatic—*Bliss*. It whirled around me and, entering my chest, flowed through me, and I was immersed in love and awareness for ineffable time.

Since 1976, when I first began my work in near-death studies, I have been the recipient of many hundreds of letters from people interested in NDEs and related experiences. In many of these letters, of course, correspondents would describe some of their own experiences and, for reasons you can now well understand, most of these accounts I read with deep absorption and appreciation. Of all the beautiful letters I have received, however, I think the one that touched me the most profoundly was written by a woman, now fifty-one, who resides with her family in the Midwest. I've never met her, but for a long time I've kept her letter in a special file in my private study because, for reasons I myself don't fully understand, I particularly treasure it.

It seems fitting that I should now share this letter, at least in part, with you. I only wish I could reproduce all of it, but since it runs fifteen pages, I will have to content myself with quoting a few passages from it and summarizing what I have to omit. I especially hope that any parents who have ever lost a child, and particularly a newborn, will derive from this letter a lasting source, not merely of consolation, but also of joy.

In July 1981, four NDErs and I appeared on the *Donahue* show, and Ann happened to see it. Doing so prompted her to write. Her letter begins:

I watched you on the *Donahue* show today with a great deal of interest because I am also one of "those people" who have experienced the peace and absolute love of the spiritual existence.

I volunteer my own experience to your study because, in addition to creating a total change in my personality, I was given information that literally saved me from suffering the terrible grief of the death of my husband and two children later on.

I was 22 years old, delivering my second child, a little girl. The date was June 18, 1954. I began to hemorrhage badly (I'm told) but I recall a great pain in my chest that was making it impossible for me to draw in more air after exhaling. I recall a sense of being pulled (up!—not down) by some great force, out of the room toward a bright light which seemed far away at first but I "flew" toward it very swiftly. The pain fell behind me like ribbons or streamers trailing me, as I "knew" I was going faster and faster. The "light" appeared to be a window of some kind and I was momentarily alarmed that I would be hurt as I crashed into it, because I could not possibly stop myself in time at such high speed. I automatically shut my eyes and braced myself for the "crash" which was unavoidable (I thought).

Nothing crashed. I suddenly stopped and felt myself lying perfectly still—like floating on water. My sense of belonging, love, peace, and well-being was (as they all say) indescribable. It was absolute—perfect—wonderful. I didn't know where I was, but I didn't care, I would be content to stay there *forever!* I was alone, but *not* lonely. Even though there was no visual means of determining my position in this environment of "nothing," I "knew" I was lying down—rather than standing up.

Then I received the knowledge (no one was there with me and no one spoke, as we speak) that I was to wait there until a person came to talk to me. Then, I "knew" he was on his way toward me from an unthinkable distance away. He (rather than a "she") came to me at an unthinkable high speed, passing through the universe, through whole galaxies to come to where I was. I was in a world (a huge world) of total nothingness, except myself. The bright light I had seen at first, as a window in a world of total darkness, was all about me now, but not bright anymore—soft now, and soothing— or perhaps no light at all (and) no darkness either. More a haze. I felt so very, very comfortable there.

I "sensed" this person's approach toward me, and I "knew" the exact instant he entered into the outer edge of the world (or state of awareness?) I was in. He came to me from my right-hand side. In a matter of seconds he entered "my world" hundreds and thousands of light years away (the edge of it, I mean) and travelled to my side (he was standing) and took hold of my right hand.

When he took hold of my hand, I immediately knew him to be the greatest friend I had. I also knew that *I* was a very special person to him. The thrill of this touch of hands exceeds anything I have ever experienced on earth, in life as we know it. Our meeting was "understood"—"sensed"—not visual.

Without vocal communication, he "told me" he had come for my child. *"My child?"* I asked, scarcely able to contain my joy and happiness over the news that one of my own children would be going back *with him!* It was, I "knew," a very high honor to be selected for this. I had the honor of being the mother of a very extra special child, and I was *so* proud that he had picked *my* child. (We were discussing her *life*, not death!) It was a fantastic opportunity for my child, and it never occurred to me to refuse to *give* my child to this man.

Thus, I "gave" my child to him, or meant to do so immediately, but I could not do this because—I then realized—with great disappointment—my child was not with me! I had no child to give him! I started to cry over the loss of such a great opportunity as this. No child to give! I was a mother with no child! It seemed such a terrible thing to have no child to give to this man. I was about to be devastated by my own sorrow over such a great loss of this wonderful opportunity for my child—if I had a child right then, to give him. But I didn't, and I didn't know why I didn't, because I knew I *was* a mother!

He patted my hand in sympathy and reassured me that I was a mother, and I *did* have a child, but the child must have been delayed somehow. Then he waved his hand across the space in front of us and the haze cleared. I could see the nurses and doctor, and my baby, back in the delivery room. The doctor was examining the baby and laying it on a scale-like machine which was supposed to indicate its life-span (rather than weight!). We could see that the machine was malfunctioning and giving the doctor a false reading. The doctor gave the baby to the nurse saying it would live 80 years. But the man with me is shaking his head, saying to me, "Men put so much faith in their own machines, they fail to notice the Truth. The machine is wrong. The child will live only 4 days."

"Would my child live 80 years, if the machine was fixed?" I asked.

"Yes, but they don't know that it is not working properly." "Then I'll tell them! When I go back, I'll tell them!" "No. You won't remember any of this when you go back." "Then I don't want to go back, I want to go with you." "No. I came for the child. It is not time for you to come with me now. You must go back."

"But what about my child now?"

"I will return for your child in 4 days."

And this statement filled me with joy again. With this promise, I was willing to go back. . . . I was perfectly willing to go back, and wait for "my own turn" while my child went *first*. I had not seen (as we "see" on earth) or held this child in my arms yet, but I felt such an overwhelming love for this child, I would have sacrificed *anything* for her. Going "back" was a sacrifice, or so it seemed to me *then*.

"I'm going to tell them about that faulty machine when I go back."

"You won't remember."

"I will! I *must!*"

"Most people never remember this place when they go back. Even if you do, they won't believe you. It is probably best that you don't remember, rather than be disbelieved."

"No, I will remember—whether anyone believes me or not doesn't matter. I *must* remember this place!"

He let go of my hand and I felt myself falling away from him, moving downward quite fast, looking back to where he was, saying over and over, "I'll remember, I'll remember."

Then someone was screaming my name and slapping my face on the cheeks back and forth, and I was still concentrating so hard on what I intended to remember that I didn't answer to my name being called. I knew I was back in the delivery room now and fully aware of the nurse bending over me, slapping my cheeks and calling me by name, but if I answered her, I'd forget what I was trying so hard to remember. Somehow, I knew that if I answered her, I'd forget everything—so I didn't answer. Deliberately didn't answer her.

Then she said, "Your baby is here," and that caught me off guard. I wanted to see my baby just once, before she left me. I answered, "But I must remember!" which made no sense to her (she said later). In that instant of speaking to her, I totally forgot it all. I wanted to see my baby!

Ann's letter continues with a description of her next few days in the hospital. Her own situation, she discovered, had indeed been critical, but the outcome for both mother and child (she did give birth to a daughter, Tari) appeared positive. Nevertheless, she continued to feel that there was *something* she was supposed to tell her physician about her baby—but simply could not remember it.

On the second day, her physician detected severe cerebral hemorrhaging in the baby, who was now paralyzed on her right side and he knew, according to what he later told Ann, that she would probably die. He tried to prepare Ann for the news but did so in a gentle, indirect manner. Nevertheless, at this point, Ann was totally unconcerned about her baby's state of health:

[I] persisted in concentrating on some elusive thing that I was supposed to remember to tell him. Still, I heard and understood all that he said to me. What I failed to do was feel worried about it, or frightened, or sad. That sense of peace and well-being seemed to come back with me, though I remembered nothing, and could not explain why "I was not worried about my baby daughter" and how I *"knew"* she was going to be all right. It was contrary to the physical facts.

On the morning of the fourth day, June 22, Tari died. That morning, Ann writes, she "woke up, suddenly, fully alert. I 'sensed' something had happened to me, but I didn't know what it was."

Because her physician had noted her strangely serene attitude about Tari's impending death, he had given the staff strict orders that none of them should break the news to Ann; he himself would do it.

It didn't work out that way, and Ann found herself ready to be discharged. She was explaining to one of the nurses that she had to sign certain papers first when it was apparent that

. . . the nurse was devastated. She *knew* Tari was dead and I didn't. "Oh, God!" she wailed. "Your doctor should have been here by now! I'm not supposed to tell you, but I can't let you go on believing Tari is alive. She died early this morning."

In the time it took her to get up from her desk and come to me, taking hold of my shoulders, I completely remembered it all—in detail. Relived it, almost. I suppose I looked strange to her.

"Are you OK?" she asked.

"Yes," I told her much too *calmly* under the circumstances.

"This is the fourth day!" (I felt *joy!*)

In the weeks following, I felt no grief of my own loss, but I felt sorry for my friends and relatives who didn't know where Tari was, and couldn't believe—*really* believe—that my "experience" was anything more than a vivid dream.

Her husband and her doctor (who had other patients who experienced NDEs—though they were not, of course, called that in 1954) did acknowledge, however, that something "real" had happened to Ann, but not so her minister, who

pronounced this experience as an hallucination common to persons undergoing great stress. There was no such thing as leaving this life, going to another, and coming back here again. It was a psychological defense mechanism, he said, and I would be better off to simply forget all about it, so that my natural grief period could begin, and [be] gone through, so that my life could get back to "normal" again. . . . This conversation with [my] minister almost wiped me out . . . but I obeyed him without question—or tried to, at least. In a matter of months, I had not been able to forget it, and was well on my way to thinking myself to be some kind of freak. It would have been easier, I think, to try to forget my own name, than to forget that wonderful feeling, surge of sheer joy I had felt when he took my hand, and told me he had come for *my* child. That was the greatest moment I've ever known.

I still don't know *who* he was, nor do I care! I know he exists at least.

Well, I soon realized that my acceptance back into this world depended upon "pretending" to forget, and "pretending" to grieve the loss of my baby. So I did this for everybody else's sake—except my husband, who believed me, and gained some comfort from it, second-hand. It was a dropped "subject," but never forgotten.

Ann concluded her letter by saying:

So, you know, I listened very intently to the people you appeared with on the *Donahue* show and, of course, I don't simply believe they had some kind of *real* experience—I *know* they did. It all rang so true to me, and I also understand the terrible difficulty in trying to verbalize it afterwards in a way that others can believe it too. You have to water it down so much. I have not been very successful at this. . . .

Thank you for listening—by reading all this. I'm sorry it got so long, but there's a lot more I skipped saying—trying to keep it shorter.

And then she added this postscript:

I had 3 more children after Tari's birth.

My beloved husband died in my arms at home 16 years later. My first-born son lived to be 25 and was killed in a car accident (*instantly*—no time for pain or suffering) seven years after the death of my husband.

My grief was softened and shortened each time. People said, "She's in shock now, she'll grieve more later." Later they said, "She must be a very strong person to live through what she's had to live through so calmly." Neither statement was true. It feels good to tell the truth to someone. They aren't dead. They are all alive, busy and waiting for me. Our separation is only temporary and very short, compared to all of eternity.

Conclusions

After this lengthy exploration of the core NDE through the case histories I've presented, I think at least something of the tremendous spiritual energy that appears to be an inherent feature of these experiences will be evident. In one sense, the experiences speak for themselves. From another angle, however, there is a need at least to tie together a few threads that we started to weave at the beginning of this chapter.

Recall that we started out seeking to understand better what lay at the core of these deep NDEs and why they have such profound effects on those who experience them. Though you now have the beginnings of the answer to these questions—as much, anyway, as words can tell—it may be helpful in seeing more keenly the implications of these core NDEs, to make certain matters explicit. This we can best do by returning to three questions posed at the outset of this chapter (see pages 51–52).

The first of these was: What are the features of the core NDE that apparently make it an overwhelming, if numinous, spiritual experience?

To answer this question, we first need to recall—but in an empathetic way—the recurrent themes mentioned by our panel of experiencers. And then to be aware that even though there is no *time* in these experiences ("It was eternity," says Joe. "It's like I was always there and I will always *be* there. . . ."), there is a certain feeling of progression.[8] In fact, I intentionally placed these accounts in a certain sequence to try to bring out this sense of progression. Therefore, in recalling the features of the core NDE, we should be mindful of its developmental aspect as well.

And so, we remember (1) the incredible speed and sense of acceleration as one approaches (2) the light that (3) glows with an overwhelming brilliance and yet (4) does not hurt one's eyes. We remember that one feels in the presence of the light (5) pure love, (6) total acceptance, (7) forgiveness of sins, and (8) a sense of homecoming; that (9) communication with the light is instantaneous and nonverbal and that the light (10) imparts knowledge of a universal nature as well as (11) enables one to see or understand his entire life so that (12) it is clear what truly matters in life. We also remember that one may be aware of (13) transcendental music, (14) paradisiacal environments, and (15) cities of light as one progresses farther into the experience. And that, finally, (16) once having encountered the light, one yearns to remain with it forever.

Now, obviously, I have to some degree arranged these features to convey a coherent picture of the entire core NDE, and just as obviously I have omitted from this composite description certain elements that might have been included. Nevertheless, I think you will agree that the picture I have drawn is at least representative of the main outlines of the experience.

If it is, then simply by remembering (or actually rereading) the descriptions in the accounts I have presented that correspond to the features of the composite narrative I have given here, you will have, in summary form, the answer to the first question. Or at least something as close to an answer as any conceptualization can give.

The second question was: What is the kind and the form of the knowledge conveyed to the core NDEr?

As we have seen, the knowledge is sometimes of general universal principles ("consciousness is life [and] this consciousness we know that is behind our personality will continue"), and sometimes it has direct personal relevance ("'my life passed before me' . . . And I had done a terrible job") to one's past life or (as in cases of Janis and Ann) to events still to come. And then there is Tom Sawyer, who—in agreement with other core NDErs—says that one is in touch with "absolute, total knowledge."

Whatever this may mean experientially, it is at least easy to understand why people who have had these core experiences feel that they have been given access—at least once—to something that transcends human knowledge and that may approach universal knowledge.

And yet, while all this may be true, it still misses the heart of this question. Perhaps this point could be seen more clearly if we asked: What is it that the core NDEr has knowledge *of*?

Think this question over for a moment before reading on. And then ask yourself if there can truly be any debate about it.

Isn't it obvious that what core NDErs experience when they come close to death is what the rest of us would call God, or if not God, then surely some aspect of the infinitude of God made manifest to the mind or spirit of the NDEr? To what other agency is it, after all, reasonable to ascribe the attributes of the core experience: the brilliant light, the all-consuming love, the feeling of total acceptance, the sense of total knowledge, all the other elements I've already enumerated? If this experience is *not* of God, then what else could it possibly be?

Of course, one could argue—and some persons undoubtedly would—that these experiences are nothing more than transcendental hallucinations. But even if one took this position, it would still appear evident that whatever these NDEs be labeled, NDErs themselves would have directly penetrated into the experiential source of humanity's universal belief in a higher religious dimension. It may be that such a belief is false, but I think there can be little doubt that core NDEs give one direct access to the experiential point of origin of religious faith, whether it be truth or superstition.

This, in turn, implies that core NDErs in particular (and NDErs in general) have received an immediate, undeniable, and absolutely unforgettable experience of the existence of God and that, furthermore, they learn through this experience that, as Jayne put it, ". . . nothing could happen to you and you're home forever. That you're safe forever. And that everybody else was." Consider for a moment the impact of that knowledge on an experiencer. Not merely to believe as a matter of religious *tradition* but actually to know incontrovertibly, from one's own experience, that God exists and to feel directly his pulsating, all-embracing love. Is it any wonder that NDErs such as Ann (and many others) return from this experience and later claim that they have undergone a "total change in my personality"?

And not only this, but since NDErs also learn that it is death (though not only death, of course) that affords this contact with an all-loving God force, it is understandable why any previous fear of death would be instantly dissolved. For NDErs, the equations Death = God = Love are obvious.

In drawing out these implications, it is certainly mandatory to check this reasoning against the views of NDErs themselves. Just what level of belief do they have in God?

Two observations are relevant here.

First, to head off the objection that the core experiencers I've selected were chosen because of their prior partiality toward religion, let me repeat here that this was decidedly not the case. Several, in fact, were either atheists or agnostics before their NDEs; still others were indifferent to religion or only nominally religious. And some, of course, were religious to begin with. Furthermore, of those professing some religious preference, even this small sample had its Catholics, Protestants, and Jews. This religious diversity cannot be overlooked when considering the uniformity of perceptions and understandings common to the core experience. Plainly, whatever adherence to a notion of God we may find in such people following their NDE cannot be attributed to their prior orientation.

The second observation is based on some data from one of the questionnaires in my Omega study which, so far twenty-five NDErs have completed, including some of my core experiencers. One item simply asks the respondent to indicate on a five-point scale his belief in God before and after his NDE. The scale ranges from -2 (strongly doubt) to $+2$ (strongly believe). Every single NDEr, *without exception*, checked the $+2$ (strongly believe) alternative following his or her NDE. Behavioral scientists, more than most people, will know how rare it is to have absolutely no variability in response to a questionnaire item even with a sample as small as twenty-five. Thus, NDErs unanimously express the strongest belief possible in God following their experience.

Lest it be contended that probably most respondents would check the same alternative whether or not they had an NDE, let me hasten to add that the evidence does not at all support this view. Fully 60 percent of my NDEr sample, for example, indicated that their belief in God prior to their NDE had been something less than strong (i.e., they checked alternatives -2 through $+1$). From what we have already seen (in Chapter 2), there is every reason to believe that NDErs—before their experience—are no different from anyone else.

There is, finally, one further aspect of this question about knowledge that needs to be addressed here. It will be recalled that a number of core experiencers state or imply that there is a being or presence of some kind associated with the light or that sometime after their experience with the light, they encounter a "being of light." Naturally, one is curious about the identity of this being or beings (there is sometimes more than one reported, as we have seen). What do core experiencers have to say on this point?

First of all, it is clear from unquoted portions of the transcripts or letters I've drawn on for this chapter that there appears to be something like a hierarchy of luminous beings. Some are perceived to be relatives of the NDEr; others are not known at all to the NDEr. Still others are not really visible in a way that corresponds to earthly sight and their identity remains altogether unspecifiable (recall, for example, the being Ann was aware of).

Of course, it is the presence most clearly identified with the light itself that arouses the greatest interest. Is it Jesus?

Only one of my core experiencers—a Mormon—made this particular identification; two others—both had Christian upbringings—

implied it, but one of these two was most reluctant to be specific in this way. Most core experiencers do not or do not choose to give this being any particular identity tag. This even includes Carol Parrish-Harra, who is a Christian minister by profession. She simply calls it a "Light Being." Ann's observation here is typical. She said, "I still don't know *who* he was, nor do I care! I know he exists at least."

To these brief comments, I would add only two brief remarks of my own. First, in my six years of research into NDEs, I cannot recall even one instance in which a being of light was said to have identified *himself* as Jesus. Second, although the data are lacking, I strongly doubt that persons from religious traditions different from our own would be likely to report seeing an image of Christ during their NDEs. This opinion is seemingly seconded by Belle, one of those whose depiction implied Christ to me, who said:

. . . no matter what religion you are in, of the five major religions . . . you are still worshiping the one God, no matter what you call it: Allah, God, Jesus, or whoever. And if you are of the Jewish inclination you will recognize him as Abraham or an angel. . . .

On this matter, then, there is simply not only no clear-cut answer but some indication that there never could be one. In any event, we will return to related issues when we reach Chapter 6.

And finally, the last question: What is the basis for the transformative effects said to be inherent in core NDEs?

The answer is again suggested by one of Joe's comments when he's speaking of the light. Recall he said in this connection:

It's something which becomes you and you become it. I could say, "I was peace, I was love." I was the brightness, it was part of me. . . .

The implication is that qualities of the light somehow infuse themselves into the core of the experiencer's being so as to lead to a complete union with the light. In apparently the sense in which medieval theologian and mystic Meister Eckhart spoke of man becoming God, NDErs may experience this merging of their own individuality with the divine. In any event, the testimony from more than one core experiencer indicates that there is a direct transmission of the light's energy into themselves and that what is absorbed in that encounter with the light in that moment outside of time remains with them when they return to the world of time. In short, the seeds of transformation appear to be implanted during the NDE, but the degree to which they mature and show themselves here depends entirely on factors outside the experience.

This thesis is consistent with what some of my core experiencers assert. For example, Rev. Carol Parrish-Harra has already remarked

. . . an intensity of feeling rushed through me, as if the light that surrounded that Being was bathing me, penetrating every part of me. As I absorbed the energy, I sensed what I can only describe as bliss.

Later, however, she goes on to say that afterward

I longed to understand, to find that feeling of love again. Some part of it remained in my heart, however, and that part continues. It is sometimes expanded and sometimes decreased, but it remains a sign to me of another dimension of Love, Life and Power. I think of the feeling as one of Love, although that word lacks its total import. It is certainly much more than that.

After my interview with Janis, she sent me a long letter amplifying on some issues she felt she had neglected in the conversation we had together. In connection with the light, she wrote:

I mentioned the golden light. It should be Golden light and you ask me if it burned my eyes. No, it did not. Fact being, I gained strength gazing upon it. It's as if by gazing upon this beautiful golden light the power that it was was revitalizing something within the depths of me. There was a transmission of a higher power, knowledge, understanding, and the "oneness of everything" through gazing upon the light.

*   *   *

Thus we see that it appears not merely that core experiencers have an overpowering experience of the energy of the light but also that the light *projects* its energy into them and fills them with its love. It's for this reason that the core experience—and NDEs in general—can never remain, as I have already said, simply "a beautiful memory." It is an experience that continues to pulsate within and, when the circumstances are right, to shine without afterward.

At this point in our inquiry, then, we have been able to acquire, I trust, something of an appreciation of the essence of NDEs and why they often affect NDErs so totally. It remains for us to consider how the tremendous energies encountered and apparently stored during an NDE are handled once an individual returns to the world of ordinary reality and what changes begin to take place in his or her life after recovery. It is to these matters that the next five chapters are devoted.

CHAPTER 4

· · · · · · ·

NDEs and Personal Transformation

÷

To experience the ecstatic intensity and noetic illumination of the NDE and then to have to return to the mundane world is a source of sorrow, sometimes bordering on anguish, for many NDErs, particularly those who have had core experiences. The realm that the NDEr enters at the time of the experience is one of timelessness, infinite space, and total freedom. One feels enormously expanded in all ways and filled with divine love and knowledge. Usually, with all one's heart, one desires to remain in this state forever.

Suddenly there is a pulling back. One's footing in this blissful realm begins to give way. Paradise, having once been attained, is about to be lost. Awareness of the journey back may or may not be present, but the return itself is all too real. Physical pain is felt again along with the body, the latter now experienced as a cage and possibly a source of torment. One has returned to the old world of time and space with its legion of restrictions. One's consciousness has once more contracted so as to live within the tiny confines of the ego. Seemingly, everything that one was and could ever have yearned to be has been lost. Who is there in this world who could ever comprehend the measure of one's despair? Who could ever begin to understand what one has left behind?

Nevertheless, the journey of self-transformation has already begun, and to trace its path from the start, we need to examine first this process of coming back.

Coming Back

Even before returning, NDErs are aware of the dimensions of their coming loss and may have an emotional reaction proportional to the magnitude of their desire to stay.

In Darryl's case, he was informed by a being of light that he must go back to do "this work." Darryl's response was:

"What work?" The next thing is that in thirty years, I experienced the worst feeling I ever had. The most depressed, the most severe anxiety I've ever had was at the moment I realized I must return to this earth. That is the greatest depths of depression I personally have ever had since that time or before. It was so devastatin' that I cannot think of anything bad that has ever *happened* to me and put it in the same parameters—the distance is a million miles. I did not want to come back. And now that I'm back, I'm absolutely assured of the fact that I did not want to come back. . . . This [earth] is a wonderful place to live if you don't know anywhere else. I know somewhere else. . . .

When Stella recalled her experience for me during my interview with her, all her feelings poured out when she related to me her coming back. I'll resume her account by continuing with where it left off in Chapter 3 (see page 74).

I began to realize that I was going to have to leave and I didn't want to leave [begins to cry]. . . . I began to hear my name called. And the first time it happened, the drawing, the pulling force, and then I heard a second time [she is still crying] stronger and then I was [sobbing] outside the *wall* of the city and I was trying to hold on there. I didn't want to *leave* [sobbing]! *Trying to find some way to stay there!* . . . Then, all this light that had all this vibrant color coming through from the light that was inside and touching the wall, I could still feel the warmth of that light, and the peace of that light, and the love in that light, but I couldn't hold onto it. And I turned and I saw, like a grassy hill and at the low portion of it, there was a river and it had a tree by it and I heard my name again in my ear (still sniffling throughout) and I realized that I was back in this *body,* this physical form. And all the pain was there again. . . .

[How did you feel when you came back?] Ah, angry! Angry, angry, angry. [For how long?] Oh, for a good year. First of all, at having to come back—that I saw such a *beautiful, beautiful* place and, once again, I have no word to describe the beauty in the forms, in the peace, in the love, in the languages, in the music, in this being, in the wall, in everything. And the speed, the movement at will, without the limitations of this body! And to gain that kind of knowledge and then—it's like taking a backward step, you know? To have to come back to these limitations.

And to try to explain to someone what your intentions are, what your feelings are, about them, about this experience, especially to try to talk with somebody about it and they only stare at you . . .

Not everyone, of course, has such a strong reaction to coming back—and many people will eventually if not immediately express gratitude for being back, particularly those who have not had core experiences, but some difficulties in readjusting are the rule, not the exception. These difficulties are often compounded by the failure of hospital staffs and other professionals to understand the momentous nature of the NDE and by their frequent attempts to dismiss it. A good illustration of this is in the case of thirty-nine-year-old Barbara Harris, whose out-of-body experience in the hospital's laundry room I related in Chapter 2 (see page 44).

[Did you try to communicate to anyone anything of the experience?] Yeah, I told the nurse the next morning that I left the bed, that I came out into the hall and she told me that it's impossible, that I was hallucinating and just dropped the subject. And had no time for silly things like that. [Did you try to tell anybody else?] Yeah, I tried to tell my internist. When nobody would listen to me about all this, I asked my internist if I could see a psychiatrist and he told me, no, that I was doing just fine. They just kept telling me that I was doing just fine. . . . They were just passing over the experience. I was the only one that wasn't just passing over it. I wanted to see a psychiatrist very badly. [For what reason?] Because things were happening that I just couldn't understand and I thought that maybe the psychiatrist could help me to understand. . . . I really thought the psychiatrist at that point would be the answer to all of my confusion and nobody understood, nobody wanted me. [How did that make you feel?] I just kept withdrawing more and more into my own world. I really didn't have much desire to go on living. I really wanted to go back to the tunnel. . . . I really wanted to die. . . .

While recovering from her operation in the hospital, Barbara relates that she made several further attempts to see a psychiatrist, but they were all dismissed or refused. Finally, after her release but while she was still in a body cast, she was able to convince her brother to take her to a psychiatrist (her husband had also refused). As she related the incident:

I was on a walker, I was really a pathetic thing. . . . He [the psychiatrist] had a stack of records this high [and] . . . the first thing he said to me was, "Barbara, if I'd been through what you've been through, I'd need to see a psychiatrist, too." He just calmed me down. . . . There was a lot of static about [my] wanting to see a psychiatrist. My family was really against psychiatry; that was something to be ashamed of. . . . I tried explaining the tunnel to him . . . and . . . he just stopped it. He put it at a complete halt. He didn't want to get into it because he felt I didn't have the strength. My place at the time was to be quiet and to heal. You know, to take the medication the doctors wanted to give me, to cooperate completely. [To be a good girl?] Yeah . . . just to behave . . . If I could have sat and explained it [her NDE] the way I just explained it to you, that would have been everything that I needed. . . . Instead, he just wiped it away; he just told me to forget it, which I did. And therefore deprivation was what I had for those six months.

Barbara's experience is perhaps a somewhat extreme version of a fairly common type of reaction of professionals and family members to NDEs. Nevertheless, it is certainly not the only such case I have encountered in my research. Perhaps an even more dramatic and poignant example of this kind of unsympathetic dismissal of an

NDEr's experience happened to Nel, a woman in her late forties, who nearly died of a bleeding ulcer in 1972. I happened to meet Nel at a workshop in Boston in February 1983; this provided an occasion for her to divulge her experience publicly for the first time. A week later she wrote me a full account of it, including its sorrowful aftermath. Nel has since told me (and others) that the response she received immediately after her NDE triggered an underlying fear that she really was crazy and plunged her into a ten-year-long depression from which she has emerged only in the past few months, something attested to by her own psychiatrist. Here is her account of what coming back was like for her:

I was exhilarated! I wanted to tell my story before my insides burst. What a magnificent wonder I had seen! Oh, but to share my joy, to tell about my heavenly experience of being in the presence of The Holy Spirit and of talking with It! I had to try to describe the light with its infinite power and grace. I put my right hand to my chest and thought to myself, "How lucky I am to have brought a piece of it back with me; I will always have it inside, right here."

A nurse came in to check my blood pressure. I looked at her and began to tell her of my experience. She listened until I was finished. As she unwrapped the cuff she said, "Well, dear, that is very interesting, but you are very ill and you had an hallucination." I thought she had really not understood what I had tried to communicate. She went on to tell me that my vital signs were normal; the bleeding had stopped. She said that I would be OK.

A little while later a second nurse came in and I told her my story. When I finished she told me that the drugs they were giving me often caused people to have strange dreams. But I knew what I had seen; I knew what had happened to me and it was *not* a strange dream! How could anything so vivid and so real be a dream?" I thought I had better wait a longer time before I told anyone of my experience again.

When the night shift came on I tried for the third time. When I finished this time the nurse told me in a cold, matter-of-fact manner that if I continued to talk that way a pychiatrist would be called in. With that pronouncement I became very frightened. I figured that if the medical profession thought I was crazy I had better keep my silence about the whole affair. I realized that the best thing I could do was to hold onto the light, never let it go, but keep silent, very, very silent. And so I did—for ten years.

Sometimes, of course, there is a person who may demonstrate some openness, but even then there is often little understanding— and there are still likely to be others whose lack of sensitivity may override the sympathetic response, as we have already seen in Ann's case recounted in Chapter 3 (see page 81).

To provide another instance, let me introduce still another core experiencer, a woman in her mid-fifties I'll call Sonja. Sonja was first interviewed in November 1977 in connection with the study I did for *Life at Death*. As with many other NDErs I met doing that re- search, we became and have remained dear friends and she has vis- ited us many times at the Near-Death Hotel. For this research I decided to reinterview her, using a new set of interview questions specifically designed to elicit information on aftereffects (see Appen- dix I). At this time she explained to me in full how others had treated her NDE.

Her own physician was interested to learn about it. Though Sonja says that his response tended to focus on the clinical aspects of her NDE, especially its "hallucinatory" character, he did encourage her to talk to others about it. She next approached her two priests,

Father X and Father Y, and they kind of shushed me, just like, you know, don't talk about it, just don't talk about it. And when I men- tioned it to one of the nurses at the hospital, her reaction was . . . very negative. She said . . . "don't even talk about it, we don't want to hear about it." So everyone I talked to at the hospital seemed almost afraid to discuss it. I tried talking to my children about it, and they just seemed to be humoring me by listening, but I knew they weren't really convinced at the time. When I talked to [my hus- band] about it, he would listen as though it was a dutiful thing to do. And then, after a while, he would say, "I don't want to hear anything about it." So everywhere I went . . . I felt I would just explode from that thing that happened to me. And I wanted to, I guess, have it confirmed, that this is possible, that this sort of thing happens, and that I wasn't, you know, losing my marbles or something.

In Sonja's case, she finally divorced her husband, and though there were multiple reasons for this, her husband's inability to relate to her NDE was one of them. In general, I have observed—though I've undertaken no formal study of this—that primary relationships are often subject to great strain following an NDE, and a considerable number of NDErs end up by divorcing their spouses, or at least wanting to. At the same time, of course, many relationships do endure, but even they can be buffeted by the afterwinds of an NDE.

Joe Geraci's marriage did remain secure, but in his case, real understanding from a priest was the key to his coming to terms with it. Again, in his words:

It was at least, at least six months after the incident that I, that I could even speak to my wife about it. It was such an emotional, beautiful, swelling feeling inside that every time I tried to express it, I think I would just explode, you know; I would break down and cry. And she, for the longest time couldn't figure out what was wrong with me. . . . [In the hospital, immediately upon regaining consciousness, he recalls] I remember being very angry that they brought me back and my wife ended up asking me why later. "You seemed angry, how come?" I just couldn't tell her.

That was probably the most frustrating six months of my existence. After experiencing perfection and something so beautiful, I wanted to hold onto it. I didn't want to let go. And it wasn't easy. After I had recovered the second time [i.e., after his NDE] and went home, everything seemed to change. It was almost like starting my life over. I was a baby, I hadn't had the mistakes that I had made in my life. . . .

And, I can recall in my attempt to hold onto this feeling and to hold onto this peace, I began to bump into earthly things that you know, of course, aren't going to escape from you—they're there. My first frustrating experience was with the television. I couldn't watch television. There would be a commercial, a cosmetic commercial, I couldn't—I'd have to turn it off because it was something false, it was unnecessary, it was fake. It just didn't belong, [it was] insignificant. Any type of violence, if there was even an old Western, an old Western movie, I'd have to turn it off because to me that was total ignorance. There was just no reason on earth to show people killing people. That was frustrating, especially when the family was sitting down trying to watch television and Dad gets up and turns it off all the time! So I finally learned just to go to my room.

It got to the point where I had a great deal of trouble readjusting. And it was at that time—I have a very, very close friend who is a priest, we call him Father Jim—who sat down with me a few times. *Very* understanding. Here was a man I know did not experience what I did, but he seemed to know. He knew what I was talking about, very understanding. Perhaps the most important thing he did for me was to help me to readjust, to accept life, to understand that you *are* living, that, you know, *that* is there, it will come again. And that there is much more here, and that I was here for a reason.

And, as Joe laughingly and somewhat ruefully concluded his story, he was able to readjust eventually.

. . . it did help. I'm back to watching television. I even like the boxing matches. I've come a long way.

In the last instance I'll present here, we see many of the now familiar features of the immediate post-NDE state, but in still another variant of the pattern: This time the support comes from a family member. And, in the end, the outcome is similar to Joe's but points to an even more complete stabilization. Perhaps this is, in part, because Jayne has had thirty years to make her adjustment, whereas Joe has had only a few years.

Recall that Jayne, a core NDEr, had her experience while giving birth. Afterward, as she describes it

Then when I did become conscious and was wheeled back into my room and all that, I was in such a state of awe. As far as I knew, I was the only person in the entire world that this had ever happened

to, because this was thirty years ago. I'd never heard of such a thing
. . . and I just couldn't imagine what it all meant. I knew it was the
blessing of my life, but I didn't know what I was supposed to do
with it.

I tried to tell this experience to my mother and father who were
there. They didn't want to hear—I think I got out one and a half
sentences and my father said, "Put your head back, close your eyes.
You've had a very bad time. Don't think about it." So I dropped it
with Mother and Daddy because they thought I was delirious or
something.

My husband, fortunately, didn't think that way at all . . . he
was very supportive. . . . He knew that it was real. . . .

I kept saying to him, "I would give anything to be able to go
back," because when the man told me I couldn't stay, I felt terribly
disappointed. And yet I was quite willing. I just knew and realized
that this was part of the pattern; I had no thought of arguing. It was
just, "Oh, all right, yes; I'll do that," but I was very disappointed
that I had to. I would have loved to stay. I kept saying to my husband, "I wanted to stay so badly," and I would see this look of hurt
cross his face. So finally, I stopped saying that because there's no
way he could understand that there was nothing *personal* in this at
all! And for weeks, I would have gone back any moment. And then,
gradually, happily, that feeling leaves. You become more a part of
this world. For years I would have gone back almost any moment.
Now I'm so entrenched here, I'm willing to wait my turn. I mean, I
really like it, I'm having a good time!

These, then, are some of the common feelings and experiences
NDErs have upon coming back and a sampling of some of the typical reactions their "stories" elicit. Obviously, many experiencers do
have a difficult time adjusting to "ordinary life" again, especially in
the first year following their experience. But, as Jayne's example
shows, either through sympathetic understanding from a significant
other or merely the passage of enough time, NDErs can and, it
appears, usually do come to terms with their experience and are
able to integrate it into their daily life. Of course, some do not and
remain in a state of longing to return—but they are the exceptions.

In any event, coming back is obviously a necessary first step, and how it is handled by both the NDEr and those persons close to him or her (not excluding, of course, health-care and religious professionals) may very well influence the form *and* the timing of the transformative process that the NDE sets into motion.

Personality Changes Following NDEs

In the previous chapter, Ann mentioned in her letter that her NDE brought about a total change in her personality. In this avowal Ann is hardly unique among NDErs. My files are dense with similar testimony from other NDErs. Just to take one case with which we are already familiar, Mr. Dippong has written:

Although this event occurred a long time ago, it marked a very crucial point in my life. I began a new chapter; a chapter which was to continue for the rest of my life. This moment and the following minutes and hours changed my life entirely. I was transformed from a man who was lost and wandering aimlessly, with no goal in life other than a desire for material wealth, to someone who had a deep motivation, a purpose in life, a definite direction, and an overpowering conviction that there would be a reward at the end of life similar to the pot of gold at the end of the rainbow. . . . The changes in my life were completely positive. My interest in material wealth and greed for possessions were replaced by a thirst for spiritual understanding and a passionate desire to see world conditions improve.

Letters from correspondents[1] unknown to me personally support the results of my interview data.

From a woman who attempted suicide in 1977:

I can't tell you what happened to me because I don't know, but something happened as I've never been the same since. People describe me as being "high on life." And they are right. I'm thankful for every new day God gives me and I never take one minute of my day for granted. I wish I could explain how very much that one experience changed me, but I just can't find the words to express myself. But I'm sure of one thing: there is a peace that remains with me always now—it has the strangest calming effect on me.

From a recovered alcoholic who nearly died of liver failure, also in 1977:

I know I am an entirely different person. For someone who was so miserable and self destructive, I am more serene and calm and happy and live each 24 hours trying to do a little bit for mankind, if only a smile at an unhappy looking person.

As I have implied, there is abundant material of this kind in my files, but such self-reports have only suggestive value in the absence of other corroborative data. Even so, the consistency of such reports with additional findings I have gathered firsthand from both NDErs and those who know them well means that what these informal accounts suggest is representative of the personality changes I will later document from my own interviews and questionnaires.

Naturally, the purported changes in personality attributed by my respondents to their NDEs are often apparently specific and limited. For example, one that repeatedly cropped up in my interviews appears at first to reflect a change in self-assertiveness and extroversion. Here is a sampling of such statements just from the interview material I've collected. Bear in mind that these statements were made either spontaneously or in response to a general question—i.e., I was *not* specifically asking my respondents about either assertiveness or outgoingness or any other similar behavior.

I think I used to be a very superficial person, always breaking my butt to please or be accepted or to be liked. Now I just don't give a damn anymore. It's really a delicious feeling. . . .

I was easily intimidated. . . . I'm not like that anymore. . . . I can talk with anyone now. . . . I have more confidence in myself. . . .

[Before] I was insecure, always. . . . [Now] if somebody doesn't like me, I don't fret about it. . . . I [had] always been—believe it or not—shy and reserved and you could not get me up in front of any group of people to speak out. Well, I did a complete one-hundred-eighty-degree turn. . . .

Well, I know my whole personality changed. I was always very shy. I'd rather read a book than go to a party. Not that I became a partygoer, but I was much more active [afterward]. I joined more things and I went to classes. I did all kinds of things where before I would sit in the back of a room and not raise [my] hand until [I] had to. . . .

I have changed three hundred sixty degrees, from a very shy, introverted person to an extrovert. All the way out! I now talk in public. . . . I could never have made a speech in my life [before].

You're talking to an ex-stutterer, ex-whisperer, ex-stammerer. . . . [So you really had a basic personality change?] Oh, definitely. I'm aggressive now where I was very passive [before]. . . .

. . . before I could not talk to anyone. Maybe if there were three people in the room I didn't know—you couldn't hear my voice if you were sitting next to me. . . . [Now] if a person is the longest way [off] in the largest room, [he or she] can still hear and understand what I am saying. I have talked [to many large groups] and but for this experience I would not have been able to participate in that at all.

What is the source of such changes? One doesn't have to be a psychologist to suspect that these qualities are not so "specific and limited" as they may seem but are a surface expression of a deeper, much more basic personality orientation. If you think about it for a moment, you can appreciate that people can behave in these ways because they have a strong sense of self-confidence. Someone who has confidence in and likes himself or herself doesn't need to remain shy or care what others think of him or her. And if you were to examine the transcripts of the interviews I've done for this study, you'd see that this is precisely the case with NDErs. When I asked them to address the question of how they now felt about themselves, their remarks would usually refer to their greater feelings of self-acceptance, self-confidence, self-worth, and so on.

In short, one of the strongest findings of this research with respect to personality changes is that after their experience, *NDErs like themselves more.*

This conclusion not only is supported by my interview data but also is overwhelmingly seconded by NDErs' questionnaire responses. In an item on one of my questionnaires—the life changes questionnaire (see Appendix II), which we will be discussing at length later in the next chapter—respondents are asked to indicate if there was any change in their feelings of self-worth following their NDE. Thirteen persons said it had strongly increased, an additional nine said it had increased, and only two respondents reported that it had declined (two others reported no change). Despite the small size and nonrepresentativeness of the sample, the trend seems clear enough. Further research is desirable to secure this finding, of course, but the magnitude of its effect here suggests to me that this conclusion is very likely to stand up. Supposing at least for the time being that it does, we can push the analysis of these personality changes to a still deeper level. If it is true that NDErs afterward manifest a greater degree of self-worth (or self-acceptance), why is that? From what we have so far seen, it doesn't appear likely that it is a simple reflection of the esteem they receive from others. Indeed, on the basis both of findings already presented and those to come, it would appear that, if anything, NDErs are *less* responsive to the opinions of others after their experience. Again, whence does this increased self-acceptance arise?

One possibility I'd like to advance—though for several reasons that will soon be evident, this interpretation does not lend itself easily to empirical verification—is based on the NDE itself, particularly the encounter with the light. Recall what is experienced in the presence of the light: total love and unconditional acceptance. If the light, and possibly the general ambiance of the NDE as a whole, can confer such a complete sense of loving acceptance on the individual and if, as I've already suggested, something of the light's energies are directly absorbed by the NDEr, is it not reasonable to suppose that the individual would emerge from this experience with a definite feeling of worthiness? Or for those who would feel comfortable

with religious phraseology: If one has felt experientially the truth of
the maxim "God loves you," could he fail to love himself?

Though, strictly speaking, this argument may be untestable scientifically, there certainly are some NDErs who would endorse it.
Consider, for example, Nel's testimony on this point. Of her encounter with the light, she has written:

. . . it was accepting; it was forgiving; it was completely nonjudg-
mental; and it gave me a sense of total security the likes of which I
had never known. I loved it. It was perfection; it was total, unconditional love. . . .

And, regarding the effect of this experience on her sense of herself,
she has said:

This is probably the greatest lesson that I have learned for myself,
after a difficult life-long struggle. I have learned to accept myself as I
am. If the Light and the presence could accept me with all my
weaknesses and my faults, then I must be an OK person.

There is still another way of grasping the meaning of this overall
change. When we turn from isolated, if similar, fragments of many
NDErs (the method of this chapter so far) to an in-depth examination of a few instructive cases, we see from another perspective why
we would expect these changes to occur. It is not merely that one is
better able to accept himself or herself. It is, rather, that one dis-
covers just *who* one is and thereby reclaims one's true identity. It is
thus a new self, not the old personality, that elicits an increase in
self-esteem. Just how this happens will be illustrated in the case
histories that follow.

Changes in Self-Concept and Personal Identity: Three Case Histories

The individuals whose stories will be told here are all persons I
know well. I have spent a significant amount of time with each of
them—three or more occasions—and all have visited the Near-
Death Hotel at least twice. In addition to our face-to-face contact,

there have been many long telephone conversations between us, abundant correspondence, and audio tapes. I feel a deep sense of friendship with each of them, and know it is reciprocated.

I make no claim here that the personal development each of them has undergone since his or her NDE is "typical" or "representative" of NDErs in general. Indeed, in some ways it is apparent that each case has idiosyncracies. In one sense, these cases are presented here simply because I have had the opportunity to study them in greater depth than most others. In another sense, however, I am convinced that, quite apart from their special individual features, these episodes offer us a deep insight into the *process* that leads an NDEr to adopt or return to a mode of being truly consonant with his essence as a person. It is in this sense—rather than with respect to the "content" of the personal transformations—that these cases appear to be especially illuminating and that their internal dynamics may prove to be true of NDErs in general.

We have met each of these people in earlier chapters. One woman is Barbara Harris; the other I have called Stella. The man is Tom Sawyer. We will begin with Barbara.

Barbara

Barbara was also one of those people (though her own case wasn't cited in this connection) who before her NDE lived to please others. She was raised in the upper Midwest, the daughter of middle-class Jewish parents; she married young to a successful businessman and in short order produced three children. Her life, as she describes it, was by and large devoted to her family and to the maintenance of its comfortable, bougeois style with its attendant values and patterns of sociability.

As a result of an accident in the mid-seventies, when she was in her early thirties, she suffered serious injuries to her back, and in 1975 she underwent a spinal fusion operation to correct her problem. It was after that operation, while she was still recovering in the hospital, that she had her NDE.

Barbara has told me that when, much later, she heard of my earlier work on NDEs where I had used the term "core experience" to denote what I've here called simply the NDE, she immediately related to that expression. To think of her episode in the hospital—for which she had had no label or framework—as a "core experience" made a great deal of sense to her for reasons you will soon be able to understand, for what her NDE did for her was to strip away the layers of a false self she had been maintaining ever since childhood and to reveal what was, to her, her core personality.

To appreciate the significance of Barbara's experience during her NDE, you will need to be aware of one fact in particular: When Barbara was a child, her parents would punish her quite severely whenever she wet her bed. It appears that she carried, but was not conscious of, the psychological scars of this treatment for many years. Then when she was recovering in the hospital in a circle bed,[2] completely unable to take care of her own needs and still critically ill, she felt herself again to be like a child. One day, when she was left unattended for a time, she found that she had to urinate and, under the circumstances, was forced to wet her bed. Shortly thereafter, she had her NDE. For her, its cardinal and ultimately transformative feature (but far from its only one, of course) was the life review she experienced. She describes it as follows:

At that point, I left . . . it's not clear to me which happened when, but I went back into the tunnel and I really wanted to die. . . . And I saw myself in bed, crying, the way I had just left myself, only I was a little child. And my mother was there and my father was there. . . . This was such an intense experience, it was like I was there again. Everything was clearly the way it was when I was that small child. I was that child again. If there were any aromas, I was picking up aromas. I was picking up all the physical sensations of my mother hitting me again, yet at the same time, besides my feelings, I understood *her* feelings and I understood my father in the hallway . . . I was saying "no wonder." No wonder you are the way you are, you know? Lookit what's being done to you at such a young age. I mean, I look at my kids now and I think if I'd done that to them every night how would they feel? You know, I could see it from all angles now as an adult but at the same time I was experiencing it at maybe the age of four or five. And it was the kind of a thing that I knew where my dad was coming from. I knew all the connections. That was it. I could feel our connectedness in this scene.

And then it was like I moved through, on to where I am now. . . . I don't want to give the idea that this was linear, because it wasn't linear. It was almost like that might have been the focal point and then things would branch out in every direction[3] and I was getting different connections with different people. It was like I was understanding how insecure I was and how inferior I felt because nobody had put their arms around me and given me a sense of value. Now this was my adult, my real adult observer. Then I was able to see my whole life unwinding from that perspective of this poor, neurotic little girl who was, you know, not really coming from the same place all the other little kids were coming from. I was a very, very lonely child. I was watching this whole childhood unfold and realizing that my head was in the wrong place and I was able to refocus so that I had a better understanding of all the rejection I had felt. All that rejection was in my own head. It wasn't everybody else rejecting me. Everyone else was just coming from their own problems and hangups. All of that stuff that had been layered on me was because my vision of what was going on was really screwed up. [So it was like a corrective review of your life?] Yeah. It was like the most healing therapy there could be. . . . Years and years of intense psychoanalysis of the most intense type of external therapy could not have brought me through what I was experiencing rapidly. I was forgiving myself for not always being good. I was forgiving myself for being as neurotic as I had been. [And I felt] a great deal of forgiveness and compassion for people that I thought were being mean to me. There was just a great deal of understanding that we had formed a bad pattern because of my defensiveness in my entire life and I had put them into the mold they were in of treating me the way I thought they were treating me to the point where I actualized that treatment. And I could understand their beauties and their qualities. And it was like all the slates were being wiped clean. . . . It was the kind of a thing where I just wasn't the victim anymore; we had all been victims . . . the structure was becoming stronger and stronger of us victimizing each other and it seemed like I was able to just very objectively observe it . . . we were just establishing more and more walls. And I was able to just understand everything that was going on.

[Did you actually see these scenes like images, or were you just aware of this?] OK. This is very, very hard to explain . . . what I was really sensing was that I had layers and layers and layers of this stuff. Like the domino effect, the sudden realization from the beginning was just going through and everything was shifting. Like each electron was jumping into another orbit. It was like a healing. It was going right through me. And I was sensing this entire evolvement of my lifetime through my feelings and, wherever I wanted to, I could sort of zoom in on different huge events in my life maybe I felt were good or bad—but there was no good or bad, just me reexperiencing stuff. . . .

The whole overall effect was that I had relived my life with a much healthier attitude that had healed me. And by the time I got to the end I had the first sense of wanting to live, of wanting to turn around and struggle again in that bed.

Later reflecting on what this experience had taught her, Barbara commented:

I was acting. My whole life I was acting because I always had the feeling that if people found out who I really was they wouldn't like me, that I was really very bad. I had walked around for thirty-one years hiding the fact that I was bad. Every time I got spanked, I felt I was bad. And the few times something good happened to me, I was aware, "Well, they don't know the real you." So up until that point in my life it was an act, an act to be good so people would know that I was a good person and if I could win everybody over, then I would finally like myself.

But when I came back from that [her NDE], I really understood. I had a real feeling of understanding that I was a good person and all I had to do was be me. . . . It was a feeling all of a sudden that if people would get to know the real me . . . that they would have to like me. [And you really did experience the real you in this state, it seems.] Yeah. I knew at that point that I had met myself.

. . . Without sounding corny, that was the most important incident of my thirty-nine years and the rebirth of who I am now. That was really being born again. I can vividly go back to who I was before that time; I can put myself into that mental state . . . but it's a totally different human being than I am now. If I still had to be that other Barbara, I wouldn't want to be walking around. I would probably find something else that hurt just as badly as my back and I would probably have a tremendous need for all the pain medication and/or drinking and/or pot and/or something to fill that emptiness that was so much a part of me. That experience made me whole and that experience wiped away all the scars that I collected and that experience gave me all the tools to struggle through these seven years and get to the feeling now that I'm always here. You know, it took me a long time to recapture that person because everybody around me, I felt, was restricting me from becoming that person because of who they were. So the experience itself gave me the spirituality that I need and the tools that I needed to be who I am now.

The reasons why Barbara is now able to accept herself as she is are of course evident from her own comments, but referring back to my own speculation on this effect (see page 102), it is noteworthy that Barbara also mentioned this:

[In that experience] I sensed something so strongly that I just came back knowing there was a God. And it wasn't God like I had ever pictured God. When I was a little girl, I held strongly to the-old-man-with-a-beard-concept. . . . I saw *nobody* . . . yet I would stake everything I have and wish that I could prove that there was something with me that was just wonderful. It was an all-encompassing energy. Even if everything I saw would have made me out to be evil, it would have been OK. Whatever this was that was with me just loved me the way I was.

We would need a full chapter to begin to do justice to the changes that have occurred in Barbara's life and in her personal character since her NDE. Although we will return later in this book to consider more of them, suffice it to say here that Barbara is now a bubbly, vivacious, extremely loving woman with enormous energy and infectious enthusiasm. She shows all the characteristic value and behavioral changes of NDErs that we will be examining in the next chapter. In her case we have her husband's statement that her self-reports (and my own impressions of her) are accurate. Although one needs to be with Barbara really to appreciate her zest and sparkle, her own words convey at least partially a bit of the contrast between her pre-NDE life and her life today:

Before love was important to me, but not the kind of love I understand now. Oh, I liked materialism and I went after it, but my values before were a lovely home and the community where I felt status . . . and to be accepted. I never felt accepted. I never felt like I was like everybody else. I felt that I was different and I didn't want to be different. I wanted to be normal. . . . I didn't want to be crazy. . . . Those were the things that I was trying to grab ahold of. A sense of being loved, and a sense of being sane, and a sense of being normal.

Now my values are in my smile! . . . My whole *being* is transformed. I don't feel time like I felt time before. . . . My [life] is one of calmness, and love, and that's what I'm really all about. . . . The true value of existence is the connectedness that you have going with every other *living* thing. . . . Everything that happens to me now is a sense of awe. . . . What everyone talks about heaven being, is right here and now. You just have to open up and see what's really going on.

On the basis mainly of her own testimony, it certainly appears that in Barbara's case, her transformation was set into motion by the torrent of insights her life review unleashed. If we can trust her words, a lifelong process of conditioning was undone in a moment, and in that moment Barbara was able to reconnect with the essence of her self as it was reflected in her childhood personality before she internalized her parents' view of her and constructed a false self-concept around it. From our subsequent conversations, at least, it is clear that Barbara's own understanding is that she has now been able to evolve into the adult person she would have developed into had not her parents' conditioning detoured her onto another track.

In short, her NDE put her on track again, and when she experienced it she knew, as she herself put it, that she had met her true self.

Under the circumstances, it is obvious why Barbara regards her NDE as a healing—a making whole—that years of conventional psychotherapy could not have produced. In fact, however, some forms of radical psychotherapy[4] *can* bring about similar profound transformations and sometimes very quickly. Barbara's own case—stripped of its NDE context—might well serve to illustrate some of the powerful insights that such intense psychotherapeutic procedures may trigger in patients. Indeed, from a psychodynamic point of view, there is nothing in Barbara's transformation that cannot be accounted for by basic psychological principles known to every psychotherapist.

In the next case we are going to examine, however, something more than conventional "basic psychological principles" are required to understand the peculiar chain of circumstances that led to a self-transformation no one could have foreseen.

Stella

Stella's story, as she related it to me, proved to be one of the most remarkable episodes I've ever encountered in my research into near-death experiences over the past six years. Although in Stella's case I have so far only her own word that her account is truthful, I have found no reason to doubt it in any respect. In any event, it is one of the most thorough and improbable personal transformations following an NDE in my files.

I'll let her describe her family background, which turns out to be crucial for what follows:

I was adopted when I was nine months old and I grew up [in the Deep South] in a fundamentalist background. My grandfather was a Baptist minister. I grew up in the Nazarene church, very restricted, very narrow. I did exactly what I was told to do. I didn't do any of the "don'ts." I thought that surely hell would open up immediately and swallow me if I did. Extremely fearful, controlled totally by other people. Never allowed my own thoughts or ideas. Just "this is the way it is" and never even to express your own feelings or anything . . . Never any self-expression; never knew there was any such thing.

When she was eight, she was told by a playmate at school that she had been adopted. Stunned and disbelieving, she—for the first time in her young life, she now attests—disobeyed the rules and rushed home to find out the truth from her mother. The latter, herself shocked to find her hysterical child at home in the middle of the day, finally admitted to Stella that she had been adopted but refused to tell her anything about her biological parents.

Like Barbara, Stella grew up continuing to conform closely to the values of her family and community. She also married young, had five children, and, as she now admits, played out the role of the "ideal wife." She chauffeured her kids around, became dutifully involved in a variety of community activities, and subordinated herself to her husband. As to her marriage, she described herself as "obsequious" and also happened to mention to me on the occasion of our first meeting that she was so shy and retiring that she even had difficulty writing a thank-you note.

Not long before her NDE in June 1977, she had what seems best understood as a waking vision. It occurred one night while she was in bed but before she had gone to sleep. In this vision she saw a series of written characters. She did not recognize them but could see them so clearly and distinctly that she was able to copy them down. She has told me that much later—after her NDE—she discovered that the characters were Hebrew and, translated into English, they constituted a phrase that could be rendered "Beyond the Vanishing Point."

During her NDE itself she, too, encountered a being of light at one point. This is her description of him:

Almost as though two faces in one. One with the beauty and the peace and the light that was in that place in the face and yet, somehow contained in the same face the form had been beaten. It almost looks like one side [was] out of shape. One totally peaceful and yet one with the pain of the other. [Did this being communicate anything to you?] Yes . . . [that] there was a purpose to my being sent back here and the purpose had to do with bringing knowledge, particular knowledge. One, of the experience and that there is life after this on a much greater level. . . . We're so much more. That we have the ability and capacity to know . . . [Did you have any sense of the identity of this being?] I don't attempt to make any identification for anyone else. [Inwardly, what do you think?] I feel very strongly that he, too, had a purpose. Whatever his purpose was is not totally clear to me, but it also was to bring a knowledge, an understanding to mankind. . . .

In an earlier portion of her transcript that I have not quoted here, Stella also mentioned that the feet of this being appeared to have suffered wounds. Remember that Stella was raised in a fundamentalist tradition, and yet she still is reluctant to identify the being she saw as Christ.[5]

At this juncture, however, Stella's story takes a most unexpected turn. While communicating telepathically with the being of light, she was told that she was Jewish! As she put it,

You ready for this? He told me. [How was this communicated to you?] This was part of what I needed to do, part of a process to be able to do what I will ultimately come to do. This was something that was a blockage that I didn't know anything about. But it definitely was a key to understanding. It has great meaning to me. There wasn't anybody who could have told me that.

Last year she finally

. . . started a search on my own without my family knowing about it to find my biological heritage that I found out didn't exist on paper. It was just gone, I didn't exist, period. . . .

Her leads took her to her birthplace, but she was unable to discover any further information. Despondent, she took a walk on a nearby beach.

I walked up and down the beach and said, "OK, I'm trying to do what you said to do and it can't be done by what I'd consider to be normal means. The paperwork's not there, so if this is what you want done, you're going to have to help." And I went back [to town] and sat down in the restaurant there that night and was trying to think of another way I could go about this and two policemen walked by the table and I thought, "I bet there's a clue" [laughs].

One of them had forgotten something and had to return to the table where he had been sitting. Stella seized the opportunity to tell him that there was somebody she was trying to find and solicited his help. The policeman put her in touch with a couple who had run a local newspaper for many years and they, in turn, directed her to a now-retired judge who had been a resident of the town for a long time. When Stella met him [the judge] was taken aback. "It was like turning back the clock when he saw my face. . . . [He] took one look at me and, after, he put me in touch with my grandfather, who had retired and moved down to Florida."

She goes on to describe a very dramatic meeting with her grandfather in which he showed her the family album and other memorabilia and confirmed for her *another* fact that had been conveyed to her by the being of light—that she did indeed have a brother. She subsequently spent some time with him and his family in Texas as well. She was also finally able to meet briefly with her own biological mother, but that visit, unfortunately, was not pleasant. Her mother was still not interested in Stella and had no wish to establish any kind of relationship with her.

Despite its emotional tone and the personal rejection Stella felt, that meeting was extremely important to her. She says that it "removed a tremendous emotional blockage" and it facilitated the already accelerating process of Stella's awakening to a full realization of her own authentic identity—first suggested to her by the being of light.

Since that time there have been many changes in her life. Not only has she formally converted to Judaism (which proved quite a shock to her fundamentalist family) and divorced her husband, but also this formerly shy and "obsequious" woman has become a successful businesswoman, has served on the White House Council on Children and Youth, and has become actively involved in local politics. She has a special interest in the problems of adopted children and she, who formerly cringed at having to write a thank-you note, is now writing a book on the problems of adopted children. That is just *one* of the books she is working on. Another is an autobiographical memoir featuring her NDE and the developments to which it led. She's planning to entitle it, *Beyond the Vanishing Point*.

It would be a mistake to conclude from this brief account of Stella's life since her NDE that it has been one never-ending series of improbable successes and emotional highs. Although there have been these, there have also been setbacks and moments of despair. She still encounters a great deal of resistance from her family and friends to her new mode of life, and the transition, though she is grateful for it, hasn't been easy.

But at least, she says, she is now finally free—as Barbara also became free—to be who she truly is:

My life is totally different now. I realize now why it [her earlier life] was so restricted. I didn't do my own thinking. I never came to those points. I realized as I went through this process last year of finding my biological family that somehow implanted in that nine-month-old child was the knowledge that my biological mother had rejected me and that if I didn't adhere to all these rules, regulations, requirements—whatever—somehow it had been my doing—as a child would think. It has to be me, something I've done, to be this totally rejected. And it set up a barrier that I didn't know, didn't understand, and yet a very definite wall that kept me from going past anything that was required of me in order to not be rejected in that way again. And I was going through this process last year, I began to realize that, I began to see those challenges set up all over the place. . . .

Now I stand toe-to-toe and say, "Reject me, if you will." I have the same power over you. And now, you see, they don't control me that way anymore.

Tom

We come, finally, to the case history of my friend Tom Sawyer, whose core experience was presented in some detail in the previous chapter. I mentioned some pertinent facts about how we met and our subsequent relationship but also indicated that there was much more to say about Tom. We've now reached the point where the remarkable aftereffects of his NDE can be related. As you will see, his personal development has been quite different from those of the foregoing cases, but Stella's encounter with the being of light has prepared us for at least some aspects of it.

Before tracing Tom's development since his NDE, I have to emphasize again that I now know both Tom and his family quite well, as do Norma and various members of our own IANDS family. This is important to mention here because of some of the highly unusual features of his case I will soon have cause to describe. Therefore, I want to make it clear that all of us who know Tom are absolutely convinced from our own direct contact with him that the events he has related to us are substantively accurate. In some cases they have been directly confirmed by his family; in other instances his conversations, tapes, and writings are consistent with his claims. Even his wife, in one of her letters to me, made the point that "the one thing that Tom has always been is completely honest." In addition, I have the medical documentation of his NDE-inducing accident in my files.

As with the preceding cases, to appreciate what has happened to Tom since his NDE you have to know what he was like before. From what Tom himself and his wife (a childhood sweetheart) have told me, the following pre-NDE portrait emerges.

In high school, Tom was an undistinguished student with an avid distaste for reading. In fact, he claims never to have finished a single book during his high school career. His chief avocations during this time seem to have been driving cars at excessive speeds (he received many speeding tickets) and bicycle racing. In his youth, Tom was a superior athlete and competed in the 1968 Olympics trials as a cyclist but was eliminated when his bicycle had a flat tire. After nearly a year of arduous training, his failure to make the Olympics team was the major frustrating experience of his life to date.

After graduation from high school, Tom worked at first as a garbageman and, seemingly always more a "hands" than a "head" person, then as a carpenter for some years before being employed in his present occupation as a driver of heavy equipment, mainly bull-dozers, for the city in which he now lives. All his adult life Tom has worked as a laborer.

Like the others we have considered, Tom married young; he also became the father of two boys.

In 1978 he had his NDE—and that marked the great turning point in Tom's life and mind.

If you review Tom's core experience (see pages 57–59) you will see that he was one of those NDErs who claimed to be in touch "with absolute, total knowledge." He also claims he asked many questions in this state and received instantaneous answers to all of them, even on matters where he asserts he had virtually no back-ground.

One morning not long after his recovery from his NDE, Tom awoke next to his wife in bed and blurted out the word "quantum."

"What?" his wife asked.
"Quantum," repeated Tom. "Quantum."
"Tom, what in the world are you talking about?"
"I don't know," said Tom, as if to himself.[6]

Neither Tom nor his wife knew what the word meant.

Two weeks later, Tom and his wife were watching television one afternoon. Suddenly Tom was heard to say: "Max Planck—you'll be hearing about him in the near future."

Again, his wife responded with perplexity, wanting to know what *that* was supposed to mean.

Tom, however, was as much in the dark as she was.

By now, Tom reports, he was beginning to become aware dur-ing the day of what seemed to be fragments of equations and mathe-matical symbols. One of them, of which Tom sent me the original sketches, was the Greek letter psi (Ψ), a symbol widely used in psychology, parapsychology, and physics and that often denotes "the unknown." Tom, however, was not familiar with the symbol and asked a friend to try to discover its meaning. When the friend later told him that it was the Greek symbol for the number "700,"[7] that did not make sense to Tom, and he remained puzzled by it. When I saw his sketches, it was apparent to me what he was attempting to depict, and I explained its significance to him. That clicked.

At about this same time, Tom says, various brief passages that appear in books—although Tom didn't necessarily experience them as book quotations—would also come into his mind. One of the passages that presented itself to him at this time Tom later showed to me. It seemed familiar to me and, sure enough, it turned out to be from Max Planck's *Scientific Autobiography,* a book of which Tom claimed never to have heard, much less read.[8]

Things now took a dramatic—and yet often amusing—turn.

As Tom tells it, he became so perplexed and intrigued with these occurrences that, unaccustomed to libraries though he was, he nevertheless took himself to one. The following account of the events and conversations that took place there are, to the best of Tom's memory, accurate.

Tom approached the reference librarian and said tentatively, "Quantum? Quantum, like in quantum energy. Is there such a thing?"

The librarian hesitated just a moment and then replied, somewhat doubtfully, "Well, we have many books on physics in our science section. Why don't you try there?"

When Tom had found his way to the appropriate place, he still didn't know which books to select and, never an avid reader, tried a shortcut. He espied a man standing nearby who appeared, to use Tom's words, "like he was college-educated." Tom went up to him and said:

"Excuse me, sir, but I wonder if you could help me. I want to learn what the quantum theory is and I only have a high school education."

Taken aback, the man warned Tom: "Well, I'm afraid, young man, that what you've done is to pick a subject that requires a college education just to understand it." Nevertheless, he did direct Tom to a few books he thought would provide some introductory material.

As Tom leafed through one of these books, he happened to stumble across the passage "Max Planck, the father of quantum theory."

Click!

As Tom read on—eagerly, for once—things rapidly fell into place. The various fragments of knowledge he had been receiving ever since his experience with the light were obviously all connected. They all related to quantum physics, a subject Tom had absolutely no prior knowledge of or interest in.

That day in the library marked a critical stage in Tom's personal development. He now began to read—and finish—books. Books on physics that, despite their unfamiliar jargon and concepts, he seemed to understand intuitively.

He would come across these books in curious ways. Once, for example, he was in a bookstore to purchase a book for one of his boys whose birthday was upcoming. When he went to the counter to buy the book, he noticed that directly *under* it was a book on physics. Tom told me he had no idea how it had gotten there, but seeing that it was and by now being used to peculiar events in his life, he felt he had no choice but to buy it, and he did.

Tom eventually decided he would have to enroll in college if he was to learn more and deepen his knowledge of physics (and mathematics). The story of his initial meeting with the professor who was to be his adviser is worth retelling, not only because it is amusing but also because it somehow symbolizes the astonishing synchronistic[9] pattern that was dominating Tom's life at this time.

As Tom explained his interest in (if not his full reasons for) pursuing his education by taking up the study of physics, the professor listened carefully, if perhaps a bit incredulously. At the end of their conversation he made out a list of four books on physics he felt Tom ought to read at the outset of his studies.

Naturally, they turned out to be exactly the four books—and the *only* four books—that Tom had already read!

When he saw the list, Tom turned to the professor and said dryly with an air of mock-nonchalance, "Oh, I've already read these. Is that OK?"

Not long afterward, I received a letter from Tom's son, Todd. It read in part:

My dad's name is Tom Sawyer who I'm sure you know; he is starting to talk more like Einstein with more letters than words. Some of the stuff is boring but some is interesting. . . . P.S. My dad is doing good in school.

Comments from his wife's letters from about the same time paint a similar picture:

Many times he says a word he has never heard before in our reality—it might be a foreign word of a different language—but learns . . . it in relationship to the "light" theory. . . . He talks about things faster than the speed of light and it's hard for me to understand . . . when Tom picks up a book on physics he already knows the answer and seems to feel more. . . .

Since these letters were written, Tom has continued his studies, though for the most part without the dramatic results that characterized his beginning ventures. He also spends a lot of time reading on his own now and not just books on physics, but also studies in parapsychology, metaphysics, and higher consciousness. His psychic abilities, too, seem to have expanded enormously since his NDE, as have—he avers with great earnestness—his sensitivities to nuclear reactors and sites where radioactivity may be unusually high or where chemical technology is possibly being used for classified purposes. In addition, Tom sometimes discourses impressively on topics that would seem to be very far afield from his pre-NDE range of knowledge—e.g., religious teachings, ancient history, and cosmology. Much of what he has shared with us in these informal conversations derives, he says, not so much from his reading as from his contact with "the light" itself which, as he understands it, is the fount of universal knowledge.

In his own city, Tom has by now become something of a local celebrity. He has appeared several times on television there, is in demand as a speaker, and is beginning to be sought out by various individuals who sense in him a kind of power or knowledge—or simply an incredible capacity for love and compassion—that they feel they want to draw on.

Throughout all of this, Tom seems to have retained his boyish good humor and modesty; in the years I've known him at least, I have not detected any major change in his personality. He still works for the city and, although his peers find it odd that he now totes around books by the likes of such luminaries as Heisenberg, Einstein, and Bohr and sometimes "razz" him about his television appearances, he still seems to be esteemed by them as much for his muscles and proclivities to horse around good-naturedly on the job as for his mind. Tom remains married and devoted to his wife and family, even though, in common with the families of other NDErs, his wife and children are sometimes puzzled or even disturbed by the new identity and knowledge Tom acquired through the core experience.

It will be interesting to follow the course of Tom's continuing development over the next few years. In the meantime, however, it seems safe to say that this unusual young man is certainly worthy in his own right of the name that his fictional counterpart made famous.

Conclusions

In this chapter, we've seen how the NDE not only changes an individual's life but often completely and radically transforms it. On the basis of the research reported here, it seems that what the NDE does, at least in some cases, enables the individual to come into a new and more authentic sense of self as well as to help actualize inner potentials to a sometimes astonishing degree. It would appear justified—again in some, surely not all, instances—to claim that NDEs tend to confer a new personal identity upon the NDEr as well as bring about major changes in behavior.

That, of course, is by no means all that NDEs do to alter an individual's life. One of the most important kinds of changes they induce—and one that is inseparable from the personality transformations we've considered here—is changes in *values*. Even in this chapter we have occasionally had to allude to some of these changes. In the next chapter, however, we will concern ourselves with this issue. These findings will give us an even clearer idea of the full scope of the personality transformations undergone by NDErs and will illustrate the inextricable bond between the core NDE and its aftereffects.

CHAPTER 5

· · · · · · ·

Value Changes Induced by NDEs

÷

Early in Chapter 3 I enunciated "the spiritual catalyst" hypothesis for NDEs, which states that NDEs at their core *are* deep spiritual experiences that tend to accelerate one's spiritual development. This hypothesis provides the overall framework for the interpretive line that will be taken in this book, but the hypothesis itself is not without its ambiguities. For instance, although the spiritual nature of the NDE was exhaustively illustrated in Chapter 3, one may still ask just what constitutes evidence of spiritual development. In my view, there are several distinct types of criteria that are relevant to a comprehensive answer to this question, and each of the next three chapters addresses a different dimension of the spiritual growth reported by-NDErs. In this chapter, the *value changes* that tend to follow upon NDEs will be treated in detail.

Surely, if NDEs do trigger spiritual development, it would seem reasonable that NDErs ought to embrace more spiritual values following their experience. But what would such values be?

Here the teachings of the world's great religions and spiritual traditions will obviously guide our inquiry at the outset. Despite diversity in their specific beliefs and practices, there tends to be an impressive commonality among them in their moral and social injunctions. For instance, most religions and spiritual traditions emphasize such values as love and compassion for others; lack of concern for self; honoring the spiritual dimension of life at the expense of the material; and striving to know and to love God. Values, of course, are simply statements of what matters, and the aforemen-

121 . . .

tioned concerns are certainly high on the list of what matters most from a general religious or spiritual perspective.

If our hypothesis is correct, we should expect to see value shifts by NDErs in the direction of the values I've just mentioned and toward similar values as well. Moreover, the predicted shift should cover a spectrum of such values and not be limited to one or two.

To evaluate this hypothesis, we will examine simple quantitative data presented in a series of easy-to-read graphs. In order not to clutter the text with statistical tables and charts, however, all the quantitative material for this book is in Appendix III. Those of you, like myself, who dote on such statistical information will find it convenient to consult this appendix in conjunction with this and the next three chapters. If, on the other hand, you would rather skim or skip the numbers and rely on the text for your understanding, you may rest easy because my findings will always be illustrated by ample qualitative material designed to bring out the value changes under consideration. Thus, by quoting directly my respondents and correspondents once again here, we will be able to appreciate more readily the personal meaning of the value changes reported.

In this and the next three chapters, then, we will have this mix of statistical and individual data to give a rounded picture of our general findings. In each of these same chapters we will rely primarily, if not exclusively, on one questionnaire specifically constructed to obtain the necessary information to evaluate a different aspect of the spiritual catalyst hypothesis. In this chapter we will be referring repeatedly to the "Life Changes Questionnaire," or LCQ, which is reproduced in full in Appendix II. You might wish to glance through this questionnaire before reading further, though the following brief comments should prove sufficient to understand the findings that will be presented.

The LCQ is a simple forty-two-item test that asks an NDEr to indicate whether he or she has experienced any change in a variety of personal domains since his or her NDE. Some sample domains are:

1. Tolerance for others
2. Religious feelings
3. Ability to express love openly
4. Desire for solitude

Respondents are asked to select one of five possible alternatives for each item: strongly increase (SI), increase somewhat (I), no change (NC), decrease somewhat (D), or strongly decrease (SD).

A total of twenty-six NDErs completed the LCQ, and statistical information based on this sample will be summarized in Appendix III in the various graphs for this chapter.[1] It needs to be emphasized, however, that the LCQ is not the only source of data here. Illustrative data for the trends charted in the graphs will be taken from our sample of forty-two interviewees (of whom eighteen also completed the LCQ) and our sample of sixty-two correspondents. Thus the total number of NDErs who furnished data for this chapter is 111.[2]

Appreciation of Life

The first value shift revealed by the LCQ that we'll consider is one I've called "appreciation of life." It is comprised of a cluster of just two items (numbers 3 and 17 on the questionnaire), but as you can see by a quick glance at Figure 1, the trend is unmistakably clear[3] and almost identical for the two separate items, one having to do with appreciation of "the ordinary things of life" and the other with appreciation of nature. Both of these items show a pronounced increase in appreciation following NDEs. The comments quoted below from Omega NDErs will give a qualitative feel of this value orientation.

From a correspondent:

This experience has really changed me and my whole attitude toward life. . . . I appreciate the beauty of this life. . . .

And from another:

I have a fierce desire to live every wonderful moment of as many days as I can manage to be gifted with. . . . My life is unquestionably even richer than before for having had the near-death experience. . . .

From an interviewee:

[After I came back] I was very, very happy, filled with some tremendous energy. The wonder of everything about me. I loved everyone and everything. . . . People were beautiful. This time we have—make the best of it. Don't waste it!

Patrick, another interviewee, whose NDE was used for illustrative purposes in Chapter 2, brings out an implicit facet of some of these comments—the importance of appreciating the moment:

. . . Another thing that it [his NDE] did for me was to give me the information that all you have to do to have a life of great interest . . . is simply to stay in the present moment. . . . If you stay there, you will live in eternity, I believe. I *know* this; this is not just a conjecture on my part. . . . I have never ever heard a boring person during all this time [since his recovery]. . . . That's one of the reasons why every day of my life now seems far better than every yesterday.

Harold, still another interviewee, whom we met in Chapter 3, emphasizes the increased appreciation of the *natural* world that many NDErs seem to feel:

After my release from the hospital I found that certain senses which I had paid no attention to were more alert and sharper. For example, the sky was so much more blue, a tree and its leaves were more green, everything was so very more beautiful. I could almost smell and taste the air and wind. I became cognizant of things which I had previously taken for granted. . . . The sunset sinking on a prairie, a lake in the wilderness in the early morn, a mountain range in the distance—anything of this nature stirs my soul.

Harold's reflections were hardly unique in my sample. Another interviewee commented:

I also learned to sit still [afterward]; to find a power in silence. . . . I learned to see the physical world in a new, highly detailed way. I noticed the changing colors of lichen on tree trunks, the shape and direction of the bark's twists. I sat by a pond and watched a reed blowing in the wind; watched the iridescently red or electrically blue damsel flies' flashing, dazzling flight. . . .

Is this kind of appreciation a spiritual value? Of course, in any individual case, this determination might be difficult to make, but in my judgment what many NDErs are implying often comes close to expressing not simply an appreciation of life but rather a reverence for life. There is, I think, for many NDErs a heightened sense of the preciousness of ordinary life, the beauty in human relationships and feelings, the awesomeness of nature. If you reread the foregoing quotations, I believe you will detect these more spiritual qualities.

The values reflected here are integrally related to those in the next section—which could be called "appreciation for others"—where the spiritual aspects of NDErs' orientation toward people will be clear.

Concern for Others

The next cluster of items on the LCQ centers on what is surely one of the key values of NDErs: their caring concern for and acceptance of others. In contrast to the last value cluster, this one is much more complex and involves eight items (numbers 1, 2, 4, 8, 14, 16, 22, and 39 in the questionnaire) dealing with the following aspects of concern for others: helping, compassion, patience, tolerance, love, insight, understanding, and acceptance. If you examine the trends in Figure 2, you'll see that there is a marked increase on each of these items following NDEs. The consistency and strength of this effect are certainly noteworthy and indicate that the NDE has a substantial effect on human relations.

To illustrate some of these features through recourse to our Omega sample is a problem, however, for two reasons. One has to do with the sheer massiveness of relevant material; one could almost quote at random from my stack of transcripts and letters and find comments covering most of these issues. The second problem relates to the form of the comments: Typically they do not refer to a single facet of human relationships (as do the separate LCQ items) but weave several of them together. Thus, if I were to try to illustrate individually each of the eight aspects distinguished by the LCQ items, I would be forced to do unacceptable violence to the integrity of a comment by stripping away the context in which it was embedded. Accordingly, I have deliberately chosen a number of observations here that individually may include reference to multiple features of this value orientation and that collectively will exemplify all of them.

Perhaps as representative as any single expression was this series of statements from one of my original respondents in *Life at Death*, a woman I'll call Celia. She was certainly one of the dearest and most loved of our friends and one Norma and I saw most often before Celia's death in 1982 of a heart attack. A year or so before she became ill, we sat outside her house on a warm, summery day while I tape-recorded her reflections on how her life had changed following her NDE. Much of what she had to say concerned her feelings for and relationships with others.

Now . . . I find that everyone I meet, I like. I *very* rarely meet someone I don't like. And that's because I accept them right away as someone I like. . . . I don't judge people. . . . And people respond to me in the same way and I think that they can *feel* this [in me]. . . . I'm a very demonstrative person in showing my feelings. [Have you always been?] No. I was with my children. . . . But since I had that experience, I kiss everyone I meet. It's just a natural thing, an expression of love. For me it is now, yes.

Celia had spent the last five years of her life working as a volunteer, mainly with dying people and their families, and was much sought after for this purpose. Concerning this aspect of her life, she said:

. . . Everything went into place and I just knew what I had to do. It was as simple as that. And I had this *urge*—and I don't know where it came from—but I *knew* that I *had* to help people who were terminally ill. I read articles that just sort of came to me . . . and I said, "That's it!" And it kept happening. And so it's been growing ever since. It's a nice feeling to work with them. You love them. I know sometimes when I go see someone, I go out of the room and I cry. I cry with them because you feel so bad, but you love them and you want to help them.

The themes Celia addresses here occur with astonishing frequency in the testimony of other Omega NDErs.

Another interviewee said:

My joy comes from another's smile. I also notice that I reach out and touch people more. . . . I seem to make people feel better. I know this—that when there's a family problem, everyone turns to me. . . . I have more insight into other people [now]. . . . It's very difficult for me to lose my temper anymore. I can see the pain in other people's eyes. That's why they hurt other people because they really don't understand. . . . The most important thing that we have are our relationships with other people. . . . It all comes down to caring and compassion and love for your fellow man. . . . *Love is the answer.* It's the answer to everything.

When I last talked with this woman, she was about to start working as a volunteer at a nearby hospice.

Again, many of these same features are echoed in the accounts of others. More evidence could be cited here of other NDErs claiming that they never (or rarely) lose their temper, that others with problems tend to seek them out, that they feel an inward desire to work with or for others in some capacity, and so on. But perhaps more than any other aspect, it is the feeling of love and compassion for others that seems to lie at (or in) the heart of many of the Omega NDErs in my sample. Here, for example, are some representative comments:

First, from Patrick again:

I think it's far easier just to want to love everybody than I ever loved before, that's for sure. . . .

From another interviewee, not previously quoted:

Well, to me, a lot of things people think of as important are just not very important. I find that love, giving of love, is sufficiently important . . . to me the human heart is what it's all about, and the rest isn't very important.

From a frequent correspondent who lives in the Deep South:

Now I'm able to love others and not be afraid of being hurt. To take every opportunity to show love, with God's love in mind. With no thought of worldly gain whatsoever. To use my arms to draw my loved ones closer to me, instead of holding them at arm's length. To give others something of joy, if nothing but a smile. Most of all, to share your love . . .

From a man who had his NDE in 1963:

I love people very much [now] and wish I could help everyone who needs help.

In our interview, Barbara told me:

. . . the only emotion I feel [now] is love. . . . I don't get caught up [very] much anymore in anger with my kids or my husband. . . . Jealousy and all those other things have been gone for years.

A number of other NDErs also mentioned that they have come to feel more compassionate toward others. Two of my interviewees, neither previously quoted, expressed their views here in a fashion consistent with what we have already seen:

From a suicide attempter in her mid-twenties:

The emotion of hate is not very good . . . and I just found [afterward] I really don't hate anybody. Instead, I replace that emotion with one that I didn't think was that bad, such as, "Gee, I feel very sorry for her." More of a pity, sympathetic-type outlook. I used to have a very bad temper and I was also a very mouthy [i.e., fresh] person. Maybe I still am, but not quite as bad as I used to be. I tend to listen.

From a woman in her mid-fifties:

Well, I think it [an NDE] makes you more tolerant of other people, a little bit more understanding. . . . I don't think I judge people quite as harshly as I once did. . . . Maybe I have a better sense of humor than I once had.

Certainly there is an abundance of evidence here that NDErs care more for others following their experience and that they are more open about expressing the love they now feel inside themselves. That these claims have some basis in actuality we will later see, but for the time being it seems safe to conclude that the spiritual injuction is to "love thy neighbor" (no matter how that value is stated in different religious traditions) is one that is keenly and more strongly felt by NDErs subsequent to their NDE.

In one sense, the value shifts discussed in these first two sections represent two ways of viewing a single effect: Whether it is appreciation for life *or* appreciation for others, NDErs return filled with the conviction that these things matter. Looked at in this light, one is led to ask: If these are the things that matter to NDEs, what ceases to matter? That is, in what domains are these value shifts in the opposite direction? We'll look at this question next.

Concern with Impressing Others

We have already seen in Chapter 4 (see page 102) that, as a rule, NDErs think better of themselves (i.e., have more self-esteem) following their NDE, but in the same chapter evidence was also presented (see pages 100–101) that NDErs are not particularly concerned with what others think of *them*. Our data from the LCQ reinforce that finding.

This value shift is tapped by three items (numbers 9, 29, and 36 in the questionnaire) that deal with the following topics: making a "good impression," desiring to become a well-known person, and an interest in what others think of me. The data corresponding to these items are shown in Figure 3.

Our NDErs tend to evince a sharp decline for all three items, but especially the last two.

These findings imply that although NDErs may feel a greater

sense of self-worth following their experience, that change is not typically accompanied by an increase in self-inflation. Indeed, in my experience, NDErs do not tend to regard themselves as anyone special. Considerations of relative status and other social-comparison games are no longer of interest. Just as they tend to accept others as they are, so they accept themselves in the same way, and they present themselves to others as they are.

These points come out nicely in the comments made by some of the NDErs in our sample, a couple of whom I had occasion to cite in the previous chapter.

Sonja told me:

I think I used to be a very superficial person, always breaking my butt to please or to be accepted or to be liked. Now I just don't give a damn anymore. It's really a delicious feeling. . . .

A woman who is paralyzed from the waist down as a result of a brain tumor informed me that in contrast to her pre-NDE behavior, she was no longer intimidated by others. At one point, in speaking of discussing her NDE in public, she said:

I don't really care if I'm laughed at. The few who don't laugh are the few who will learn.

Another interviewee confided:

[Before] I was insecure, always. . . . [Now] if somebody doesn't like me, I don't fret about it.

A female correspondent wrote:

Now at 49 and a half years, I'm starting to see that God didn't want me as a professional psychologist, dragging in the big bucks, getting all involved with the big words and labels for other people's conditions, and me getting all puffed up with my importance. He has made me a candle, lighting the place where I am. He has given me the ability to communicate who I am and my knowledge of God in gentle ways. . . . He has kept me human in my understanding of others' problems.

In my own personal experience, perhaps the most striking example of this lack of concern with impressing others was that provided by a Near-Death Hotel guest—Patrick, who, following his NDE, had retired from his well-paying position as a professor and, in his late forties, had become something of a Whitmanesque character, hitchhiking from one end of the country to the other and sharing his being with whomever he met along the way. In Patrick's hierarchy of values, the chief thing was simply to remain fully open to the present moment. For him, that was not merely sufficient; it was all there was.

Of course, Patrick is not typical of most NDErs. Most of them do not make such drastic changes in their lives, nor do they give up all personal ambition. Nevertheless, it appears that in this context at least Patrick may represent an extreme instance of a tendency many of them feel but few choose to act upon.

Materialism

Just as the first two value domains—"appreciation of life" and "concern for others"—could be understood as reflecting a single facet of appreciation (either for life as a whole or for people in particular), so also the "concern to impress others" and the "materialism" clusters may be seen to be linked to each other by another common thread, that of acquisition. One wants to acquire either the good opinion of others or material goods. In either case, such ambitions are fueled by personal insecurity, and however "much" one has, it is never enough to allay the desire for more.

As we have already seen, because of what NDErs experience while close to death, they return to life by and large bereft of the kind of insecurity that motivates most of the rest of us. As a result, the reduction in their concern with impressing others should also be found for their interest in amassing the symbols of worldly success. Let us now see whether these expectations are supported by the findings from the LCQ.

The materialism cluster is composed of four items: two of them (numbers 7 and 38) are concerned with material things, while the remaining two (numbers 15 and 24) have more to do with living well. Figure 4 presents the data based on all four items.

If you're following the statistical charts, you'll observe that the data are generally in accord with our expectations, but not perfectly. On the items directly concerned with materialism (numbers 7 and 38), the decline shown on the chart is straightforward and in the predicted direction. The same trend is present for item 24, though not so strongly, but item 15—the one that asks respondents to assess the importance of "living the good life"—lacks any clear-cut direction. Why should this item have failed to conform to the overall pattern?

Quite a few respondents complained directly on their LCQ form that they found this item ambiguous and implied that they did not know how to interpret it. This lack of uniformity in meaning would produce the variable responding pattern we observe here. Hence we have some grounds at least for discounting the results based on this one item alone. The antimaterialism theme then emerges clearly and harmonizes perfectly with the other findings we've previously considered in this chapter.

Certainly the qualitative data from our Omega sample amply buttress the antimaterialistic orientation suggested by the overall LCQ findings. Just as these NDErs spoke often in their letters and interviews of their positive feelings for others, so again their words given abundant evidence of their indifference to things. A few examples here will speak for the many recorded in my files and transcripts.

A female interviewee said:

Before I was living for material things. . . . Before I was conscious of only me, what I had, what I wanted. . . . I have gradually sloughed off the desires to have and to hold earthly possessions, material possessions to any great degree. I don't worry about tomorrow . . . because I know that the Lord will take care of me.

Another female interviewee commented:

. . . Material things . . . have completely faded into the background; material things aren't important.

And recall in this connection an earlier remark of Barbara's:

Oh, I liked materialism and went after it, but my values before were a lovely home and the community where I felt status. . . . Now my values are my smile!

A sixty-five-year-old correspondent who had her NDE nearly forty years ago went even farther in saying:

I've not put any importance upon gaining material things since my death experience. I've shared or given away much of the worldly goods that have come to me. I am a donor; my eyes, kidneys, skin, etc., are available for use for whomever may be in need at my demise.

And, finally, we have the powerful testimony of Mr. Dippong, who wrote:

My interest in material wealth and greed for possessions was replaced by a thirst for spiritual understanding and a passionate desire to see world conditions improve.

Such, then, are the sentiments of NDErs regarding the importance of things in themselves. Of course, it would be an error to assume that most NDErs are contemptuous of material goods or that, like Tolstoy, they typically seek to give away to the poor their own possessions. The correct understanding here is best expressed, I think, by saying that while NDErs like the rest of us, enjoy their possessions, they are not particularly attached to them. They certainly don't live for them. They are there and they have their uses but in the hierarchy of NDE values, they are not of great worth. Matter is not what matters.

Quest for Meaning

Because NDErs tend to be disinclined to seek either the good opinion of others or simply the goods of this world, you should not infer that they are altogether without desire. NDErs *do* have goals, but the things they aspire most to attain are not in either the social or the material worlds. On the contrary, as a group NDErs are likely to strive after meaning; they seek to know the purpose for which they live and are to live; they quest for a deeper understanding of the nature of life and for a higher consciousness by which to penetrate to the hidden significance of things.

I call this general value orientation the "quest for meaning," and on the LCQ it is represented by six items—numbers 13, 19, 20, 26, 32, and 40. How intense this quest becomes for NDErs following their experience is revealed by the data in Figure 5.

As you can see, for each of these items there is a pronounced increase for NDErs as a whole. The NDE appears to trigger a strong, inner drive for understanding as a result of which one's prior value orientation shifts away from the acquisition of conventional sources of self-esteem and moves toward the attainment of knowledge.

This quest is, of course, carried out on various levels, and there seems inherent in it a progression I will attempt to illustrate in the quotations that follow.

This quest can be said to begin with an attempt to understand just why one had the NDE in the first place. Perhaps surprisingly, this is a question that "makes sense" to almost all NDErs, and in my interviews I attempted to probe this issue with my respondents. All of the observations given below come from my interviews.

Sonja reflected on her NDE in this way:

You know, one thought I've had quite a few times . . . is that the near-death experience I had—I wonder if I created this. . . . I think that certain people are able to create their own "shock treatments," and I almost have a feeling that this clinical death experience is your own [form] of shock therapy to make you aware.

. . . 134

*   *   *

Another person used the same metaphor:

[It was] a learning experience. It's a crude form of shock therapy. To make you more aware . . .

Still another respondent spoke in a similar vein:

As I look back on it, it seems to me that the reason for its happening was for God to come into my life because I wouldn't let Him come in any other way. He used a dramatic method to get my attention. . . . I was playing games with Him. . . . I was diddling around with this, into this and into that, this boyfriend and that boyfriend, just kind of messin' up my life and not paying any attention, making a lot of people unhappy. . . .

Janis was even more explicit here:

I was lucky. I was lucky it happened. Because had it not, I could very well be dead now. 'Cause I wasn't headed in the right direction. I was on a self-destruction kick. Only I was doing it very slowly. [The] people I was associating with . . . the people I hung around with were always . . . inferior [she qualifies this here to indicate that she does not mean to be judgmental]. . . . They were a sordid group. Pushers, prostitutes. I was streetwise. I was getting too streetwise. I think if it wouldn't have happened, I wouldn't be here. . . . I would have been dead.

These excerpts suggest that to the NDEr not only is the experience purposive, but also it may well exert some kind of "self-correction." It is as though it serves to turn the NDEr in a different direction and, once heading that way, the individual tends to awaken to a new view of life. Of course, by no means does this happen in every case, but it seems to occur often enough among my respondents that we should pay attention to it and ponder its possible significance.

When one pushes this line of inquiry a little farther, the next stage of the progression is obvious. It is usually summed up in the form of a pithy realization. The respondents I quote below are not the same persons just cited.

The first respondent here hints at what others will make clear:

Well, I really believe it happened to me for a reason because . . . I believe I've learned a lot [spiritually from it]. I don't mean that egoistically. . . . It did cause me to progress in a certain direction that I would not have otherwise.

Jayne said simply:

It [her NDE] was a very spiritual experience and I have been very spiritual, but not particularly religious, ever since.

And finally here is Celia's more extended statement on the meaning of her NDE and its implications for the NDEs of others:

I think we *all* have had this experience for a reason. Because there is something *we must do* [said with emphasis]. We were given a special calling. I truly believe it's like a calling. . . . I think God knows what He's doing and we don't, so the gift is accepted without any question. But there is a purpose for us and if you want to know why, I think it's because God has called you to do something and you have to grow as a person. . . . And I know that God's been the center of my life ever since that experience.

How these interpretations are acted upon and the extent to which they are realized vary enormously, of course, but whatever the subsequent developmental path the individual may follow, it tends to have a decided spiritual or religious direction. Some NDErs may become more involved in the affairs of their church; others prefer some alternate form of fulfilling this same spiritual impulse, such as counseling or doing healing work; some become speakers or writers; still others express their spirituality within the confines of their own family and network of friends; and so on. But each person seems to be led to try to actualize what Celia called "the gift" by using it. Several NDErs have told me that it is chiefly by using or sharing one's experience that it continues to grow and makes its purpose more evident. For example, in his interview with me, Patrick spontaneously remarked:

The other thing that astonishes me . . . is that this experience is not just a memory that gradually fades and vanishes. No, it's something that seems to grow all the time. It gives you various hints. Then you try these and they are so stupendous, it makes your life far better than it's ever been before. . . .

In many cases there is still another distinct stage to this progression, and this involves an intentional search for what can be called higher consciousness. I cannot provide an exact statistic for how many of the NDErs I've met are motivated by this search, but I can say that "many" is indeed the correct word. Of course, one would also expect that it might take a while before some NDErs reach this stage in their own development. Here, however, I will limit myself to just two examples: Barbara Harris and Mr. Dippong.

In her interview, Barbara described to me how radically altered her life was following her NDE:

My purpose and my outlook on life became from that point on a searching. . . . Books became my friends [before this, she said, she tended to read only escapist literature]. . . . I found myself on a college campus, which was somewhere I had always wanted to be when I was younger, but I never got to do. . . . I went back to school. . . .

While there she took a two-week personal growth course—again her first such experience—which had a powerful effect upon her and clarified many of the insights she had had during her NDE. Later

someone handed me this book called *A Handbook to Higher Consciousness*, and this was the first time I had my hands on one of those kind of books and I just couldn't stop reading it. I think I've read that book, cover to cover, about eleven times. . . . And from that point, it's been a constant reading of these kinds of books. Just a total evolvement to feeling, sensing, and being the type of person that I felt I merged with in that tunnel.

And in Barbara's case, her activities have been by no means confined to reading. She has traveled widely to conferences, spoken personally to many of the foremost researchers and scholars in a variety of consciousness disciplines, and has become close friends and maintains regular contact with quite a few of these individuals.

Barbara's development is more marked—at least by externals—than that of other NDErs whose interest in higher consciousness takes on a less exuberant form. But in Mr. Dippong's case we have, if anything, an example that would be difficult to excel. He writes:

The impact this experience made on me is evidenced by the remarkable changes that occurred in my lifestyle. The entire direction of my life turned completely around. Almost immediately after my experience, I began to ask questions. First I became interested in reading about and talking to people who had death or near-death experiences. While I found our experiences had some similarities—the joy at being free from the physical body, the vision of beautiful colors, and at least some impression of light—they differed vastly for the most part in terms of the overwhelming intensity I had experienced.[4]

I could also find no one who could answer the many questions I had about the experience. A burning thirst to understand what I had undergone drove me around the globe in search of someone who could satisfy my intense curiosity with a scientific explanation. After a time I began to realize that every road I started out on eventually led to the same thing: the knowledge contained in the original, untampered words of the world's great spiritual teachers—men and women who had a first hand awareness of a divine state of consciousness.

Mr. Dippong ultimately arrived at what he found to be a satisfying interpretation for his experience, and he now heads an international organization and publishes an attractive magazine, *CHIMO*, through which his own views on higher consciousness are expressed. Oddly enough, entirely independently of Mr. Dippong's writings and following a different route altogether, Barbara has also arrived at a very similar understanding of her own NDE. The specific—and highly compatible—views of both these individuals are not relevant here, but we will be returning to them in Chapter 9 when we consider the possible biological basis of NDEs.

For now, however, we may bring this section to a close by noting that this quest for meaning—whatever form it takes—is precisely what gives a continuing sense of direction to the lives of many NDErs. And, just as obviously, that direction tends to follow a spiritual course that at least for a minority of NDErs becomes a conscious search for illumination. In the world of NDErs, this is ultimately what matters.

The Validity of Self-Reports

Throughout this chapter and the previous one I have provided a great deal of information concerning personality and value changes following NDEs. Without exception, all the findings I have discussed were based entirely on the self-reports of the NDErs themselves—i.e., we have only the claims by NDErs that they have changed in the ways they describe. That being so, this very obvious question arises: How do we know that the NDErs are describing themselves accurately? Raising such a question does not necessarily imply, of course, that most NDErs would consciously lie about themselves, but it is certainly not unreasonable to wonder if they, like most of us, wouldn't succumb to the temptation to depict themselves in more flattering terms than might be justified by the facts.

Fortunately, we do have evidence on this question. And the evidence, though it is only preliminary, consistently suggests that NDErs' self-reports are accurate.

In conjunction with administering the LCQ and some of my other questionnaires to my Omega sample, I asked respondents whose NDE had not occurred too many years ago (no fixed number of years was specified) if they could identify up to three persons who knew them well both before and after their NDE and who might be willing to complete anonymously a brief questionnaire for me. I supplied copies of this questionnaire in envelopes and requested two things of the respondents: (1) that they not look at the questionnaire and (2) that they not discuss it in any way with the person who was to complete it. The envelope containing the questionnaire was already stamped and addressed to me so that when the questionnaire was completed, all that was required was to enclose it in the envelope and mail it.

I called this questionnaire the Behavior Rating Inventory (BRI), and I have reproduced it in full in Appendix II. It simply asks the rater to indicate whether the NDEr in question had shown a decrease, an increase, or no overall change in eleven characteristics since his or her NDE. Ten of the characteristics included on the BRI were selected so that they coincided with certain LCQ items. These referred to (1) spiritual interests; (2) expressing love; (3) ability to enjoy "the ordinary things of life"; (4) fear of death; (5) sense of self-worth; (6) interest in material things; (7) acceptance of others; (8) closeness to family members; (9) religious involvement; and (10) self-understanding. These ten items corresponded to LCQ items 10, 14, 3, 28, 5, 7, 39, 27, 11, and 32, respectively. The eleventh item dealt with psychic abilities, and for that item alone correspondence was assessed by reference to another entire questionnaire, the Psychic Experience Inventory (see Appendix II).

Fifteen of my respondents were able to obtain at least one external rater—usually a close relative or friend—to fill out the BRI, though only four NDErs were able to procure BRI ratings from as many as three persons. Given the unreliability of single ratings, the variability of knowledge about the NDEr on the part of the external rater, the informal nature of the study, and the simplicity of the questionnaire—to say nothing of the very small size of the sample—it would not have been surprising if no clear-cut results had emerged from the analysis of these preliminary data. On the contrary, the overall pattern was, under the circumstances, remarkably consistent.

The modal number—that is, the most often occurring number—of identical ratings was eight of a possible eleven. Altogether, eight persons in my sample, slightly over half of them, achieved this modal value, and only *two* (of fifteen) fell below seven. What this means, of course, is that overall, the changes that NDErs attribute to themselves are also perceived and corroborated by individuals who knew them well (and, presumably, usually best) both before and after their experience.

The findings here must naturally be regarded as highly provisional, and a more rigorously controlled study with a larger sample is plainly necessary before we can have full confidence in them, but at least we can tentatively conclude that there is no indication whatever that the self-reports of NDErs are biased or in any way invalid.

Conclusions

The general findings of this chapter can be summarized quite succinctly. After NDEs, individuals tend to show greater appreciation for life and more concern and love for their fellow humans while their interest in personal status and material possessions wanes. Most NDErs also state that they live afterward with a heightened sense of spiritual purpose and, in some cases, that they seek a deeper understanding of life's essential meaning. Furthermore, these self-reports tend to be corroborated by others in a position to observe the behavior of NDErs.

How do these findings square with "the spiritual catalyst" hypothesis restated at the beginning of this chapter? Based on our earlier discussion of the implications of that hypothesis for value shifts, I think that the answer can only be: very well. If you recall the essential features of the core NDE—especially the sense of total love, absolute knowledge, and spiritual perfection—and examine the subsequent value changes in that light, I think you will easily see why I have argued that the aftereffects of NDEs are all of a piece with the experience itself and are natural outgrowths of it. This last point, however, requires some elaboration.

This continuity may be seen, for example, between the unconditional love and acceptance one feels during an NDE and the generalization of this effect, to a marked degree, to humanity as a whole following the experience. Similarly, the personal life review in which one clearly sees what matters in life seems to provide one source of the value matrix for NDErs who afterward come to exalt caring for life as they tend to lose interest in caring about things or the opinions of others. The deep spiritual truths that some NDErs claim to grasp during their experience likewise appears to be the origin of the hunger that motivates them subsequently to follow and value the pursuit of higher knowledge. In postulating such links between characteristics of the NDE itself and the values NDErs tend to endorse afterward, I expressly do not want to leave the impression that these connections are so specific and direct as my words may imply. The holistic NDE pattern is not a phenomenon that lends itself to atomistic dissection with clearly defined cause-and-effect chains. My only point here was to clarify by some examples just how the general NDEr value pattern may be seen to reflect the spiritual qualities of the experience itself.

Both the personality transformations we reviewed in Chapter 4 and the value shifts we considered in this chapter are, however, only expressions, albeit important ones, of the core NDE transformation itself. Remember that the core NDE was said to be, in its essence, a spiritual experience of a very high order. That facet, above all others, manifests most clearly in the lives of NDErs and that, in a sense, underlies and shapes all of the other changes we have so far encountered. Even as we discussed these other changes, therefore, we couldn't help referring, at least in passing, to some of their spiritual aspects. We are now prepared, however, to penetrate into the heart of the transformative process of NDErs by concentrating our full attention on the way their NDEs dominate their experience of religion and the spiritual life.

CHAPTER 6

· · · · · · ·

Religious and Spiritual Orientations
Following NDEs

÷

Since the NDE has been shown to be grounded in a profound spiritual encounter, we would certainly expect the NDE itself to lead to a reorientation of one's religious and spiritual life. Not only is this so, but also for many NDErs it constitutes the preeminent feature of their new life around which all other changes tend to be constellated. In this chapter, therefore, we will examine in depth various dimensions of this central post-NDE phenomenon. We will be concerned with the feelings, attitudes, beliefs, *and* behavior of NDErs that relate specifically to their religious and spiritual life.

Two aspects of "the spiritual catalyst" hypothesis are relevant to the findings to be discussed in this chapter. The first of these deals directly with the catalytic role of the NDE itself; the second—and this will be the main thrust of this chapter—concerns the particular form of one's spiritual development following an NDE. We will begin by turning for a moment to the first of these factors before taking up the major theme of this chapter.

We have already seen in the previous chapter, especially in the section on the quest for meaning (see pages 134–139), how the NDE tends to stimulate a spiritual search for the individual. Obviously, for many NDErs their experience *is* a spiritual awakening, and what is revealed to them in that moment out of time quickly comes to fruition in them when they return to the world of time and space. In many cases—and certainly in virtually all core NDEs—they realize both the implications of what they have experienced and the necessity to act upon those implications.

Because this point has previously been made, there is no need to dwell on it again here. To illustrate it, let it suffice to call on another frequent visitor at the Near-Death Hotel, a woman in her mid-fifties who is now leading a very active religious life in the Catholic Church. Though I have quoted various brief excerpts from her interview with me at earlier points in this book, let me now weave some of those remarks together with her other statements to give to her account the coherence it had originally. In the summer of 1980, six years after her NDE, Rose (a pseudonym) told me:

Before I was living for material things. . . . Before I was conscious of only me, what I wanted. . . . I went from a person who was selfish, empty, vain, *completely* vain, frightened of life, of living, of death, of anything and everything to . . . a real sense of freedom in my inmost being, a complete sense of knowledge with God; I've grown to really know what love is in a universal sense, and I'm still growing in that area. . . . As I look back on it [her NDE], it seems to me that the reason for this happening was for God to come into my life because I wouldn't let Him come in any other way. . . . I feel now that God is first in my life. . . . In all reality, what this has done also is to give a freedom that I didn't know existed. It's given me the freedom to be myself, to find myself . . ..to be what God wants me to be.

That the NDE should be a catalyst for religious or spiritual awakening is, in view of all we've considered to this point, hardly surprising. What is noteworthy, however, is the particular form that this spiritual development takes in many NDErs—i.e., the real significance of the NDE here may not be simply that it promotes spiritual growth as much as the kind of spiritual growth it promotes.

To clarify the meaning of this observation it will be necessary now to introduce the key questionnaire used in this chapter, and the Religious Belief Inventory (RBI),[1] which will be found in Appendix II.

This questionnaire is both briefer and simpler than the LCQ, which we drew on in the previous chapter. The RBI contains only twelve statements, and the respondent is asked merely to indicate whether he or she now agrees more or less with each statement (or has not changed his or her mind) than before.[2] If you read the RBI items carefully, however, you will see that they appear to fall into two distinct categories. Items 1, 3, 5, 6, 9, and 12 comprise a cluster of statements, agreement with which indicates sympathy with a *universalistically* spiritual orientation. Items 2, 4, 7, 8, 10, and 11, on the other hand, comprise a second cluster of statements, agreement with which implies a more *conventional* (Christian) religious orientation.[3] The relevance of this distinction will be clear in a moment.

The same twenty-six NDErs who took the LCQ also completed the RBI. In addition, however, 146 members of IANDS also filled out another (but equivalent) version of the RBI as part of a larger research project coordinated by IANDS' Director of Research, Dr. Bruce Greyson.[4] Altogether, then, a total sample of 172 persons responded to the RBI. Of these, seventy-six were NDErs, thirty were near-death survivors, while sixty-six had never been close to death. The data furnished by this sample constitute the principal statistical findings in this chapter and will be presented and discussed shortly.[5]

Importantly supplementing this material, however, will be additional relevant data drawn from the LCQ. Moreover, I will again use excerpts from interviews and letters to illustrate the spiritual and religious changes reported by NDErs that can be summarized only by the statistical findings of this chapter.

As you will see, the data from all these sources reinforce one primary conclusion: Following their experience, NDErs are likely to shift toward a universalistically spiritual orientation. This shift is not found—at least certainly not nearly to the same degree—for persons who have not had NDEs but who are otherwise comparable. Although these general findings need to be qualified, as will be seen in a moment, the thrust of the spiritual development of NDErs is very clearly in accord with a general spiritual—rather than religious—orientation toward life.

Before proceeding to consider the findings that support this conclusion, we must first define a "universalistically spiritual orientation." From the research instruments and interviews of this study I have found seven essential elements of this coherent world view. The bulk of this chapter will be devoted to describing and illustrating them, but we can begin simply by listing them here:

1. A tendency to characterize oneself as spiritual rather than religious per se.
2. A feeling of being inwardly close to God.
3. A deemphasis of the formal aspects of religious life and worship.
4. A conviction that there is life after death, regardless of religious belief.
5. An openness to the doctrine of reincarnation (and a general sympathy toward Eastern religions).
6. A belief in the essential underlying unity of all religions.
7. A desire for a universal religion embracing all humanity.

Each of these elements is supported by the data from one or more items of the RBI and LCQ as well as from the spoken or written comments of Omega NDErs.

Before we consider each component of this universalistically spiritual orientation, it will be advantageous to spend a few moments focusing on the broad outlines of the general findings based on the RBI. Let us start with an examination of the data presented in Table 1.

Because of a few technical matters—which for the most part are relegated to Appendix III in material intended for the professional reader—it will be necessary for me first to clarify certain features of Table 1 before we can consider the meaning of the data presented there. My discussion here will be brief and intended for the general reader, but I have included a more detailed and technical explanation in Appendix III for the professional reader who may wish to consult it following the next two paragraphs.

First, let me explain the labels. Respondents were divided into two categories based on their current religious affiliation. Those who described themselves as affiliated with either the Roman Catholic religion or one of a number of recognized major Protestant denominations (e.g., Baptists, Congregationalists, Episcopalians, Lutherans, Methodists, and Presbyterians) were labeled "mainline Christians." All others—Jews, other Christians, followers of other religions, believers with no specific religious affiliation as well as those who said they had no religious preference—were lumped together in a second, catchall category.[6] Respondents were also divided into one of three categories (arrayed vertically to the left of the table) based on their near-death status: as NDErs, near-death survivors (N-NDErs), or others (never knowingly having been close to death).

Second, let me explain what the numbers inside the table mean. The figures containing fractions represent the average spiritual universalism score for persons in that category. The higher the score, the greater the shift toward universalistically spiritual sentiments. A positive score (and all scores, you will notice, are positive) means that individuals are more inclined to agree with universalistically spiritual statements than they were before.

What is the gist of these findings? The main point to grasp is that while all groups show a shift toward spiritual universalism, that tendency is strongest for NDErs, especially for those NDErs who are not mainline Christians. The difference between this latter group and all others is well brought out in Figure 6, which presents the findings of Table 1 in graphic form.

Clearly, this shift cannot be attributed simply to the fact that one is not affiliated with a mainline Christian religion; if that alone were responsible, we would expect the other nonaffiliated groups to show a similar shift, but they disclose, if anything, a smaller shift than do the mainline Christians themselves. Rather, it would appear that NDErs who find themselves strongly disposed toward a universalistically spiritual orientation following their NDE were either unaffiliated with mainline Christian religions in the first place or, as some have attested, could no longer feel at home there. In any event, the lack of those ties seems to free the NDEr—but only the NDEr, as a rule—to gravitate toward a religious world view that may incorporate and yet transcend the traditional Christian perspective. We will see this point illustrated in some of the comments of NDErs later in this chapter, but for now note that it is chiefly the nonmainline Christian NDEr who is characterized by the strongest universalistically spiritual leanings. (There are reasons to believe that mainline Christians are more anchored in their religious beliefs, so they would not be expected to shift as much.)

Another and simpler way to highlight the differences among NDErs, near-death survivors, and all others in universalistically spiritual orientation would be to count the number of persons in each of these categories who give evidence of a *strong* universalistically spiritual shift by scoring 8 or more (of a possible 12) on the index for universalistically spiritual orientation.[7] This count reveals that 49 percent of all NDErs are strong shifters compared to 30 percent of near-death survivors and only 15 percent of all others. Again we see that these figures reveal a consistent trend among these three groups, and the differences are highly significant statistically—i.e., not due by chance.[8] Once more, NDErs—subject to the qualification just stated—show the greatest propensity to endorse strongly a universalistically spiritual world view.

So much for our general findings. We now need to examine the specific elements of this universalistically spiritual orientation to appreciate just how these NDErs come to understand and honor the spiritual dimension of life to which their experience has sensitized them. For this analysis two more statistical tables summarize much of the information to be discussed in the remaining pages of this chapter. To allay any anxiety you may have—if you suffer from "statisticitis"—let me assure you that there will be nothing technical in either of these tables. They consist either of simple averages or head counts, but they will reveal to us the various facets of the universalistically spiritual orientation of NDErs.

The first of these tables gives the average percent of agreement for different categories of respondents to each of the twelve items of the RBI. Just a few words are needed here to clarify the main headings at the top of Table 2.

Because NDErs who are not affiliated with mainline Christian religions show such a pronounced shift toward a universalistically spiritual orientation, they have been differentiated from the general category of NDErs, and their averages are given separately in the first column of Table 2. The next three columns list each of the major categories of respondents followed by their average percent agreement for each of the RBI statements. The "n" underneath each column head stands for the number of cases in that category.

If you now glance at the last *row* in the table you will see the average percent agreement for *all* RBI items for each of the four categories of respondents listed. The trend here, of course, is necessarily precisely what we have observed before, since this is simply another way of presenting the same data. Nevertheless, we are no longer interested in this general trend but rather in some of the individual comparisons that appear in the body of Table 2. These will be specifically discussed throughout the chapter.

In Table 3 I have presented some frequency counts (for NDErs only) from LCQ items that deal with religious or spiritual orientation. I've abbreviated each item to the left of the table, but the full wording is, of course, available in Appendix II. The column headings have the same meaning as in the previous chapter (e.g., SI = strongly increase, etc.).

As with the data in Table 2, we will here be interested in certain specific items in conjunction with the discussion to follow.

But now buttressed with these statistical data as background for that discussion, we may finally proceed to delineation of the universalistically spiritual orientation of NDErs by drawing directly on their own words that will, as usual, eloquently color the painting that abstract statistics can only outline.

Spiritual Rather Than Religious

One of the themes that runs repeatedly through the testimony of NDErs is that, though they believe in God and may continue to attend church, they are apt to describe themselves as spiritual rather than religious.

Says Jayne:

It [her NDE] was a very spiritual experience and I have been very spiritual, but not particularly religious, ever since.

And Janis echoes this:

I'm not religious, but I'm spiritual.

These seem like straightforward statements, yet they clearly lack precision. What does it mean to be spiritual but not religious?

Though the various shadings of this distinction will surface in the sections to follow, one of the most obvious seems to revolve around the distaste for the formal aspects of religious life, the doctrinal disputes, and the layer of dogma that often encrusts the religious impulse. Some of these points are addressed in a letter from a woman who had her NDE in 1974:

It might be important to add here that I stopped attending church regularly when I was in my early teens [before her NDE] because I felt at odds with what the Baptist church was preaching. I did not feel at odds with God, only with the interpretation of the church people. . . . I have never been one to read the Bible very much. Until recently I usually got bogged down . . . if I tried to read it, the scriptures just didn't have any meaning to me personally . . . [but] one of your case studies [in *Life at Death*] put it beautifully . . . she said something to the effect that she no longer needed the ritual and trappings of religion. It just wasn't necessary anymore. I've felt that way as long as I can remember, but more so since my experience.

My sense of the gist of these and similar comments is that they reflect an experience of God (or Spirit) that is more keenly felt inwardly than it is encountered in the many outward forms of religious worship. Such a view will be amply supported by the testimony given in the following two sections.

Before turning to those remarks, however, we should at least glance at the one questionnaire item that supports at least indirectly the sense of this universalistically spiritual element. Item 10 from the LCQ, listed as the first entry in Table 3, shows that the NDErs who completed this questionnaire tend to show a strong increase in their concern with spiritual matters. That they make a clear differentiation between such spiritual issues and formal religious worship will be evident shortly.

Inward Closeness to God

Many NDErs report a heightened sense of the presence of God following their experience. That this is strikingly so is evidenced by the responses to item 33 of the LCQ as shown in Table 3. This increasingly palpable awareness of God's presence is also reflected in the comments of NDErs I've interviewed.

Said one woman, not previously quoted:

That [her NDE] has not made me go to church [but] I feel very close to God. And more so afterward . . . Now I *know* He's there.

Celia told me:

. . . I go to church for one reason only—because I feel close to God there. But He's a part of me, a very necessary, essential part of me. He's my whole life. . . .

And Janis described in pithy terms her dramatic metamorphosis from atheist to believer:

I was raised Protestant. . . . I gave it up in my early teens. . . . I researched Catholicism. I found that was worse. . . . Essentially, at the same time of my accident, I was a ranting, raving atheist. There was no God. . . . He was a figment of man's imagination. . . . [Now] I know that there's a God. And that God is everything that exists, [that's] the essence of God. . . . Everything that exists has the essence of God within it. I *know* there's a God now. I have no question.

Another woman spoke in almost identical terms of her transformation:

I was never a religious person. I was almost an agnostic, you could say. [What happened afterward?] Uh, I'm not a churchgoer—we're Jewish—at the same time, I do belong to a temple now, which I didn't . . . Now I'm religious. I have faith that there is a God. I *know* there is. Before . . . I wasn't sure.

In much the same way, some NDErs speak specifically of their sense of the immanence of God, as witness Sonja:

[Now] I think of God as a tremendous source of energy, like the nucleus of something enormous and that we are all just separate atoms from this nucleus. I think that God is in every one of us; we are God. . . .

* * *

Sonja's statement is also very much in keeping with the findings of our questionnaire data—viz., item 9 of the RBI. In Table 2, you can observe that NDErs tend to be more likely than others to shift in the direction of agreement with the statement "God is within you." Indeed, among nonmainline Christian NDErs, this item has the *highest* level of increased agreement of any of the RBI statements: Fully 94 percent of these NDErs are more inclined to subscribe to this belief than they were before their experience, almost double the corresponding figures of IANDS members who have never come close to death.

Not surprisingly, this inward sense of God's presence sometimes gives rise to an increased desire to pray, as is apparent from the responses to LCQ item 30 in Table 3. A nurse who had an NDE told me in this connection:

Since then [her NDE], I can't say that I've gone to church any more, but I feel I'm a more religious person. I find myself praying, not in a structured kind of way, but just praying more than I even did when I went to church. I mean, you went to church because it's kind of the thing to do, but now I find that I pray just because it just comes out of me. . . .

Rose, whose testimony was cited near the beginning of this chapter, also related this to me:

I have grown in a prayer life. . . . My prayer life was zilch before except when I wanted something or I was scared or frightened, but I didn't pray in a consistent manner. That changed, where I really enjoyed praying or talking to God.

Rose then went on to describe some of the many spiritual and religious experiences she has had—and continues to have—since her NDE and the powerful emotions that often accompany them. Though I won't describe these here nor those of other NDErs that have been shared with me, Rose's post-NDE religious experience is not atypical of those of NDErs I've met. This assertion is also supported, as you will note, by the data from LCQ item 18, which indicates a marked increased in religious feelings following an NDE.

The upshot, then, of what has so far been presented to illustrate the universalistically spiritual perspective of NDErs is that these individuals are characterized by an awakened spiritual sensibility that apprehends God as an undeniably omnipresent force. How far removed this sense of God is from many of our houses of worship—at least in the opinion of NDErs—will be examined next.

Deemphasis of Formal Religion

Although many NDErs continue to attend religious services following their experience, results from the LCQ (see item 11, Table 2) suggest that the NDE itself has no consistent effect on interest in. organized religion. Findings based on the RBI also reveal that persons who have survived a near-death experience tend to deemphasize the formal aspects of religion compared to those who have never been close to death (see items 4, 5, and 10, Table 2). Furthermore, it is precisely this contrast between inner religious *feelings* and outward, formal religious *behavior* that is repeatedly mentioned by NDErs in their comments about their post-NDE religious life. The preceding two sections have served to illustrate the first point; here, the contrast will become evident as we document the second by citing representative testimony from my interviews with NDErs.

Recall, for example, the nurse I quoted in the previous section who said, before speaking of her tendency to engage in spontaneous prayer:

Since then [her NDE], I can't say that I've gone to church any more, but I feel I'm a more religious person. . . .

Sonja expressed a similar view but adds (in her second sentence) an observation I've heard from several of my close NDEr friends in informal conversation:

I don't think [my NDE] increased my desire to be in church. It's just that when I was in church, it had more meaning to me.

A woman now in her late forties and who was raised in the South described the changes in her religious orientation as follows:

153 . . .

I was brought up in the Bible Belt and when I was a child I was very religious. . . . I mean I was taught certain things and I believed them as a child and adhered to them . . . just out of rote. But *after* this [her NDE], it made me *less* religious formally but probably more religious inwardly. . . . I don't think I was in church one time since [my NDE], but I think I'm spiritually stronger than I ever was before.

Jayne also described her pre-NDE religious views but then goes on to recount her frustrating experience afterward in seeking a formal religious outlet for her new beliefs, something that again is not uncommon in the testimony of Omega NDErs:

[At the time of her NDE in 1952] I was not a religious person per se. I was raised in the Episcopal Church, had gone to church with my parents, but when I went away to college [I] dropped any pretense of going to church. I did believe in God. I thought the rest was probably mythical, if I thought much about it at all. I hoped very much that there was a heaven, but I had no belief system that said, "Oh, yes, there is."

After her account of her NDE, a member of the audience asked Jayne if afterward she practiced religion more enthusiastically. Jayne replied:

Less . . . I'm really sorry to say that because what it did was propel me back into church to find one that spoke to the things that I knew and I didn't find one. And I gave up rather quickly, I must say. I got so turned off . . . I tried to go back to my Episcopal church and I have found, it isn't the church. If you happen to get into a church that has a minister who's on your track, it doesn't matter what the church is. Finally, four years ago, I found a Presbyterian church in———[a mid-Atlantic state], where the minister was totally on *my* track and I went every Sunday while we lived there. And then we moved up here [to a northern city] and I haven't found anybody. . . .

*   *   *

In some cases, NDErs' views of churches are even less charitable than those cited so far. A woman in her mid-twenties told me:

Well [before her NDE], I wasn't too sure if God actually existed. . . . I was never a great churchgoer. I still am not. However, I do know . . . that there *is* a God. [You know this from your experience?] Yes. I'm quite more religious than I was [but] I don't exactly believe in what the churches do. I don't like their methods. They're into scaring people. Everything they preach I don't feel is exactly true, so I have my own beliefs.

And, of course, there are some persons who were and who remain openly hostile toward organized religion. Janis is one such person, and so is the forty-eight-year-old woman whose extensively detailed out-of-body experience was cited in Chapter 2 (see pages 42–43):

Before [my NDE] I was already totally alienated from religions per se. I don't like them [and] I have a real antipathy for them. . . . I just don't want to have anything to do with them. . . . [Afterward] it didn't make me run out and join a church. As a matter of fact, it drives me away from them. I wouldn't go to any of them. . . . I think they are the antithesis of what I experienced there [i.e., during her NDE]—with the possible exception of a church like the Quakers or Unitarians. . . . I don't think it [i.e., church-based religion] has anything to do with what Jesus was about. . . .

This individual, incidentally, was clear that her own NDE was a "religious" experience, but for her, as for Jayne, she had a difficult time finding a formal religious setting that conformed to her own NDE-based understanding of the divine.

In this section I've presented a sampling of a range of representative universalistically spiritual-inclined views of NDErs concerned with formal religious practice. As I've already indicated, however, the observations given here should be read bearing in mind the material of the previous two sections, since what is illustrated here is essentially the other side of the same religious coin we have been examining and therefore inseparable from it. On one side of this coin, NDErs are averring that they are spiritually inclined and have a deep inward sense of the presence of God, while on the other side they seem to be claiming that their spirituality is independent of and unrelated to the practice of institutionalized religion.

Life After Death Regardless of Belief

One of the strongest and most reliable findings from previous research in near-death studies is that NDEs tend to lead to an unassailable conviction that there is life after death. This same result was obtained once again with Omega NDErs, as you can see by examining LCQ item 35 (see Table 3). My correspondents were particularly insistent on this point, without any prodding from me. Here are just a few brief samples from their letters:

I *know* there is life after death! Nobody can shake my belief. I have no doubt—it's peaceful and nothing to be feared. I don't know what's beyond what I experienced, but it's plenty for me. . . . I only know that death is *not* to be feared, only dying.

I have a message to others living an ordinary earth life to tell them, "there is more." Our identity will continue to *be*—in a greater way. Friends will not be lost to you. You will know a beauty and peace and love [and] that loving light that encompasses and fills you is God.

This experience was a blessing to me because I now know with certainty that there is a separation of body and soul and there is life after death.

It gave me an answer to what I think everyone really must wonder about at one time or another in this life. Yes, there is an afterlife! More beautiful than anything we can begin to imagine! Once you know it, there is nothing that can equal it. You just know!

Those assertions are typical of NDErs,[9] but they fail to address themselves explicitly to the issue of just who will experience this beautiful life after death or whether the experience itself depends in any way on one's religious-belief system or commitment.

Fortunately, we do have quantitative data from the RBI that speak to these questions. The most pertinent of the RBI statements is item 3, which reads: "No matter what your religious belief, there is a life after death." As you will see from Table 2, over 90 percent of nonmainline Christian NDErs say that they are now more inclined to agree with this statement, while the overall agreement level for all NDErs is better than 85 percent. These figures are, moreover, substantially higher than for the remaining groups. Item 8, which declares that eternal life is available only to those who believe in Jesus Christ as savior and Lord, is obviously also relevant here. NDErs (especially those who are not mainline Christians) and near-death survivors are nearly twice as likely to state that they are now more in *disagreement* with this proposition than are those persons who have never been close to death. Thus, both items suggest that Omega NDErs on the whole take a very universalistic view of who "qualifies" for life after death. In a phrase, their collective position is "no one is excluded and particular religious beliefs are irrelevant."

Because I didn't specifically probe this point in my interviews with NDErs, I cannot furnish here any direct quotes from my sample to illustrate this position, but the question *was* raised by an audience member at an IANDS conference in Charlottesville, Virginia, where Jayne, herself a Christian, had given a very moving account of her NDE to which the audience had responded with considerable warmth. Jayne's reply was unequivocal:

Nobody said to me, "What do you believe?" Nobody. The universe is not set up—I *know* this, my friends [laughter]—it is not fair to say if you believe in Jesus, you've got it made, and if you don't, you don't have anything made.

Openness to Reincarnation and Eastern Religions

It is to be expected that whereas NDErs might agree that there is a life after death, there would be divergence of opinion concerning the form that this postmortem life will take. In this connection, one possibility that recurrently crops up in the literature on NDEs is that of reincarnation—the doctrine that a person (or a person's soul) may have more than one physical existence in human form. Although variants of this doctrine were acceptable to and promulgated by the early Church Fathers, reincarnation was declared heretical and expunged from Christian dogma in the sixth century. In the public mind, therefore, it has come to be associated primarily with Eastern religions such as Hinduism and Buddhism.

My own previous work, reported in *Life at Death,* suggested that NDErs—compared to nonexperiencers—were more likely to be more open to[10] the concept of reincarnation following their NDE than they had been before. To follow up on my own preliminary data, I inquired more systematically of my present sample concerning their views about reincarnation.

What I found here paralleled and reinforced my earlier findings: NDErs do appear to be more inclined to a reincarnational perspective following their experience and, not surprisingly, appear to be more sympathetic to Eastern religions as well. Furthermore, my findings seem to be consistent with the data of other researchers.[11]

To examine these trends more closely, let me first furnish the relevant statistical data, following which some representative comments from NDErs will be arrayed.

We'll start with our questionnaire findings for NDErs only. LCQ item 31 specifically asks about "openness to the notion of reincarnation." Table 3 demonstrates that there was a general increase in openness toward this concept among NDErs following their experience: Seventeen said openness did increase, compared to only three for whom it declined (six NDErs reported no change).

Additional data from another questionnaire—the Psychic Experience Inventory (PEI), mentioned in Chapter 3 and featured in the following chapter—are consistent with this finding but provide further information. Toward the end of the PEI, these same NDErs were asked to rate their pre- and post-NDE beliefs in various concepts, including reincarnation, using a five-point scale that ranged from strong belief $(+2)$ to strong disbelief (-2).

Again, the findings revealed an overall increase, this time in *belief in* rather than openness to reincarnation. In this case, fifteen

NDErs increased in belief while four declined (and six persons again reported no change).[12] Interestingly, whereas only 3 respondents had believed (all weakly = +1) in reincarnation before, fourteen NDErs professed belief afterward, including eight respondents now with strong convictions (= +2).

Nevertheless, it should be noted that overall final level of belief for this NDEr group as a whole was only slightly above the neutral point on the scale (+0.32). Thus, though there was indeed a shift *toward* belief in reincarnation, the average level of belief in reincarnation was still quite moderate.

Finally, let us look at the comparative data available from the RBI, specifically item 7. Unfortunately, the wording of this statement seems to have been confusing to some respondents, and for that reason the findings here may have been blurred. The item asks respondents to indicate whether they now find the doctrine of reincarnation more implausible than they once did. As you can observe in Table 2, there is a consistent but not strong tendency for NDErs to be more in *disagreement* with this item (and thus to have a higher spiritual universalism score) compared to other respondents. Thus these data can be said to give only relatively weak support to the other findings in this section, but at least the RBI results are not incongruent with those findings.

When we turn to the comments of the NDErs themselves whom I interviewed, we usually find little more than a simple assertion of belief, as the following brief excerpts (without identification) will attest:

I think that I feel more likely that it's true.

Yeah, it seems to me that it's clear that's what actually occurs to us.

Oh, yes, I believe in reincarnation. [Had you believed in it before?] I never thought about it.

I believe in reincarnation also. I believe in it, very definitely. [Did you believe in it before?] I'd heard about it . . . but I didn't actually believe. But now I do believe.

* * *

Obviously, such statements in themselves add very little to the statistical data we have just reviewed. One wants to know just what is it about the NDE that inclines experiencers toward the idea of reincarnation. This was not a matter I was able to delve into in any systematic way either in my questionnaires or my interviews, but occasionally NDErs would discuss the origin of their views regarding reincarnation with me. Though I do not feel that I have enough material to present anything formally here—this needs to be addressed more carefully in future research—I can at least offer a few suggestive tidbits from these conversations.

In some cases—and Belle was an instance of this—NDErs seem to have what is not merely a past life, but a past lives, review—i.e., they claim to be aware of events from their previous incarnations or simply of the fact that they have lived before. Since I have not attempted to determine how often such perceptions occur (my guess would be that they are quite rare), I would not want to claim that they are by any means a principal basis for post-NDE belief in reincarnation, but it may be a factor in some cases. Janis has given me a detailed account of the "mechanics" of reincarnation. All this, she claims, was disclosed to her by what she saw during her NDE and by the responses she received to her own questions from a being of light she encountered. In still another case I recently learned of, the being of light communicated to an NDEr specific information after his NDE clearly indicating that reincarnation was a reality. How common such reincarnation-relevant experiences are among NDErs is a question that can be answered only by subsequent research, however.

Of course, there is no reason why an NDEr's openness toward reincarnation must stem directly from his NDE. In fact, I am quite convinced that in many cases it is more likely to be a response to an NDEr's reading and other life experiences *following* an NDE. Some of the findings to be presented in the next chapter are also consistent with this belief.

Before concluding this discussion of leanings toward reincarnation among NDErs, two qualifications, though of different orders, need to be mentioned to keep all of this material in perspective.

The first is that of course a substantial number of NDErs are *not* inclined to believe in reincarnation, and some quite emphatically disbelieve in it. Remember, my aim in this chapter is to provide an overall account of the universalistically spiritual orientation of NDErs, of which the inclination toward reincarnation is one component, but there are certainly many NDErs who do not have this orientation. It is just that NDErs are more *likely* to conform to it than are others.

The second qualification is a warning not to construe reincarnation too simplistically. NDErs who assert that there is such a thing as reincarnation are not necessarily saying, for example, that it should be understood as a procession of successive incarnations that one lives out in linear, historical time. A recent conversation with Tom Sawyer will illustrate this point. When Tom was asked whether reincarnation was a reality, he deliberately paused before answering. He then gave an elaborate preamble, lasting about five minutes, concerning why his answer was going to take the form of a highly qualified "yes." This was followed by a two-*hour* discussion in which he attempted to give just a bare exposition of the complexities of what we refer to as reincarnation. Suffice it to say that no one who heard that conversation and was persuaded by its plausibility could ever again entertain a simple and straightforward conception of reincarnation. Of course, the enormous published literature on reincarnation and allied topics is proof enough that it is a subject of extraordinary depth and subtlety much too far beyond the scope of this discussion to consider.

However that may be and whatever the basis of content of NDErs' own views of reincarnation, it is also true that the specific shift toward this doctrine is sometimes accompanied by a general endorsement of Eastern religions. This was not only my own informal observation, but also it has been supported by other independent research.[13] Again it remains for future investigations to determine the extent of this tendency among NDErs, but for the time being here are a couple of comments by core NDErs.

Sonja (whom I'll be quoting again shortly), in speaking of the beauty she found in all religions, nevertheless concluded:

. . . but I think the Eastern religions have the greatest purity.

Patrick was more specific concerning the parallels he felt existed between his NDE and Buddhist teachings:

. . . although I've had a mild interest in Eastern religions for a long period of my life, this is the first time that I've ever carried books around about Buddhism and read them with considerable interest. . . . I was just struck with the similarity between some to their propositions and what I experienced. . . . This seems very much a spiritual experience, but it's spirituality seen from a different view than I'd ever seen before and I think the closest kind of spirituality probably is from the East far more than it is from the West. Not that I'm claiming that one is more correct than the other, but one is more reasonable to me now and the other one never will be, I'm sure.

The Unity of Religions and the Quest for a Universal Religion

Eastern religions, far more than Western faiths, are known for their openness to and tolerance for various forms of religious expression as well as for their ability to incorporate the essence of other religious traditions into their own framework (as with Hinduism, for example). It is precisely this ecumenical orientation that most closely represents the core of NDErs' own spiritual perspective. In a sense, their embrace of Eastern religions is not so much a substitution of new doctrines for old as it is an endorsement of the ecumenical spirit of Eastern world views. Indeed, the strongest evidence of NDErs' universalistically spiritual orientation and in many ways the culmination of the qualities already discussed is their belief in the underlying unity of all religions and their desire for a universal religious faith that will transcend the historical divisiveness of the world's great religions.

Writes Joseph Dippong:

. . . all religions started from the same truth and there is little variation between the major beliefs of each. What a great tool this will be to at least begin to unify mankind under one God, one truth and one spiritual belief.

And Sonja speaks in the same unifying voice:

I've had the freedom to investigate many religions, and the only thing that I've been able to really understand is that every religion—the pure religion itself—is the same thing. There's no difference. . . . I think every religion has beauty. . . .

That these are not exceptional statements can be quickly confirmed by a final reference to one of our statistical tables. The first RBI statement expresses the belief that the essential core of all religions is the same, an assertion identical to the avowals of Mr. Dippong and Sonja. And Table 2 shows that the overwhelming majority of NDErs assent to this view, compared to a minority of other respondents. Similarly, the last statement, item 12, endorses the desirability of a universal religion. Here again, NDErs provide ample support for this goal, while only a minority of other respondents report a similar shift in its favor.

Clearly, NDErs as a class of persons stand out by virtue of their resounding support for the ecumenical world view these statements make explicit. It is as though the unconditional love many of them felt during their NDE swept away the last vestiges of religious parochialism and opened them up to a vision of humanity united in a faith whose shared foundation is God's limitless love for all.

Conclusions

With this chapter we have nearly completed the portrait of the NDEr's spirituality, which had been prefigured in the previous three chapters. We are now in a position to see with great clarity just how the spiritual world view of the NDEr is a gradual outgrowth of the spiritual seed crystal implanted at the time of the NDE. All the transformations in the life of an NDEr—the changes in personality, relations with others, values and beliefs—take place and are given meaning within the context of a spiritual understanding that is born in death but that requires everyday life to be realized. Every piece of this transformation is part of this spiritual whole, and every piece can be fully comprehended only by reference to this whole. Now that it has emerged in the form of the universalistically spiritual model presented in this chapter, we can begin to appreciate how completely the NDEr's life comes to be dominated by this organizing principle. Thus, the NDEr's spirituality is the core of being from which all else flows.

Obviously, what I have just sketched is the general case. In any particular instance there are bound to be deviations from the ideal form. There are certainly many NDErs for whom the universalistically spiritual orientation is weak or altogether lacking; there are those in whom it takes a long time to emerge; and there are those whose personality may give it a most peculiar, almost unrecognizable, imprint. But it is unmistakably *there*—as a tendency, as a potentiality seeking to manifest itself as a plant seeks to burst through the surface soil and penetrate into the sunlight-filled air. Empirically, we have seen that this potential is realized to various degrees in many NDErs and that, proportionately at least, NDErs —especially those who have moved beyond the constraints of conventional religion or have found ways to imbue their religious faith with their own brand of spirituality—are the most likely of all groups to express a universal spirituality that transcends the divisive interests of religious sectarianism. Some of the collective and evolutionary implications of this kind of transformation may now be dawning, but these issues must be deferred until the complete portrait of the NDEr has been drawn.

Though we have arrived at a point of reasonable understanding of the psyche of the NDEr, the most provocative revelations have vet to be divulged.

CHAPTER 7

· · · · · · ·

NDEs and Psychic Development

÷

Toward the end of her interview with me, an elderly woman related this post-NDE vignette:

I was awakened one morning with a vision of a woman's forearm holding a box, translucent. And, in the box, there was a beautiful white gardenia. And it wasn't the type of gardenia that we see in this world; it was a spiritual flower. And I heard a voice just as clearly as my own saying, "Take this flower, take this to Mrs. Henry, my mother, and tell her I am always with her."

Now, Dr. Ring, I didn't know any Mrs. Henry, but I had the habit of going to the corner of the cafeteria [at work] every morning for a cup of coffee and I sat at the counter. And I was the only person there except for a woman that sat at the opposite end of the counter. There was no one else there but ourselves. And I heard the waiter say to her, "Would you like another cup of coffee, Mrs. Henry?" And I said [to herself], "Do I dare?" A perfect stranger. A *perfect* stranger!

I went up to her afterward and I said, "I beg your pardon. Your name is Mrs. Henry?"

"Yes."

"May I tell you something?"

"Yes."

And I told her what I had heard. She looked at me with stricken eyes, and she said: "A gardenia was my daughter's favorite flower and she has just been killed in an automobile accident."

*   *   *

Over the years of my near-death research, I have heard from the lips of NDErs many such unusual and intriguing anecdotes, which appear to involve paranormal elements. Of course, it is hardly necessary to have had an NDE before one begins to experience such psychic phenomena as clairvoyance, telepathy, and precognition. Obviously, many people, probably most people, would claim to have had such experiences. Nevertheless, as my interviews continued, I could not help noticing the frequency with which psychic events were spontaneously reported by NDErs and how often these experiences were said to have occurred following the NDE. I remember making a mental resolve, more than once, to look into this matter more carefully when I had the time.

In the Omega study I have tried to do just this. In this chapter I will begin to describe the remarkable findings that this turn in my research has produced. Actually, as the results of that research were taking shape and my own interpretation of the NDE as a core spiritual experience was crystallizing, I came to see why psychic phenomena should not only sometimes appear in conjunction with NDEs but also why they should be *expected* to occur.

The basic statement of this effect as well as a hint concerning its explanation were incorporated into "the spiritual catalyst" hypothesis, first stated in Chapter 3. There I argued, as you may recall:

Finally, as a by-product of this spiritual development, NDErs tend to manifest a variety of psychic abilities afterward that are an inherent part of their transformation.

As you will see in this chapter and the next, the empirical evidence supporting the first part of this statement is very impressive indeed, but before turning our attention to that evidence it is important and necessary to understand the rationale of this part of my hypothesis. Why, in short, should we expect NDErs to manifest psychic abilities as a by-product of their personal transformation?

For the answer to this question, we must turn for a few moments to the literature concerned with the world's great spiritual traditions, especially those that had their origin in the East, where the relationship between spiritual growth and psychic phenomena was well considered. If we examine this literature even superficially, we will nevertheless quickly discern the outlines of the rationale.

In Buddhism, for example, the classic treatment of the entrance into higher states of consciousness—a rough synonym for what I have previously called "spiritual development"—is widely held to be found in the fifth-century Pali text *Vissudhimagga*,[1] or, as it is known in English, *The Path of Purification*. In his extended commentary on this text, psychologist Daniel Goleman[2] has written:

The section on supernormal [i.e.,psychic] powers is the one part of the Visuddhimagga most dubious from the standpoint of the West, since it treats as real certain events that overleap the bounds of even the most advanced physical sciences. The Vissudhimagga enumerates among these supernormal accomplishments: knowing the minds of others, knowing any past or future event, materialization of objects, seeing and hearing at a great distance, walking on water, flying through the air, and so on. More interesting, the Visuddhimagga describes in technical detail how these feats are performed, while Western Science at present cannot reconcile their possibility. *Yet every school of meditation acknowledges them as by-products of advanced stages of mastery* [my italics], if only to warn against their misuse.[3]

Goleman goes on to say:

From the Buddhist point of view, the attainment of powers is a minor advantage, of no value in itself for progress toward liberation. Powers in one who has not yet attained the nirvanic state are seen as an impediment, for they may endanger progress by enhancing his sense of self-esteem, thus strengthening attachment to self.[4]

These two points—the linking of psychic phenomena to the unfolding of higher consciousness and the warning against being attached to psychic phenomena—occur repeatedly in the literature of the great spiritual psychologies.

So, just to take another example of many that could be offered, in the codification of the principles of Yoga undertaken by legendary

Indian sage Patanjali[5] sometime between the fourth century B.C. and the fourth century A.D., it is stated that various powers (siddhis) of the same kind noted in the *Vissuddhimagga* tend to emerge with continued yogic practice. Comment the translators:

When the mind has reached a high state of purification, the psychic powers may come to it spontaneously and unbidden. . . .[6]

In commenting on another sutra, they also sound the usual warning with great emphasis:

Patanjali now begins to describe the various occult powers and the methods by which they are acquired. All authorities, including Patanjali himself, regard occult powers as the greatest stumbling blocks in the path to truth. "Heaps of rubbish," Sri Ramakrishna [a great Indian saint] calls them. Buddha told his disciples very definitely never to put their faith in miracles but to see the truth in eternal principles. Christ spoke sharply against those who "seek for a sign," and it is unfortunate that his strictures were not taken more seriously to heart by his followers. Occult powers do, however, exist, and Patanjali, in his comprehensive treatise of yoga psychology, obviously cannot ignore them. . . . The sincere spiritual aspirant can have very little concern with such matters.

They conclude their commentary with this exhortation:

So let us stop hankering after the psychic powers and turn back to the true path toward spiritual growth, remembering Patanjali's warning: "They are powers in the worldly state, but they are obstacles to samadhi."[7]

Not only do the ancient texts recurrently make such pronouncements, but so also do modern scientifically minded authorities who themselves have had extended personal experience in states of higher consciousness. To cite just two such individuals, whose views will inform the later chapters of this book, consider first Japanese scientist Hiroshi Motoyama. In his book *Science and the Evolution of Consciousness,* Motoyama, in speaking of psychic phenomena, observes:

In ordinary life, such manifestations of nonordinary perception may seem haphazard and uncontrollable, but mystical tradition asserts that they are a normal function of nonsensory states and, as such, follow certain universal laws. Once one understands these laws, the range of possible manifestation far exceeds one's image of "psychic power." Such super-power is available to the spiritually mature. . . . As the by-product of the evolution of consciousness, paranormal abilities need to be dealt with in a more objective, matter-of-fact manner. . . .[8]

Significantly, Motoyama is making these statements not merely on the authority of the spiritual traditions but on his own personal experience and scientific research. He states, for example:

The awakening of nonordinary abilities is not uncommon among those practicing strict meditative discipline. I myself have had a great deal of direct experience with the paranormal, as have many people I have come in contact with over the years, including a large proportion of my research subjects.[9]

Neither is Motoyama basing his position entirely on subjective impressions. He offers as well objective, quantitative evidence that psychic ability is directly correlated with one's level of consciousness.[10]

In several places, Motoyama also issues the usual injunctions against attachment to psychic abilities, but I will not burden you with further quotes of this kind, since the point is already clear.

Second, let us cite briefly the views of Gopi Krishna, the world-renowned authority on kundalini—a form of subtle biological energy that has been postulated to underlie certain experiences in higher consciousness. In one[11] of the many books Gopi Krishna has written in which he draws on his own abundant kundalini experiences, he states:

The moment transcendence occurs, the aspirant blossoms into a genius of a high order. Simultaneously other windows in the mind open and, to his unbounded surprise and joy, he finds himself in possession of channels of communication which, acting independently of the senses, can bring to him knowledge of events, occurring at a distance, and also visions of the past and future. His utterances may become prophetic and he may acquire the healing touch.[12]

In another[13] he elaborates:

. . . one who has attained to a higher state of consciousness . . . should be characterized by four exceptional attributes, namely, genius, psychic talents, lofty traits of character, and an expanded state of consciousness. By the term "psychic talents" I do not mean miraculous or magical powers, but higher mental faculties, such as clairvoyance, precognition, highly developed intuition, and the like.[14]

Just how pertinent to NDErs these remarks of Gopi Krishna are you will be able fully to appreciate only after finishing the next two chapters, but for now it is merely necessary for me to put in a nutshell the general connection between all the foregoing quotes and the NDE.

NDEs, in my view, represent a brief but powerful thrust into a higher state of consciousness. Unlike the meditative disciplines we have alluded to, however, the NDE is not a breakthrough that occurs as a result of a long period of voluntary spiritual training. Rather it is an involuntary and sudden propulsion, usually without warning or preparation, into a realm of profound spiritual illumination. In this respect, the NDE resembles a full-blown mystical experience and—this is the key—the *effects* of that experience *also resemble those that stem from a mystical experience*. A journey into higher consciousness, I am saying, has effects that are independent of the way it is attained.

In short, if psychic phenomena tend to be by-products of higher states of consciousness, as both ancient and modern spiritual authorities declare that they are, we should also expect to see evidence of them following NDEs—and as I have already said, we do. Furthermore, the later chapters of this book will make clear the significance of the assumption that NDEs are a gateway into higher consciousness. The implications that follow from this assumption—if it is justified—are of momentous consequence for the future of humanity.

But that is getting ahead of our story and, moreover, anticipating its conclusion. Here, however, our aim is much more limited: We now need to consider the evidence that NDEs do trigger psychic development. We must first introduce the primary questionnaire used for this phase of my research, the Psychic Experience Inventory.

The Psychic Experience Inventory

Unlike the other inventories used in this study, the Psychic Experience Inventory (PEI) is a very lengthy questionnaire that probes into a variety of psychic phenomena that a respondent may have experienced. Using a mixture of open-ended and multiple-choice questions, the PEI is designed to determine whether there have been any changes since one's NDE in the relative incidence or quality of such phenomena as clairvoyance, telepathy, precognition, *déjà vu* experiences, OBEs, and a host of other, related experiences. In addition, the PEI measures changes in *beliefs* concerning a number of concepts pertaining to psychic, spiritual, or occult matters. The full PEI is in Appendix II.

The same twenty-six Omega NDErs whose data from other questionnaires we have previously reviewed completed the PEI. Their responses to this inventory will be summarized next, but these data will comprise only the beginning of the findings presented in this chapter. Besides supplementing these cases with the usual qualitative materials from our larger Omega sample, I will be drawing on some recent research by other investigators that will buttress the case that NDEs do lead to an efflorescence of psychic phenomena.

To introduce you to the general trends that this chapter will illustrate in detail, though, let us first examine the PEI data.

The PEI Data: A Summary

If you peruse the PEI, you will see that it covers an extensive range of both psychic and psi-related phenomena. For a unified and simple method of scoring responses to such a diversity of questions, I calculated a *composite* psychic experience index based on reported changes in fourteen key PEI items.[15] A respondent's score on this index was determined by counting the number of key items for which an increase in incidence was claimed following an NDE. Thus, scores on this composite index could range from a low of 0 (indicating no increase on *any* of the items) to a high of 14 (showing an increase on *all* items). To be designated as one who showed a significant increase in psychic activity, however, a respondent needed to report an increase in incidence for more than half (i.e., eight or more) of the key items.

The overall results showed that fifteen of the twenty-six respondents, or 58 percent of Omega NDErs, reached or exceeded half. Barbara Harris, whose history we examined in Chapter 4, has a middling score, 10, among those reporting a significant increase in psychic activity following an NDE, so I'll choose hers to illustrate a typical "psychic profile."

Barbara stated that she has had more clairvoyant and telepathic experiences since her NDE and has more often known what someone is going to say before he or she says it. Barbara also reports more precognitive flashes, more *déjà vu* experiences, and more frequent synchronistic occurrences. In addition, she reports that she is now more often likely to be "rescued" from a situation where things are going badly for her (see item 12). Finally, she says that she is *much* more intuitive than she was before and more in touch with an inner source of wisdom and has increased contact with spiritual guides.

All of these increases were also acknowledged by many others in my sample. In most instances, about half or more of the total sample agreed with the same items Barbara did. The only exceptions were those (items 9 and 10) pertaining to *déjà vu* experiences, for which only slightly more than one third of the sample reported an increase. Among all the PEI items, most noteworthy for consistency of increase were those dealing with intuition and inner wisdom (items 13 and 14). Twenty-one persons (80 percent) said they were now more intuitive, and all but one (96 percent) claimed to be more in touch with an inner source of knowledge or wisdom.

We have just summarized the findings relating to psychic *experiences;* obviously, among this small sample, the overall increase in such experiences following NDEs is evident. But the PEI also provides some data about NDErs' *beliefs* about psychic and related matters.

At the end of the PEI, respondents were asked to rate nine concepts on a five-point scale (ranging from −2 to +2) according to how strongly they believe (or disbelieve) in them. Respondents were asked to provide two sets of ratings: what they believed *before* their NDE and what they believe *now*. The results of their ratings are summarized in Table 4.

The numbers in the first three columns represent the direction of the shift in beliefs before and after. The values in the last column are the average (i.e., mean) levels of *present* belief in each of the nine concepts on the scale that ranges from −2 to +2.

Obviously, for many of the concepts there is a strong shift toward increased belief following NDEs. This tendency, you will note, is especially marked for those concepts that these respondents are likely to feel they *experienced* directly during their NDE itself. Indeed, their near unanimity of strong conviction on these matters suggests, as I have implied before, that for them this is more a question of knowledge than belief. If, for example, you have had an out-of-body experience yourself, you know it is real.

Reinforcing the interpretation that NDErs' beliefs about psychic, spiritual, and occult concepts are chiefly experientially based are the findings at the bottom third of the table. There you will see that NDErs do *not* show a general drift toward occult concepts. There is some tendency, as we have already seen in the previous chapter, to be more open to reincarnation, but the overall acceptance of the concept is still weak. And with respect to such notions as astrology and demonic possession, there is no marked shift one way or the other.

In summary, then, Omega NDErs do have a strong acceptance of certain psychic and spiritual phenomena following their experience, but it is highly selective and seems to be rooted in the features of their NDEs. There is no evidence here that NDErs show a general disposition to embrace occult concepts.

As usual, however, words speak louder than numbers, and it was often the answers to the open-ended items of the PEI or scribbled-in marginal comments that caught my eye as I was coding them.

Representative Psychic Experiences of NDErs

As the data from the PEI suggest, many NDErs simply claim that their psychic sensitivities have developed strikingly since their NDE. Sonja, who has experienced a gamut of psychic phenomena, especially precognition, since her own NDE, is typical when she asserts that her psychic abilities:

[have changed] dramatically. My psychic abilities have increased . . . they're just there now, where they weren't before. . . .

On his PEI, Hank went farther and made a direct connection between his search for higher consciousness and the occurrence of psychic phenomena:

I find that as I strive to achieve a higher sense of consciousness and a better awareness of all things, more and more psychic things happen.

Although in some cases the course of post-NDE psychic development is not especially eventful, in a few instances it can be so sudden and dramatic that it can cause serious adjustment problems. An instance of this kind was described to me by a middle-aged woman I'll call Georgia, whom I interviewed recently while on the West Coast. Georgia was just seventeen when she nearly died of pneumonia. After describing her NDE to me, she said:

When I woke up and looked around, I can remember knowing everything. And that was the hardest thing. . . . [what exactly did you know?] I knew what you were thinking, I knew who was coming into the room, I knew there was someone coming up the hall, and I knew what they were going to say; and before you turned on the radio, I knew what was going to be played. But I didn't tell anyone this and I thought, "I have to try to eliminate this; this has to get out of my head." . . . So anyway, that took a long time. [Afterward] it was terrible. I mean, it was terrible. I would walk in and I would hear all this, it would come into me. . . . I never told a soul what was happening, I didn't know who to talk to. Oh, I did everything to try to eliminate that. . . . It stayed really strong for about a year, I would try to block it out. . . . And then one day I walked into a room and maybe I would [only know what one of them was thinking] and then one day someone knocked on the door and I didn't know who they were and I thought, "Oh, that's great!" It took about two years and then it eventually began to fade.

In fact, as our three-hour interview and subsequent conversations were to make clear, Georgia was not completely able to suppress her psychic awareness, and her life has been replete with psychic events ever since. She was, though, finally able to integrate these sensitivities into her life without being continually subject to them, as she was immediately after her NDE.

If we turn our attention now to some representative instances of *types* of psychic phenomena that NDErs encounter, we will be able to exemplify a number of the abstract categories of experience summarized by the PEI.

For example, consider this occurrence, which began as a premonition, described by a thirty-seven-year-old woman not previously quoted, who had her NDE in 1967:

When my son was six to seven months old, I woke up and felt drawn to check him in his crib. My fear made me wake my husband and tell him something was wrong. I got as far as Tony's room when my husband called to me that I was being silly and to come back to bed. As I headed back, my eye caught the Boston Rocker in Tony's room rocking with Nana D'Angelo in it. She had died that prior Christmas. I dashed to Tony and he was smothering in his crib corner! Nana had lived to see Tony on Christmas Eve before she died and promised me she would always protect Tony. I can't believe my imagination to be so vivid as to wake me from a sleep and to envision a moving rocker. I can't believe I almost didn't go check my precious son.

Seeing apparitions of dead persons is by no means as rare as many people think, as Carl Becker's recent review[16] makes clear, and there are several such cases from my own files. Often these forms seem to coincide with the time of their death. A suggestive example of this was furnished by one of my correspondents who had her NDE in 1953. She writes:

Five years ago, my brother, age fifty-two, passed away. At 4:00 A.M. that day, I was awakened by a soft, luminous light at the foot of my bed. It slowly ascended upward and disappeared. Half an hour later, I was notified of his passing, exactly at 4:00 A.M. While the light was present, I felt extremely tranquil and didn't move.

Another and even richer case of this sort was described on his PEI by a forty-one-year-old man, again not previously quoted, who had his NDE when he was seventeen. He states:

Latter part of July 1980—[A] friend with leukemia came to me in a sort of vision. I could see me with him. He said, "Come, my friend, walk with me." And we walked through a beautiful forest and came upon a ridge that looked into the most beautiful valley I've ever thought about seeing. It sort of glowed and sparkled. He said, "This is as far as you can go," and he walked off into this valley and I felt immensely peaceful. It still brings tears to my eyes; I will never forget it. The next day his daughter-in-law called and told me he had died the night before.

Sometimes an NDEr will feel that he or she "travels to" the site of another's death rather than seeing an apparition of a dead person. Another woman I met on the West Coast, Reinee Pasarow, who has subsequently published an account of her NDE,[17] provided such an instance on her PEI when she was commenting on her out-of-body experiences:

Again, out-of-body experiences have been a common phenomenon throughout my life. They have increased since the death occurrence and do not seem to be limited to a particular state. It seems they have occurred in dreams, in the waking state, and frequently in a trancelike state. Frankly, until recently, I did not consider them to be out-of-body experiences: They were simply "visions" to me. They also have not been limited to a time frame. A few years ago I saw a friend's death three hours before it occurred; however, I felt I was there because the minutest details of the setting were unmistakably clear to me, even though I have never actually been to the place where the death occurred until a short time after the funeral.

Reinee goes on to relate another, more extraordinary OBE, which I will quote below. A caveat, first, however: Although such cases are to be found in some profusion in the parapsychological literature, Reinee's is only one of three that I can recall from NDErs I have met. As you'll see, it takes us full circle:

Recently . . . I found myself [mentally] walking through what seemed to be the Sierras. I encountered a casual acquaintance sitting at a stream and conversed with him about a situation he was disturbed about. I forced myself back into the everyday world, feeling quite foggy, and thought no more about the experience until I bumped into this acquaintance the next week. He immediately pulled me aside and, asking me not to think him strange, confided in me that the week before, while he was sitting at a stream in the Sierras musing over a personal problem, I simply appeared and we had a very comfortable discussion about his situation! He said I was very, very real to him, although he realized I could not physically be there. He was quite confused about how this could happen, as was I, but he could not deny the experience. I cannot say which of us was more amazed, but this was the first undeniable confirmation I had ever received about actually being somewhere else during one of these visions, and I found it quite unsettling.

Thus, according to the accounts we have reviewed, NDErs may see the apparitions of others, or they themselves may become the apparitions *for* others as they appear in a quasiphysical fashion and even carry on a conversation of sorts! What Reinee is describing is, of course, a classic instance of *bilocation* and, as such, it is one of the more unusual psychic phenomena experienced by NDErs.

To be sure, NDErs also report such garden variety—if no less puzzling—psychic experiences as clairvoyance, telepathy, and precognition. Here's an example related to me by one of my interviewees whom I'll call Gwen. As she tells it, she and her then husband were driving to visit her husband's uncle, who lived in a town Gwen had never been to. The uncle bought and restored old houses, and the husband was confused as to which house was the right one. Gwen directed him correctly to it. When they entered, Gwen was able to tell the uncle many things about the original structural features of the house, some of which this man knew to be true, and he was astonished, Gwen says. She concluded this account with the following words:

He had just been to all kinds of places and verified the year it was built. And under lock and key, he had this paper that verified that it had been built in such-and-such a year. And he said to me,
"Were you ever in this house before?"
And I said, "No, never."
And he said, "Can you tell me when it was built?"
And I said, "In 1645."
And he went and got a paper and it was built in 1645.

As an example of claimed precognition, an anecdote from Janis will suffice:

When Reagan took office in '80, I told my then husband that he was going to be lucky if he lived until June. I see an attempt on his life. I says, "He's going to be lucky to live until June." Damned if he wasn't almost killed! Before June. I saw that. I *saw* it. . . . I just knew that he was going to be close to death before June. And that an attempt would be made on his life.

In some cases, the development of ESP following an NDE can be put to good use in one's professional life. A particularly instructive instance of this was given to me by a nurse I met at one of my workshops. She did a considerable amount of work with patients who were threatened with or facing death. I was not surprised to learn from her that she herself had had an NDE (when she was twelve). I *was* surprised to learn just how she related to her patients based on her own knowledge of NDEs. After the workshops she sent me a written account of her experience and added the following observations:

. . . now that I no longer fight it, I seem to be quite psychic. I have a talent for just tuning in to the energy of the hospital and being able to appear in the places where I am most needed without needing to be paged. Even in the middle of the night, if the condition of one of my patients changes and the hour of death comes, I am often awake and on the phone before the hospital has time to call me. In conversations with patients and families, I find myself tuning in to levels of understanding and comment that would not occur to me on a purely intellectual level. The whole thing is most exciting. . . .

I find my own NDE helpful in my work. . . . In my work with patients who die slowly, I am aware of when they are "in their bodies" and when they drift "out." I even use various relaxation techniques with them to help them "get out" when uncomfortable procedures such as a suctioning are being done. . . .

When I'm in the emergency room, serving as a link between a patient who had [been] "coded" and the family, I'm often in tune with the part of the patient who is "over in the corner by the ceiling" during an NDE and telepathically send a message that he or she will just have to excuse our need to try and bring them back and that I'm aware of how nice it is "out there." I also let him or her know that I'm supporting the family. Frequently, in cases where the patient lives, when I visit later in the ICU, a patient may say, "I remember talking to you in the emergency room," or, "You look familiar. Do I know you?" or, "You're the one who was with my family." Of course, during the contact to which they refer, they were completely unconscious. I find that most patients seem comfortable in sharing their NDEs with me, perhaps because in some sense they are aware that I was aware of what they were experiencing.

*　　*　　*

If only other nurses and health care professionals could be *trained* to respond as this nurse, through her NDE, does intuitively! How much apprehension and confusion in near-death survivors could be eliminated by such a knowingly caring attitude. This one example is certainly sufficient not only to provide a health care model to others but also to show that psychic sensitivities may be directed toward very practical ends.

We could easily continue this recital of ESP in NDErs, but enough examples have, I think, already been adduced to support my allusions to their reported frequency among Omega NDErs. Nevertheless, my own data in themselves are plainly insufficient to clinch the argument I advanced at the beginning of this chapter. To do that, one would need to be able to demonstrate at least two further points: (1) that Omega NDErs are representative of NDErs in general and (2) that the NDE itself generates psychic phenomena, not merely the coming close to death. Fortunately, two very recent studies by other researchers speak precisely to these issues, and we must now lean on them if we are to bolster our case that NDEs stimulate psychic development.

The Greyson and Kohr Studies

Bruce Greyson is a psychiatrist at the University of Michigan and is also IANDS' director of research. In 1982 he undertook a survey of IANDS' own sample of NDErs to determine whether NDEs have any systematic effect of psychic and psi-related phenomena. To measure these factors, Greyson used a standard questionnaire previously developed by parapsychologist John Palmer. Among other domains, this questionnaire examines various psychic phenomena, psi-related experiences, and altered states of consciousness in general. Greyson was able to administer Palmer's questionnaire to eighty NDErs, of whom 69 (86 percent) returned theirs for statistical analysis. Greyson has reported his findings in an article in *Theta*.[18]

The data from his study compare pre- and post-NDE incidence levels and, consistent with the findings from the PEI, Greyson discovered that there was an increased incidence for virtually all of the psychic and psi-related phenomena he assessed, although not all of the differences were statistically significant. Nevertheless, for each of the three major categories of interest to us here—psychic experiences, psi-related experiences, and what Greyson calls psi-conducive altered states of consciousness (states of consciousness, like deep relaxation, conducive to psychic phenomena), the overall increase was *highly* significant, meaning in this case that such differences as his NDErs reported could occur by chance less than once in ten thousand times.

To permit comparisons between Greyson's data and those of the PEI, I have included some of Greyson's most pertinent findings in Appendix III, where you will find them in Table 5.

Clearly, the results of Greyson's study strongly bolster the conclusion I drew from my more limited sample of Omega NDErs: NDEs tend to lead to psychic development. Although, to be sure, IANDS NDErs may *not* be representative of NDErs in general, they at least constitute a second and larger independent sample, which validated my own findings. Moreover, Greyson's findings are, as we shall see shortly, strongly congruent with those of a third investigation.

Of course, Greyson's research and mine share a common limitation: Neither has a comparison or control group. This means that although it appears that NDErs report more psychic activity after their experience, it may be that other, similar groups (such as those who have come close to death but haven't had an NDE—i.e., near-death survivors) might also if they were surveyed. In short, how do we know that the NDE itself fosters psychic development?

Here, happily, we have a second recent study to draw on, this one carried out by Richard Kohr, an educational researcher with the Pennsylvania Department of Education and, like Greyson, a member of IANDS.

Kohr is also a member of the Research Committee for the Association for Research and Enlightenment (ARE), a Virginia-based organization with a national membership of more than forty thousand that was established originally to honor the legacy of famed American psychic Edgar Cayce. It is generally regarded as an educational organization highly sympathetic to a variety of "New Age" concerns. Like IANDS, ARE maintains a research pool—a list of its members who have expressed their willingness to participate in ARE-sponsored research projects. In conducting his study, Kohr availed himself of this particular research sample.

As part of a larger study begun in 1980, Kohr distributed a lengthy questionnaire to seven hundred ARE members, of which 547 (78 percent) were returned. From the standpoint of near-death status, the sample was divided into three categories: NDErs (eighty-four), near-death survivors (105), and others (358). The questionnaire dealt with a variety of matters but included sections on psychic phenomena, meditation, dreams, and NDEs. As Greyson did, Kohr published a preliminary report of his findings in *Theta*.[19]

What Kohr found is extremely significant for our thesis. He states that in general there was little or no difference between near-death survivors and others but that NDErs tended to differ substantially from both groups. Specifically:

In all instances the [NDE] group showed a significantly greater tendency to report psi or psi-related experiences such as general ESP in both the waking and the dream state, psychokinesis, auras, apparitions, and out-of-body experiences.[20]

As I did for Greyson's findings, I have included in Appendix III an adaptation of a portion of Kohr's basic table of data so that appropriate specific comparisons can be made with my own and Greyson's results (see Table 6).

On all these general variables, the NDE group reports the highest incidence, and the difference between them and the other two groups is always statistically significant.

Thus, if we draw on the findings of the Greyson and Kohr studies together, we can conclude, as implied by the spiritual catalyst hypothesis, that NDEs—and not simply a near-death incident per se—tend to lead to accelerated psychic development. Moreover (and again consistent with my own findings reported earlier in this book), the additional data from these studies dealing with meditation and mystical experiences suggest that NDEs promote spiritual development as well. Altogether, then, this recent work by other investigators strengthens the overall thesis of this book and the particular argument of this chapter.

A Puzzling NDE Phenomenon: The Personal Flashforward

Our chapter could well have ended at this point were it not for a singular phenomenon associated with the NDE that calls for special and extended treatment. I have, accordingly, deliberately saved for the conclusion of this chapter the material I have collected that bears upon a remarkable and previously scarcely noted precognitive feature of the NDE I have called *the personal flashforward* (PF). If these experiences are what they purport to be, they not only have extremely profound implications for our understanding of the nature of time but also possibly for the future of our planet, as the next chapter will make clear. For now, however, we need to become familiar with the essentials of the personal flashforward.

In some earlier publications[21] dealing with NDEs, I suggested that a small number of near-death experiencers claim to be aware of events that they believe will take place. In some cases, these perceptions appear to take place in the context of the life review phase of the NDE. In these instances, they should perhaps be construed as possible life previews; at any rate, I call them personal flashforwards to show that such perceptions refer to events that have not yet occurred in a person's life. In my research, I have now encountered perhaps a score of NDErs who have described their PFs for me.

Personal flashforwards usually occur within the context of an assessment of one's life during an NDE (i.e., during a life review and preview), although occasionally the PF is experienced as a *subsequent* vision. When it takes place while the individual is undergoing an NDE, it is typically described as an image or vision of the future. It is as though the individual sees something of the whole trajectory of his life, not just past events, as some previous accounts[22] have implied. The understanding I have of these PFs is that to the NDEr they represent events of a *conditional* future—i.e., if he chooses to return to life, then these events will ensue. In this sense, from the standpoint of an NDEr, a PF may be likened to a "memory" of future events. For him, however, it is seemingly a part of his "life design" that *will* unfold if he returns to physical life.

In other cases an individual will report awareness of knowledge of a future event some time after the NDE itself. In some instances, the knowledge will manifest itself (again, usually visually and vividly) shortly after an NDE; in other cases, the individual will recall the knowledge *only when the actual event happens*. In this case (this kind of occurrence has been related to me by several NDErs) it seems the event itself jars the memory of it, bringing back the NDE context in which the original perception was given. At such moments there is usually an uncanny sense of *déjà vu;* the event that had already been experienced is now fulfilled in fact, and its realization is accompanied by the shock of absolutely certain prior knowledge of its outcome.

A case that will serve to illustrate several of these features was provided to me by a woman who lives in the Midwest. Her near-death crisis resulted from a torn cervix while giving birth to her youngest child, in 1959. During her NDE she was met by various beings who conveyed knowledge to her. In particular, she noted:

I learned that there is a time for me to die, and that particular time when I was giving birth was not it. Those beings showed me that if I continued down the path I was on at that time (it seems that I have complete freedom of choice) I would later be living HERE and DOING THIS. I found myself in a place that was not [the town I expected to move to] and all three of our children were grown up. My husband and I had become middle-aged, and the entire scenario went like this:

I was in a kitchen tossing a salad, dressed in a striped seersucker outfit. My hair had streaks of silver in it, my waist had thickened some, but I was still in good shape for an older woman. There was a strong feeling of peace of mind about my bearing, and I was in a joyful mood, laughing with my older daughter as we prepared dinner. The younger daughter (the newborn) had gone somewhere with some other children. This daughter was grown up too, but still there were some small children involved who were not in the picture at the moment (i.e., in 1959).

My husband had just come out of the shower and was walking down a hallway wrapping a robe around him. He had put on more weight than I had and his hair was quite silver. Our son was mowing our lawn, but both offspring were only visiting. They didn't live with us.

During this scene was the only time an exception was made regarding the five physical senses. As I gained the knowledge of what our family would be like in the future, I could see, hear, and smell. Particularly striking was the smell of the salad I was producing (cucumber) mingled with the smell of evergreens growing around the house and the odor of freshly cut grass. Also I could detect my own cologne and soap from the shower my husband had vacated. This picture was only a glimpse, but it made one huge impression on me. I must have vowed right then to never forget it, because I certainly have not.

This correspondent added this intriguing follow-up commentary:

1. We look exactly like that right now (in 1981).
2. Our kids look like that picture too.
3. The rapport in our family is now as I've already described. We have a ball whenever we get together, talking and laughing.
4. Our older daughter has been married, had two daughters of her own, and been divorced. While she was being divorced and making a new life for herself with a job, I've helped her with raising the two small girls by baby-sitting every day for two years. They are very much a part of our family.
5. Our home here in [the town she lives in] could fit that description too. I only wish I had paid more attention to the way the house was built.

Another case that exemplifies most of the characteristics of finely detailed PFs is this one, sent to me by a correspondent living in the western part of the United States. As a ten-year-old child, in his native England, he was rushed to a hospital and operated on for acute appendicitis (possibly peritonitis—he is not sure). During the operation he had an NDE during which he had an out-of-body experience (at which time he could see his body) as well as an episode involving telepathic communication with beings who seemed to be clothed in robes.

What makes this individual's experience noteworthy is what happened to him *afterward*. He writes:

After the operation, when convalescing, I was aware that there were some strange memories—and that's what they were—concerning events in my future life. I do not know how they got there . . . they were just *there*. . . . However, at that time [1941], and indeed until 1968, I simply did not believe them.

His letter goes on to describe five specific "memories" of the future he had been aware of as a child. He claims all of them have actually come about as events in his life, except for the last (which pertains to his age at and circumstances of his death). I shall quote his account of the first two of these flashforwards.

1. *You will be married at age twenty-eight.*
This was the first of the "memories," and this was perceived as a flat statement—there was no emotion attached to it. . . . And this did indeed happen, even though at [my] twenty-eighth birthday I had yet to meet the person that I was to marry.
2. *You will have two children and· live in the house that you see.*
By contrast to the prediction, this was felt; perhaps "experienced" is the correct term. I had a vivid memory of sitting in a chair, from which I could see two children playing on the floor in front of me. And I *knew* that I was married, although in this vision there was no indication of who it was that I was married to. Now, a married person knows what it was like to be single, because he or she was once single, and he or she knows what it's like to be married because he or she is married. But it is not possible for a single person to know what it feels like to be married; in particular, it is *not possible* for a ten-year-old boy to know what it feels like to be married! It is this strange, impossible feeling that I remember so clearly and why this incident remained in my mind. I had a "memory" of something that was not to happen for almost twenty-

five years hence! But it was not seeing the future in the conventional sense, it was *experiencing* the future. In this incident the future was *now*.

(He then provides a floor plan of the room he and his children were in and refers to it in what follows.)

In this "experience" I saw directly in front of me, and to the right as indicated. I could not see to the left, but I did know that the person that I was married to was sitting on that side of the room. The children playing on the floor were about four and three years old; the older one had dark hair and was a girl (adopted, as it turned out); the younger one had fair hair, and I thought it was a boy. But as it turns out, they are both girls. And I was also aware that behind the wall . . . there was something very strange that I did not understand at all. My conscious mind could not grasp it, but I just *knew* that something different was there.

This "memory" suddenly became present one day in 1968, when I was sitting in the chair, reading a book, and happened to glance over at the children. . . . I realized that *this* was the "memory" from 1941! After that I began to realize that there was something to these strange recollections. And the strange object behind the wall was a forced-air heater. These heating units were not—and to the best of my knowledge, are still not—used in England. This was why I could not grasp what it was; it was not in my sphere of knowledge in 1941.[23]

Still another striking instance of a series of PFs was shared with me by Janis in our long interview mentioned in Chapter 3. You may remember that in connection with her life review she mentioned a very curious phenomenon—something that is, in fact, unique in my records. She stated that her life review was presented to her "in black and white" but when she came to events that "hadn't happened yet" it changed into color! Intrigued by this, I naturally asked her if she could remember any of the specific events she saw that she took to be episodes to occur in her life. This is a portion of what she told me:

Well, like I saw myself in a car and the car's sinking. And water. And having a hard time getting out. Eventually getting out, but struggling, really struggling to get out of the car that was sinking in this water.

I asked Janis whether this PF (and others she went on to relate to me) had any relationship to events that subsequently did occur in her life.

Oh, yeah. Oh, yeah. Um-hmm . . . I was in Florida visiting my parents and I was supposed to cross this state to take a picture of the St. Petersburg–Tampa Bridge. And for three consecutive mornings before I was to leave, I woke up, I couldn't breathe. I was sinking. I was sinking in my car, that car; my cat was caught under the front seat. I got out, she didn't. Consequently, I didn't go. And the morning I was supposed to be there, I got up out of bed and found out that the bridge had been hit by a boat. Numerous cars and a bus went over.

Another PF Janis described to me involved a fire and an explosion.

I was far enough away to get away, but I wasn't far enough away to be *safe*. There was a real threat to my existence there. [What about that fire?] I was driving on I-94 [this was several years after her NDE] between Detroit and Ann Arbor. All of a sudden, this anxiety, this fear. I saw this gasoline tanker jackknife and explode and the flames leap up over this road that went over the freeway. And I saw all these cars burst into flame—and I had to get off. I mean, I didn't see it. I didn't physically see it; I didn't hallucinate it—I just saw it. And the next exit I took off and I took a long way home instead of the freeway. And I got home [at] six o'clock, just in time for the news and turned on the news and, sure enough, there it was. A tanker had jackknifed, exploded, three cars were demolished, the drivers and passengers, and one of the homes near the freeway was demolished. [And this is where you would have been had you not taken that exit off the interstate?] Right. Had I continued at the same rate on the same route, I would have been right there.

Janis estimated that she was presented with six or seven such specific scenes from her future life during her PF, though not all of them involved life-threatening circumstances. Of these, she was able to recall and recount five such events to me during our conversation. All of them, she alleges, had some correspondence to a subsequent life situation except for one. That one she described to me as follows:

There was myself walking down a stairway, an open stairway, white, open stairway from a second floor. I was walking down the stairway dressed in white. There was someone at the foot of that stairway. It was a man. I wasn't married to him, but he was taking me someplace to get an award, an award that I'd won for writing something. [What about the man who was your escort?] That hasn't come yet. That's still in the future.

Although Janis still hasn't received any awards for her writing, it is at least worth noting that since her NDE she has *become* a writer and is currently working on a novel as well as an autobiographical memoir. It goes without saying that I will be keenly interested to observe the response to Janis's work!

In her case, however, her PFs do not necessarily always seem to be accurate forecasts of her own personal future so much as previews of conditions to which she *might have been* subject *if* she did not take some action to avoid them. In short, her PFs seem to have shown her a possible, contingent future, not her inevitable and fixed destiny.

Nevertheless, such apparent memories or intimations of the future are certainly provocative, and it is easy to appreciate the striking effect they must have on an individual when they are later actually confirmed. Nevertheless, a sticky methodological issue must be faced here before we can proceed with our delineation of PFs. Put boldly, it is: How do we know these accounts are true? To be sure, there is scant reason to believe that all those persons who report PFs (and who usually aver that many of them were fulfilled) are simply making them up. At the same time, we must recognize that PFs typically have the form of unsubstantiated and unsubstantiable self-reports: A person alleges to have had a vision of a future event and then also claims that the event later took place. Accordingly, we seem to be left in the uncomfortable position of having to acknowledge that such reports sometimes are made but lacking the means to determine the truth of the testimony given.

In rare instances, however, a way can be found to circumvent this problem by compiling external corroborative evidence that independently supports the claim made by an NDEr. Fortunately, I have recently come across just such a case involving a PF.

This account comes from one of Raymond Moody's original respondents, Belle, whom we met in Chapter 3. As you'll recall, Belle underwent a protracted period of clinical death before being resuscitated. During her experience she, too, encountered guides who gave her considerable information about the future, some of which we'll present in the following chapter. What makes her NDE unique and of particular value here is precisely what she was shown.

Specifically, she was "shown" a picture of Raymond Moody! She was given his full name and told that she would meet him when "the time was right" to tell him her story.

Belle has lived her entire life in a small southern city, residing since 1971 in a home on a street one block long. Approximately eighteen months after her NDE, Raymond Moody, who was then beginning his medical studies, and his wife, Louise, moved to the same city where Belle had grown up. To the same street! But since the Moodys lived at the other end of the block, years passed without any meaningful interaction between the Moodys and Belle.[24]

Finally, four years *after* Belle's NDE, on Halloween night of 1975, Louise was preparing to take her elder son, Avery, trick-or-treating. Her husband had asked her, however, not to take him to any home unfamiliar to them. Meanwhile, up the block, Belle, who was feeling poorly, was saying to her husband:

Look, I placed these things [candies] there for the children when they come around, and no matter how cute you think they are, don't call me because I do not feel well tonight and I do not want to be bothered.

Belle describes what happened next:

He said "OK," and sure enough, someone knocked on the door. . . . Louise didn't listen to Raymond, [and] Bill [her husband] didn't listen to me, so when the knock came on the door, my husband said, "Belle, you told me not to call you, but you've got to see *this* one!" "Oh, boy," I said, [and] I got up and went up front. I don't normally ask the children where they are from or who they are because I usually know them, but this one I did not know and I said, "What's your name, child?" He looked up at me and said, "I'm Raymond Avery Moody, the third."[25] Immediately his father appeared in my mind and it says . . . now!

Belle turned at once to Louise and said, "I need to talk with your husband." Louise, somewhat taken aback, apparently replied with words to the effect, "Oh, did you have one of those experiences Raymond is writing about?" Belle—who had no idea who Raymond Moody was but only knew he was the man to whom she was supposed to speak—asked Louise, "What experiences are you referring to?" When Louise said "near-death experiences," Belle said that she supposed she did, since she had been pronounced dead.

The outcome of this strange encounter was that shortly thereafter Raymond Moody was able to interview Belle, whose NDE is featured in his second book, *Reflections on Life After Life*. Ironically, at the time of their meeting in 1975, Moody's best seller-to-be, *Life After Life*, was still at the printer's, and Belle herself had no idea that she had just met the man whose name was destined to become synonymous with the study of near-death experiences. Furthermore, Louise Moody[26] has independently confirmed all the essential details of Belle's reconstruction of this event.

Belle herself concluded her account of this episode with these words:

It was two days before we got together and this was in November of 1975, and they left in April of 1976. We had become very close and loving friends from that point on. It seemed to be a heck of a waste of time not to have known him from 1971!

Conclusion

Starting from the assumption found in the world's traditional spiritual teachings that one can anticipate psychic abilities as a by-product of spiritual growth, we have shown that the NDE itself does seem to lead to accelerated psychic development in many experiencers. This, of course, is consistent with our view that the NDE serves principally as a catalyst for spiritual awakening and development. Not only is my own research supportive of this interpretive line but so is the work of other independent investigators.

The phenomenon of the personal flashforward with which this chapter concluded is, however, perhaps the most significant contribution to our appreciation of NDE-related psychic experiences for at least a couple of reasons. The first is because it appears to be the one psychic phenomenon that is inherently and uniquely interwoven with the NDE itself, since it seems to be born of the life review/preview phase of the experience. In that respect it is an aspect of precognition clearly deserving of more careful investigation by near-death researchers and parapsychologists alike. The second reason is even more commanding: PFs seem to be linked to still *another* precognitive phenomenon sometimes (but not uniquely) associated with NDEs and whose implications deserve the most sedulous scrutiny. These are what I have elsewhere[27] called planetary or "prophetic" visions—i.e., it is not merely that NDEs sometimes appear to generate personal flashforwards that is alone significant; sometimes they induce in NDErs a global vision of our *collective* future as well and, furthermore, these planetary visions tend to be much the same in their main outlines in *all* the NDErs who so far have reported them. Because of all we have learned about NDErs to this point, we can scarcely do otherwise than consider and evaluate what these NDErs have to tell us awaits us in the years to come. In Chapter 8, accordingly, we will devote ourselves entirely to the delineation and assessment of this common planetary vision of NDErs.

CHAPTER 8

. . . .

Planetary Visions of Near-Death Experiencers

∻

In the summer of 1977 I first met a young man who was soon to prove instrumental in the development of the field of near-death studies. John Audette was a sociology student who, while attending college in Georgia in the early seventies, had happened to hear one of Raymond Moody's first talks on near-death experiences. Astonished by his strong and positive emotional response to Moody's talk, John became fascinated with NDEs and virtually importuned Moody for the opportunity to help him in his research on the subject. As a result of his contact with Moody and the NDErs he was able to meet through him, John—who had earned an advanced degree in sociology—became one of the earliest near-death researchers in his own right and has since carried out one of the major studies in the field.[1] In addition, John was to become a cofounder of IANDS and its first executive director.

All this was years away, however, from the time of our initial meeting. I had only just begun my own research, and in those days colleagues in this field were almost nonexistent. As John was certainly senior to me in experience if not in age, I listened to his account of his own work and contacts with near-death experiencers with rapt attention.

One of the bits of knowledge he imparted to me late one evening struck me quite forcibly. He told me that he had met a few people whom Moody had first interviewed, who all independently seemed to have had a vision of the *planet's* future in conjunction with their NDE. That in itself wasn't so astonishing, of course, but what John went on to tell me was of more than passing interest. All of them, he said, had had essentially the *same* vision and that it was one of widespread and cataclysmic destruction. Furthermore, they all appeared to agree on the year in which these events were to take place. The year was 1988.

This was quite a revelation. Certainly none of the NDErs I had by then interviewed had divulged any such prophetic vision to me. On the other hand, since my interview questions did not deal with any such matters, even remotely, it was perhaps not surprising that I had never heard of such visions from the respondents in my sample. Of course, even in those days, apocalyptic scenarios were much in vogue, but I had never paid any serious attention to them. What intrigued me about John's observations, however, were two points in particular: (1) Those prophetic visions (PVs)—as I was later to call them[2]—seemed to occur in connection with deep NDEs, and (2) there appeared to be an impressive similarity in the vision among these NDErs.

At the time, however, I had my own research to complete, and since it was demanding enough, I felt I could not allow myself to pursue this tantalizing bit of NDE lore that John had disclosed to me.

Still, I could not quite forget it, and it remained with me as an aspect of NDEs with which I felt I should concern myself when I had the time to investigate it on my own.

After *Life at Death* was published I began meeting some NDErs who claimed to have had these prophetic visions. And though I had at first lulled myself into believing that I had finished my work in near-death studies, such encounters reawakened me to my earlier intention of determining how common such reports were and what significance could be ascribed to them. Accordingly, I made plans to try to track down as many of those NDErs as I could and draw my own conclusions.

My first step was to call Raymond Moody and John for leads, which they kindly supplied to me. In the meantime, several people had written me at IANDS describing such experiences. Subsequent correspondence and interviews, when they could be arranged, provided further information. In most cases I traveled to various parts of the United States to tape-record interviews with NDErs, or arrangements were made for them to come to Connecticut to be interviewed. When personal interviews were conducted, I usually was able to spend at least two days with the respondent at our initial meeting; in all these cases, contact was maintained through correspondence, tapes, phone calls, or subsequent meetings. Finally, a few respondents completed questionnaires for me, and these furnished additional data.

Since those initial steps were taken, I have located sixteen NDErs who claim to have had planetary visions.[3] Even though this sample is obviously very small, I feel that in view of the possible significance of my findings it is justified to publish these data in this form and at this time. Nevertheless, it should be strongly borne in mind that the cases presented here have been specifically sought out and that because of both the limited sample size and the method of sampling, the results need to be independently validated before they can be fully accepted.

In what follows, then, I will present what I have learned over the past few years concerning this unusual kind of NDE-related precognitive phenomenon and, toward the close of this chapter, I will consider what we are to make of it.

Prophetic Visions

Prophetic visions differ from PFs (personal flashforwards) in two principal ways: (1) Prophetic visions relate to future events that have a global rather than a personal focus; (2) they are highly consistent from person to person. This latter characteristic makes them especially remarkable, just as it was the overall similarities among NDEs in general that captured the attention of researchers and the public during the 1970s. Nevertheless, given the consistency of these PVs, it is their specific content, as we shall shortly see, that arouses one's strong interest in their possible prophetic character.

Most individuals reporting PVs[4] claim that the details of their visions were given to them during their NDEs, often in association with an encounter with guides or a being of light. In a few instances, however, the visions seem to unfold after the NDE, and it isn't clear whether the information was encoded during the NDE. In any event, most of those who have described their PVs to me state or imply that they know they were given far more information than they can now recall. Furthermore, several of them observed that they were told they would not be *able* to recall much of this information but would be given access to some of it when and if it was needed. The following comment by Belle is typical of the way in which the information is felt to be stored and of the condition governing its retrieval:

At one point I had complete knowledge of everything, from the beginning of creation to the end of time . . . [but] I was told [by her guides] that I would remain unconscious for five days so that all the things I had been shown would not resurface, so they could be stored for future reference. . . . When given this information, you are given . . . the time . . . when you can speak of it. If you were to ask me a question now . . . [and] if the time wasn't for me to answer, I couldn't give you the answer.

In most instances, however, there is a general recall of the broad outlines of the scenario. The following remark is representative:

I also had the general knowledge of certain events . . . it's not that I can pinpoint certain events . . . it's more like a general knowledge of things that are going to take place.

What restores knowledge of the specific events in the PV scenario? One factor is the temporal proximity of the event. A number of individuals stated that within one to two days prior to an event they had foreseen, the knowledge of its occurrence would resurface. For instance, one of Raymond Moody's original respondents said:

Three Mile Island, I knew it was going to happen! I don't know *why*. Three Mile Island stuck in my mind. . . . I knew it was going to happen, I knew it was going to happen. I was telling Vicky. . . . I told her it was going to happen, and, do you know, two days later it happened.

A second factor facilitating recall is a reminder of the original event. We have already seen an example of this in Belle's recollection of Raymond Moody when his son gave his name. Individuals have remarked that being in a certain physical location reminded them of an event they had seen in their PV, and this brought it back.

A third factor is one not associated with any conscious knowledge of a particular trigger. Seemingly, spontaneous recall operates here, although it is sometimes the respondent's *post hoc* interpretation that it was simply time for this information to resurface.

The General Scenario Recounted in Prophetic Visions.

I have already indicated that the broad outlines of the PV are much the same for different individuals. Indeed, PVs—as an aspect of NDEs—are analogous to NDEs as a whole in the sense that though no two are identical, the elements that comprise them occur again and again and form a coherent pattern. Keeping in mind that the number of cases of PVs in this sample is so small that any overall account must be regarded as extremely provisional, it is nevertheless possible to give the following summary of it. It is chiefly that everyone I have talked to has given me a PV that conforms, at least broadly, to this model that emboldens me to offer it at all at this time.

There is, first of all, a sense of having total knowledge, but specifically one is aware of seeing the entirety of the earth's evolution and history, from the beginning to the end of time. The future scenario, however, is usually of short duration, seldom extending much beyond the beginning of the twenty-first century. The individuals report that in this decade there will be an increasing incidence of earthquakes, volcanic activity, and generally massive geophysical changes. There will be resultant disturbances in weather patterns and food supplies. The world economic system will collapse, and the possibility of nuclear war or accident is very great (respondents are not agreed on *whether* a nuclear catastrophe will occur). All of these events are transitional rather than ultimate, however, and they will be followed by a new era in human history marked by human brotherhood, universal love, and world peace. Though many will die, the earth will live. While agreeing that the dates for these events are not fixed, most individuals feel that they are likely to take place during the 1980s.

Shortly, I will attempt to illustrate the various facets of the PV scenario by referring to interviews, but for now let me present just a couple of summary statements from individuals who wrote to me or answered questionnaires.

First, from a man who had his NDE in 1943:

Our period of trouble has begun, it seems, certainly as far as the elements are concerned. I think you can expect to see some of the most disastrous upheavals between now and 1988 that we have had in recorded history. Most recently, the eruption of St. Helens is an example. This will not only be in the elements, but in the breakdown of interpersonal relationships, between man and man, man and family, and nation and nation. . . . My own impression is that we are not facing the end of the world but that we are facing a great deal of upheaval until we have learned to stop being so materialistic and turn to the job He gave us of truly learning to love ourselves and one another.

Next, from Reinee Pasarow, who had her NDE in 1967, when she was only seventeen years old:

The vision of the future I received during my near-death experience was one of tremendous upheaval in the world as a result of our general ignorance of the "true" reality. I was informed that mankind was breaking the laws of the universe and as a result of this would suffer. This suffering was not due to the vengeance of an indignant God but rather like the pain one might suffer as a result of arrogantly defying the law of gravity. It was to be an inevitable educational cleansing of the earth that would creep up upon its inhabitants, who would try to hide blindly in the institutions of law, science, and religion. Mankind, I was told, was being consumed by the cancers of arrogance, materialism, racism, chauvinism, and separatist thinking. I saw sense turning to nonsense, and calamity, in the end, turning to providence.

At the end of this general period of transition, mankind was to be "born anew," with a new sense of his place in the universe. The birth process, however, as in all the kingdoms, was exquisitely painful. Mankind would emerge humbled yet educated, peaceful, and, at last, unified.

*   *   *

Now that we have some sense of the overall PV scenario, let us look more closely at some of its specific features.

Sense of Total Knowledge.

In the state of consciousness an NDEr enters when receptive to a PV, it appears that there is, as we have seen, a subjective sense of total knowledge. This point has already been made by Belle, but Darryl was even more emphatic. He said that when he experienced this state of total knowledge, it was not that he acquired this knowledge but that he *remembered* it—that he *was*, in effect, all knowledge. Another respondent, Hank, commented that the being of light who was with him at one point made a gesture with his right hand and there followed a panoramic vision, impossible to describe, showing everything "from the beginning of time to the end of time." Indeed, that or a similar phrase was used by several respondents in referring to their PVs.

Geophysical Changes.

Even though these near-death experiencers often claim to have this panoramic vision of both past and future, it is future events that tend, not surprisingly, to be emphasized in their accounts. And preeminent among them are various geophysical changes that tend to be mentioned almost without exception. The following excerpts from interviews will convey both the range of the events foreseen as well as some of the conditions under which this information appears to reemerge.

Earthquakes.

The seismic activity is going to increase terribly; the United States is going to start suffering some great seismic problems.

Well, it's like that earthquake that hit last week [in Italy]. I saw that coming. I see a lot of them coming. . . . There will be a series of disasters happening.

*   *   *

I saw earthquakes in South America, and in Italy, and the one that Greece just had.

I kept thinking about Italy and I kept thinking about this earthquake, and I wrote it down on a piece of paper. . . . I dunno, I was just reading and thought of this earthquake in Italy. So, in September, this massive earthquake happened in Italy. . . . I dunno, I saw it on TV and goddamn! I thought I had *seen it before*. I knew I had seen the *picture*. I mean, I had seen the pictures before! Pictures came on the screen of this earthquake and the details and where it had happened and the map of it on TV, you know, [and] I thought, "God, I've seen this *before!*" There was no mistake in my mind.

Volcanic Activity.

I was shown [the] Mt. St. Helens eruption. . . . I was also shown other volcanoes. . . . I was shown Mt. St. Helens . . . and on May 18, Mt. St. Helens really erupted its heaviest. I turned to my husband and said, "Mt. St. Helens just blew its top," and the people there just laughed at me. Later that night we were watching TV and the very scenes that I had seen in my mind were shown on the TV and no one continued to laugh at me then.

Landmass Changes.

Because of this pole shift [there is] a kind of magnetic pull [causing] the continents to move toward each other. . . . Along the East Coast [of the United States], there will be a significant rise in the tide because of the polar melt.

They [her guides] showed Florida breaking off from the mainland, land rising and becoming an island.

There may be a pole shift . . . there are going to be polar changes . . . it's not going to kill all the races off, but we're going to have to start again from square one. . . . There's going to be a larger landmass.

* * *

It [a higher being] said that there was going to be [environmental] stress. And I saw mudslides. . . . I saw California. . . . I saw water pouring. I saw quicksand. I saw things shifting . . . [and] it looked like I was looking down on islands . . . and I watched them tip and elongate and stretch and groan. . . . I'm interpreting this now as probably an indication of this pole-shift business.

Meteorological Changes.

The geophysical changes just described would naturally be expected to bring about a host of meteorological disruptions in their wake. These changes, too, have been glimpsed by near-death survivors who report PVs.

Oh, my God, that's going to be terrible. The weather is going to go crazy. We're just as likely to have snow in the middle of the summer as one-hundred-degree weather. . . . I see droughts in other countries.

I think around 1984, 1985, possibly even sooner, [we'll see] the beginnings of droughts. I guess we are even suffering some of that now [1980].

Supply and Economic Breakdowns.

Such drastic changes in the world's physical state will necessarily disrupt commerce and, indeed, every aspect of global life. Famine, social disorder, and economic collapse will be the result. Here is just one brief summary by Hank of these foreseen effects:

We'll start getting more droughts, which will bring about shortages in crops, and the shortage in crops will cause food prices to rise, which will cause a strain on the economic situation, which is already going downhill. Also, at the same time . . . because of the shortage of food and the failing economy, I see a strengthening of arms, which causes tension. . . . These kinds of hostilities and [increasing] inflation start more hostilities.

* * *

Nuclear War?

These developments bring us, at least in the view of the individuals under examination here, to the brink of nuclear warfare. I place a question mark after the phrase, however, to indicate that these near-death experiencers do not seem to agree that there will be a nuclear war, only that the prospect of one (or a nuclear accident) will be enormously heightened during the 1980s.[5] I will offer enough quotations, I think, to reflect accurately the entire range of their views.

First, there are those who sense that there will actually be a war:

Well, it'll start in the Middle East . . . and it will be the end. It'll be the Third War.

Anyway, by 1988, that will be the point when tensions finally grow to the point [of a nuclear war]. Yeah. And just from my own feelings, I think it will happen in April 1988.

Next are those who feel that, rather than a total war, there will be either a misuse of nuclear energy or illegal underground testing and that this will imperil humanity:

I can see a magnetized target of some kind and all this energy is being focused on it. . . . It's not like an explosion, it's like an implosion. And the result of this process is going to produce . . . a tremendous amount of energy. But the important thing about this aspect . . . well, it's a series of negativisms that are going on around the earth and [as a result] the human beings on the earth will experience rather extravagant things, happenings and disruptions, and so on, starting very shortly and through this period of time . . . it will change everything.

What I saw was warfare underground tests. . . . And I saw a lot of shake-ups. Seismic activity kicked off by cheaty tests that nobody is admitting. And fallout . . . the words "nuclear skirmishes" if one can conceive of such a thing . . . I saw the aftermath. I saw the explosion places. I saw a chunk of New York City was gone. . . .

Finally, there are those who have a clear presentiment of a nuclear holocaust but cannot claim it is a certainty:

I had a sensation, a feeling that—of nuclear bombs falling and the bright flash of the bomb. . . . If people don't get their act together . . . there is going to be a nuclear war. . . . Every once in a while when I'm coming home from work on the freeway, I get the feeling of a bomb going off. I believe it might be in L.A. and there's a big flash, and I'll look over there in the west and I'll see a big mushroom cloud.

I had this series of dreams about this incredible threat of a war. . . . This dream is [pause] this threat of a nuclear war. And everyone is talking about it. There was a great deal of tension about it. Things are very desperate . . . it's extremely frightening. Extremely. And it's put me in a state of near immobility. Because it's happening . . . I think it is in an Olympic year. . . . It's all armored vehicles. It's all on land. Tanks and half-tracks. And soldiers as far as you can see them. And it's an offensive. . . . I dunno, the phones are ringing off the hook. The U.N. is in joint session. Everyone's talking about it. . . . This stuff is controlling my life right now. See, it's happening. It really is happening. This caused me to have a nervous breakdown, a nervous breakdown. And I don't know what to do.[6]

A New Era of Peace and Human Brotherhood.

Whether the earth is shaken by natural catastrophes, or nuclear warfare, or both, earth and the life upon it does survive. More than that, however: A New Age emerges and the devastating changes that have preceded it are understood to have been necessary purgations effecting the transformation of humanity into a new mode of being. By analogy, just as the individual near-death experiencer may have to endure the pain and suffering associated with the trauma of almost dying before positive personal transformation can take place, so the world may need to undergo a "planetary near-death experience" before it can awaken to a higher, more spiritual, collective consciousness with universal love at its core. Religious symbolism, and Christian symbolism in particular,[7] are very evident here. It should be emphasized that almost all the PVs I have encountered state or imply a very positive outcome following years of destruction and upheaval, however produced. The following quotations will provide the flavor of this resolution:

At the end of this general period of transition, mankind was to be "born anew," with a new sense of his place in the universe. . . . Mankind would emerge humbled yet educated, peaceful, and, at last, unified.

In 1989 . . . I see a period when those who are good-intentioned and those who have acquired a type of level of spirituality of close bondedness of human relationships, that the being of light, the Christlike figure will be able to dwell among us. [1989] was the end. I just have a general knowledge of what was in 1989. Peace, contentment.

[Christ] will come back and there will also be the Christ-like features in other people. Yes, this is true, He is coming.

It's like a renaissance. I feel really good in 2005.

These, then, are the major elements that comprise the PV scenario. Before concluding this section, however, we need to consider two ancillary aspects of PVs. The first has to do with the timing of the events foreseen; the second, with their inevitability.

When Does the Scenario Occur?

Almost all these NDErs state or imply that the major geophysical and meteorological changes forecast will begin during this decade, though a few are inclined to believe it will be later. Probably most of them would agree that the changes have already begun and will be evident within a few years at most. The following sprinkling of brief quotations will convey the common timeframes used:

I believe the war will start in 1984 or 1985.

I think you can expect to see some of the most disastrous upheavals between now and 1988.

It is to be 1988 or was to be. That [would] be the year everything would be wiped away if we didn't change.

The seismic activity is going to [be] within the next ten years.

[The war will] probably be in the next ten years.

I think around 1984, 1985, possibly even sooner [will see] the beginnings of droughts. . . . Anyway, by 1988, that will be when tensions finally grow to the point [of nuclear war].

I've been told we'll see signs of its approach. . . . There will be great natural catastrophes, an assassination attempt on the Pope, an intensification of the drug problem. Abortion will be legalized. Mercy killing will come to be accepted, both for the senile and for deformed children. Since we've already had most of those signs, I believe the three days of darkness [this respondent's term for the holocaust] will come soon.[8]

Is the Scenario Inevitable?

The common view of the NDErs who have these PVs is that not only is the scenario inevitable, but, properly understood (in the light of its outcome), it is desirable and necessary. Nevertheless, few of these individuals would argue that there is anything fixed concerning the exact dates involved or specific events. Most seem convinced of the general direction of the events they feel they have glimpsed; none of them seems to have a rigid conception of the details of that unfolding pattern. Indeed, some openly admit that it can be affected to some degree by human action and an openness to God. The following are representative views:

Yes, it's inevitable. . . . From now on, we're going to see the seismic activity all over the world, and the weather and all of it is pointing to the fact that all that I'm saying is true . . . and it's going to happen.

I really feel that the destiny cannot be changed.

I firmly believe now that there was a chance at one time but now we are locked in, that there's no chance to turn back.

[This scenario] is necessary, a necessary evil, if you want to call it that. It is part of the evolution toward this oneness.

There will be survivors, but it's inevitable.

I would be the first to say that the Christ did not give me a definite date or a definite series of events that I could look forward to but more or less events that I saw in general that would be indicative of some of the events of the future.

It [was] given to me that in 1988, the world will be destroyed by earthquakes and volcanic eruptions but if the people will turn to God and honor Him, some of these things will be put off. The time now . . . is not running as close to 1988.

Unless people start working together and stop fighting, they're gonna destroy themselves. . . . Unless people learn to get along and care about each other and care about other life on this planet, there will be no planet. Even during my near-death experience, I had a feeling that there isn't that much time left *here* unless something is done. And that's why I came back because I thought, "Maybe there won't be another chance." . . . There's an urgency about it because there isn't that much time.

PFs, PVs, and the Problem of Precognition

Beginning with Chapter 7, where we started exploring the link between NDEs and psychic phenomena, we have been increasingly concerned with a range of experiences that, like the NDE itself, defies conventional scientific explanation. Perhaps nowhere is this more apparent than in the case of the precognitive phenomena with which we have been dealing in these past two chapters. Though we can scarcely afford a digression here to review theories of precognitive phenomena in general,[9] it does seem necessary to take a moment to consider how these precognitive aspects of NDEs might be interpreted, especially since their implications appear to deserve thoughtful and critical evaluation.

In seeking to understand PFs and PVs, two separate questions need to be addressed, though the second one will pertain to PVs alone. The first question is: Since both PFs and PVs purport to represent visions of the future, differing mainly only in their scope (i.e., personal vs. global), in what sense might it be possible to have paranormal knowledge of future events? The second question is: Are the *contents* of PVs likely to be prognostic visions of our planetary future, or can they be explained on other grounds entirely? The answer to the second question may depend on the first.

Two Views of Precognition

Modern theories of precognition usually are grounded in twentieth-century physics, which has now provided us with models that allow for what laypersons would call "knowledge of the future." The interpretations of precognition that follow from these models tend to fall into two main categories, each of which is associated with a different theoretical orientation in contemporary physics. What are these general interpretations and how do they relate to NDE-based visions of the future?

First, it is held that when someone reports a subsequently verified precognitive perception, he has foreseen an actual future event. This in turn implies that the future in some sense *must already exist* and that, under certain circumstances, it is possible to discern discrete events in that future pattern.

Such a theoretical state of affairs is consistent with Einstein's Theory of General Relativity and his conception of a static four-dimensional space-time continuum. As Zohar observes in this connection:

If all events are looked at within the framework of General Relativity, they become timeless phenomena in four-dimensional space-time, stretched out along the curved contour of our spherical existence as a static, changeless whole. Such a picture implies that everything that ever "will be" now "is," i.e., that the future is already written and is as fixed as the past.[10]

If this is so, then we would seem to have the theoretical basis here—if not the understanding of the exact process—for the kind of PFs and PVs reported by NDErs.

An intuitive grasp of this kind of formulation can be afforded by the following analogy. Suppose that you are a character in someone else's novel. Suppose further that you are completely identified with that character as you go through your life. Suddenly you experience an altered state of consciousness and are "lifted up" to a higher dimension in which you are identified with the mind of the author of the novel in which you have been a character. In this moment, you have total knowledge of your past and your future, for you have a complete grasp of the character's life's trajectory (including his death on page 269). All at once, however, you are "returned" to your ordinary consciousness where past is past and future is future, but, even though you are again identified with your character, you retain a few isolated fragments of the total knowledge you had when you were conscious of a higher dimension. You know, for example, that one day you will be living in Finland. . . .

However, before accepting this viewpoint too quickly, we have to recall that there is another stance available from modern physics that we must consider. Not surprisingly, it emerges from the other major revolution in twentieth-century physics (and one to which Einstein himself never could feel reconciled), quantum mechanics.

We begin with a different assumption about the nature of precognition. Since quantum physics is rooted in a purely probabilistic conception of the universe, where nothing can be fixed or known with certainty, precognitive perceptions are held to be previews of *possible* futures. As Zohar puts it:

It does not imply that the future is already fixed, but rather suggests that there are a range of possible futures and that in some way we may be able to perceive these possibilities.[11]

This second conception is favored by most students of precognition, and it certainly is, on the whole, much more in accordance with the voluminous body of literature on spontaneous cases of precognition that parapsychologists and others have been amassing over the past century. Certainly, my own data on PFs and PVs seem best interpreted as reflecting sensed possibilities rather than rigid, fixed certainties,[12] and some further PV data to be presented shortly strengthen this position even more.

Although much serious work is being done in the field of precognition today, we still do not know just how precognition "works." Nevertheless, there is increasing acceptance of the possibility that it is a valid phenomenon. Certainly the fact that quantum physics provides a ready framework has revitalized interest in theorizing about it. Whether or not any of these theories will eventually be recognized as offering a general solution to the problem of precognition, they at least can hold open the possibility that such phenomena will one day be brought into the net of scientific theory. Therefore, it seems to me at least conceivable that the kind of phenomena reported in this book could not only be true but also could, in principle, yield to scientific understanding. At this point, however, it is simply not possible to make a definitive judgment, but we have sufficient grounds, I believe, to argue that PFs and PVs *could* reflect paranormal precognitive knowledge.

The Interpretation of Prophetic Visions

If we assume, for the sake of argument, that precognition is possible, then it follows that PVs could represent advance visionary knowledge of earth's future. Of course, there are a variety of alternative interpretations that are also conceivable, and unless there are compelling reasons to discount them, there is no compunction for us to endorse the apocalyptic visions of these near-death experiencers as holding any special prognostic significance for the human race. In any case, the interpretation of PVs—remembering also their small number—needs to be made with utmost caution, particularly given their extreme content and their capacity, if taken seriously, to generate a wide range of individual and collective reactions based on fear, hysteria, or simply passivity.

In this portion of this chapter, therefore, I will consider and evaluate six possible interpretations of PVs and will conclude by suggesting which of these alternatives appears the most cogent.

The Psychodynamic Interpretation.

One possibility that quickly comes to mind is that PVs of the kind we have considered might be of psychodynamic origin. It has been suggested, for example, that these NDErs are simply projecting their own fears of the future or their unconscious conflicts onto the world scene. Their own fears of annihilation, then, are given an external apocalyptic locus. Another variant is that the individual who was, after all, very close to death has unconsciously registered the physical symptoms of his near-death state and has generated them inadvertently to "the death of the world"—i.e., since he is dying, he somehow transforms this into "the world is dying."

Though superficially plausible, these psychodynamic interpretations have certain flaws. For example, the fact that all the prophetic visions have a similar form and content makes the first psychodynamic interpretation unlikely. Why only these PVs? Why not a greater variety of projected global futures, since near-death experiencers can be expected, like the rest of us, to have a considerable range of expectations of the future? Yet only one scenario seems to surface in the PVs we have examined. Similarly, the second interpretation has difficulty in explaining the beauty, peace, and other extremely positive features of the NDEs these individuals also report.[13] If people are generalizing their own apparent near-death state to the world at large, we would not expect the NDE to have the form and content that has been so often recounted by NDErs, including those under study here.

Accordingly, I am inclined to look elsewhere for an explanation of the PV.

The Psychiatric Interpretation.

A more extreme version of the psychodynamic interpretation is that NDErs who report PVs are themselves psychiatrically troubled individuals whose visions therefore are rooted in their own psychopathology. Although it is true that some of my sample might be so regarded, there are several reasons why this interpretation can be discounted.

First, there is simply no justification for assuming that all sixteen of these NDErs suffer from psychiatric problems. It is perhaps ironically appropriate to note here that one of my PV correspondents is himself a psychiatrist!

Second, even if a relationship between psychopathology and PVs could be shown, it would certainly be understandable that the burden of living with the knowledge that the PV apparently discloses could itself induce psychiatric problems. A case in point, you may recall, is Cliff, who stated in his interview with Moody and me that his PV had caused him to suffer "a nervous breakdown." In such cases, the psychiatric problem would presumably be the *result* of the PV, not its source.

Finally, it is no argument to say that psychiatrically disturbed people can't be sensitive to future events. The opposite sometimes seems to be the case. For instance, Jungian psychiatrist John Perry has convincingly argued that certain schizophrenic patients may be more attuned to the emergence of future trends than are most "normal" individuals.[14]

Altogether, then, it is unwarranted to dismiss PVs on the basis of psychiatrically phrased arguments.

The Archetypal Interpretation.

In discussing this PV material with me one day, philosopher Michael Grosso suggested an archetypal or Jungian interpretation for the visionary aspect of NDEs. The underlying idea here is that the typical PV scenario is a reflection of a universal death-rebirth motif that is found in mythology and religion and that, furthermore, can be experienced directly in certain profound altered states of consciousness. For example, the work of John Perry[15] has demonstrated such an archetype in some acute psychotic states, and Stanislav Grof's[16] research with psychedelics has disclosed a clear death-rebirth archetype in conjunction with perinatal (birth-related) memories. Under the circumstances prevailing at the time of the NDEs reported in this chapter, it is certainly reasonable to assume that a personal near-death drama could be experienced symbolically at this archetypal level.

In my judgment, it *is* cogent to argue that at least some aspects of NDEs may represent archetypal imagery, but such an interpretation is unable to explain two common features of PVs—their specificity and their apparently paranormal character. Therefore, it again seems that a comprehensive explanation for PVs will have to be sought elsewhere.

The Zeitgeist *Interpretation.*

There is no doubt that apocalyptic ideas are rampant[17] as we approach the end of the millennium. In addition to the Bible, popular books and contemporary Christian thought have given a great deal of salience to images of widespread destruction and devastation. The early 1980s have also seen an increasing concern with the likelihood of a nuclear war, and large-scale social protest movements have resulted, particularly in Europe. All of these fears and expectations, however, have been in the air for some time. Is it not possible, then, that near-death survivors are simply "picking up on" what many people already think and feel? If this were so, no special weight need be given these visions, as the following excerpt (from an NDEr) makes clear:

I'm acutely aware of all the "visions" and predictions of late across the globe about war, but I recognize a sameness to them that occurred once before that I can remember—and that was in April of 1969. About six months before a certain date in April [can't remember which one], psychics suddenly started declaring that on that date California would sink into the ocean and the West Coast would be destroyed. Everyone started picking up the same date in their dreams—everywhere—be they psychic or not. A hit song was written about it, warning everyone to boat up to Idaho. I picked it up too, along with everyone else I knew. . . . That crazy date was popping up everywhere. We all held our breath. It didn't happen. There was a small earthquake, but not too bad. California held.

This kind of incident (and undoubtedly many other similar contagions have occurred, without result) should give us pause that even a collectively shared vision such as the PV must have predictive significance.

Nevertheless, it remains an empirical question just how widely such a scenario is shared among the American population at large. Obviously, the greater the percentage of the American public that subscribes to a PV view of the future, the more likely is it that the *Zeitgeist* interpretation plays a significant role in influencing the PVs of NDErs.

It goes without saying that without the resources of a Gallup poll no such definitive survey is possible, but I did decide to undertake a small, preliminary study of my own along these lines simply to obtain *some* data at least on the relative incidence of the PV scenario among a cross section of individuals. To do so, I took advantage of the groups easily available to me—IANDS members and my undergraduate psychology class (to which I had lectured on NDEs). In this way I would be able to compare PV incidence rates of a new group of NDErs (who did not necessarily have a PV as part of their NDEs) with those of persons who had a general interest in NDEs or at least had some familiarity with them. If there was any significant bias in such a group of respondents, I reasoned, it would probably be to inflate the overall proportion of persons endorsing a PV scenario.

To gather my data I constructed still another questionnaire, which I called the Future Scenario Questionnaire (FSQ). Like the others used in this study, it, too, is in Appendix II. The Future Scenario Questionnaire is quite simple and consists of three types of items. First, there is a list of eight different future scenarios, ranging from quite positive to extremely catastrophic, from which each respondent was asked to select the one that "most closely reflects your own view of the earth's future, from now until the end of the century." The second set of items concerned the *basis* of the respondent's opinion (e.g., public information, an intuitive hunch, a dream, etc.), while the third item asked the respondent to state his degree of confidence in his opinion, using a scale that went from 0 (not certain at all) to 100 (completely certain).

Altogether, 174 persons completed the FSQ during the spring of 1982. Of these, ninety-three were men and eighty were women (one person failed to indicate gender). All but twenty-five of the total sample were IANDS members. Finally, the breakdown according to near-death status was as follows:

NDErs	36
Near-death survivors	33
All others	105

In tabulating the results, I took only future scenarios 4, 5, and 6 as indicative of general agreement with the PVs of the sixteen NDErs whose visions make up the bulk of this chapter.

What did the FSQ reveal about the prevalence of PVs in my sample of 174?

First, I found that agreement with it was a good deal less than I had supposed. Only 28.2 percent—a little over one quarter of the entire sample—shared this view of the earth's future. NDErs as a group were a little more likely to endorse it (33.3 percent) than were others (26.8 percent), but the difference here is not significant.

Second, the usual demographic factors (age, sex, education, and religious affiliation) did not seem to have any particular relationship to the likelihood of embracing a PV scenario.

I did, however, find some other intriguing differences between NDErs and others on some of the other items on the FSQ. For example, NDErs were significantly more likely (p $<.02$)[18] to rely on dreams, intuitive hunches, visions, and other psychic experiences for their view of the future compared to other persons in the sample. NDErs also expressed significantly higher confidence ratings (p $<.05$) in connection with their views of the future, regardless of what those views were.

What are we to conclude, then, from the results of this study?

Clearly, because there is no evidence of *general* agreement with the PV scenario in this sample, the *Zeitgeist* interpretation does not receive strong support from these findings. If "prophetic visionaries" are "picking up" on the *Zeitgeist*, their visions should show a different pattern than what we have seen. Certainly, the apparently high degree of uniformity in my sample of sixteen NDErs in their PVs would not be expected on the basis of the diversity of views found here. In any event, the findings just presented appear to contravene any facile rejection of PVs on the grounds that they are merely the reflection of prevailing apocalyptic beliefs in contemporary American life.

The Prophetic Interpretation.

This, of course, is the interpretation that most of those who have had PVs would give of their experience. Some of these NDErs, in fact, while not claiming the status of prophets, nevertheless feel that their role might be similar. For example, one person remarked:

I know in the past God has had prophets of all different religions and I'm not what you could call a prophet, but yet I have been given some message to give to the people from God.

Another individual said he felt that

. . . my job is not to bring back the message of fear and hopelessness, but a message of love and hope.

Finally, Alex Tanous, referring to his vision, says that while he has made countless predictions and forecasts, he has

. . . made only one prophecy. . . . My prophecy involves the future of mankind.[19]

Of course, a prophecy is not necessarily a preview of a certainty but a *conditional* statement (e.g., unless these changes are made, then . . . or if these conditions continue to prevail, then . . .). Therefore, a prophecy could conceivably be "true" even though the event prophesied does not occur. This makes it convenient for the prophet but difficult for the researcher looking for a clear confirmation or disconfirmation of a PV.

Since the major events of the PV have not yet occurred, there is no way this interpretation can be tested. Yet there are indications that bear on its a priori plausibility (quite apart from the cogency of other alternatives). For example, we have established at IANDS our own "premonitions registry" for NDErs. Although we have as yet not received many such formally submitted premonitions concerning global events, none of them has impressed me with their accuracy. Furthermore, some of the specific predictions that have been made by NDErs who have reported PVs have been flatly *wrong*. Finally, to my knowledge, there are only retroactive claims of successful predictions. None of these points greatly undermines the prophetic interpretation, but neither do they serve to increase one's confidence in it.

The Alternative-Futures Interpretation.

A woman once wrote to me describing a detailed and vivid out-of-body experience that had occurred to her in conjunction with an apparent near-death incident involving her pregnancy. What made this case unique in my records was her assertion that as far as she could determine afterward none of the events she had "seen" while out of her body had actually taken place! Yet her account had all of the realistic detail usually reported by persons whose recollections tally with the facts. How is such an anomaly to be explained?

One possibility is suggested by the hypothesis of *alternate futures*. This notion is based on the so-called many-worlds interpretation of quantum mechanics,[20] but there is reason to think that this hypothesis may be applicable to psychology as well as physics. Let me briefly delineate the hypothesis in the context of modern physics, following which I will try to show its possible relevance to the phenomenon of PVs.

In quantum physics it is not possible to predict individual outcomes of subatomic processes. In this realm, all one can do is predict *probabilities* of outcomes. For example, of three possible alternatives—A, B, C—one might be able to predict that the chance of A occurring is 60 percent; B, 30 percent; and C, 10 percent. But in any given instance, one would not be able to state which of these outcomes would in fact occur. Nevertheless, let us say that in this case, outcome B is observed. How are we to understand this event?

The conventional (Copenhagen) interpretation argues that each potential outcome is associated with a wave function. At the instant of occurrence, however, the wave functions associated with outcomes A and C "collapse" into a certainty. Thus the instruments of detection register outcome B.

In 1957, however, another interpretation was suggested by Everett, Wheeler, and Grahman.[21] Their view, the many-worlds interpretation, holds that all three outcomes actually occur, but in different and forever separate universes. Outcome B happens to be the occurrence registered in our physical universe and thus can be measured, but outcomes A and C *also* happen—but they happen "elsewhere." Despite its apparent outlandishness and untestable character, the many-worlds interpretation is taken seriously by not a few modern physicists.

Now recall our allusion to quantum mechanics earlier in this chapter in which Zohar commented (see page 209) that rather than assuming a single fixed future, it could be supposed that

. . . there are a range of possible futures and that in some way we may be able to perceive these possibilities.

Accordingly, it is just conceivable that an occasional NDEr will become aware not just of one but also of several alternate futures, only one of which might occur in our reality.

This theoretical possibility has recently received some preliminary support. The last interview I conducted for this study disclosed just such an outcome: a view of *multiple* possible futures.

In this case, the respondent had an NDE (her second) when she nearly drowned at the age of fourteen (in 1956). She relates that while out of the body and *above* the water, one part of her consciousness focused on the body below her and the requirements to save that body. Her consciousness *split*, however, and another part was aware of

. . . three lines of trajectories that would lead toward futures. . . . Each of them is an alternate arrangement of things I saw.

She referred to these trajectories as futures A, B, and C, respectively. I will briefly describe them here. Future A was a future that would have developed if certain events had not taken place around the time of Pythagoras three thousand years ago. It was a future of peace and harmony, marked by the absence of religious wars and of a Christ figure. Figure B was, in effect, the classic PV scenario I have delineated in this chapter. Future C was an even more destructive version of future B. Both futures B and C projected to her simultaneous images associated with these separate future tracks from about the end of the century backward toward 1956; this was also true for the future-oriented events of the nonrealized future A except that these images were fewer and less detailed than those connected with futures B and C. This woman feels that we are currently headed for future B.

This individual, then, was aware of three potential futures, only two of which had to her any present possibility of manifesting on earth (since future A was only a "might have been"). How *many* potential futures there might be is, of course, impossible to know, but *that* there may indeed be potential futures we may sometimes sense in altered states of consciousness is at least suggested by this account.

It is possible, therefore, that respondents reporting PVs may have "tapped into" only one of a set of alternate future scenarios and, not having any reason to suspect other possibilities, have mistaken their *alternate* future scenario for *the* future. In this way these PVs may convey to them a sense of absolute certitude concerning the shape of the future but still be in error. Again, to use quantum physics as the basis for an analogy, one could say that what they have become aware of is the certainty of a *probability*.

To me, this particular interpretation seems to have the most persuasiveness as a provisional explanation for the PV. Since it is grounded in the kind of quantum mechanics orientation that has been favored by others to understand precognitive phenomena in general, it also has the virtue of drawing on a theoretical framework of proven appeal. At the psychological level it is attractive as well, since it implies that the future is not a play whose story is already written but an open-ended affair with many alternate scenarios yet capable of occupying center stage.

Conclusion

This has been an unsettling chapter whose implications are, despite my own interpretation of PVs, likely still to prove troublesome to most readers. Surely no one could entertain the thought of a "planetary near-death experience" with equanimity even if the ultimate outcome were to be a golden age of some kind. We are therefore motivated to find some way to discount these images of the future, or to question the people whose visions have forced us to become aware of them. No one wants to think of their children growing up only to face a holocaust of global proportions.

And yet we must force ourselves to confront the question that even the alternative-futures interpretation cannot answer: Why only this scenario? Why is it that if alternate futures are possible, only this particular one seems to dominate the visions of NDErs? We need to seek the meaning of this ineluctable and disturbing fact rather than just casting it aside as a bizarre if frightening anomaly of NDEs.

For my part, I am convinced that there is a deeper meaning to these PVs than we have as yet discerned, and it is something that goes beyond any of the explanations I have offered for them in this chapter. Furthermore, without being Pollyannaish, it is possible to see in these visions a source of hope for humanity that is in no way tied to the aftermath of the changes foretold in PVs. The remainder of this book will be devoted to laying the groundwork for this vision of hope to which the PV itself may paradoxically point.

CHAPTER 9

· · · · · · ·

The Biological Basis of NDEs

÷

Not long after I had finished the first seven chapters of this book, I received a long letter from a previously unknown correspondent from the Midwest. Like many others who have written me, Nancy Clark had had an experience she wished to share with me, but Nancy's letter was by no means "just" another account of an NDE. Among other things, it seemed to be an outline of my book, which of course Nancy had no idea I was writing! So that you can appreciate my astonishment upon reading her letter, I'd like to quote some portions of it to begin this chapter. After describing her experience, she went on to say:

How has the experience changed my life? I was immediately transformed into a brand new person with the following characteristics:

And her letter continues with a series of sections, set off by italicized capitals, in which she describes these characteristics:

LOVE
There is a deeper love and unity with everyone and everything that I come in contact with. I seem to have a greater awareness of all living things and that we are ALL a part of one another and ultimately a part of a greater consciousness, God. For the first time in my life, my earthly eyes have opened to see—really see—life around me. The simplest sights, a leaf, a tree, a blade of grass, a frog—EVERYTHING is a marvel of creation to me and I take the time to appreciate it because I feel the bond of life between us.

INCREASED SPIRITUALITY

I feel as if I was elevated to a higher level of spirituality. This manifests itself in several ways. Prior to my experience I did not attend church or have any formal religious training during my adult life. Following the experience, I joined a church and am very interested in learning about Biblical teachings, etc. However, I must stress that there is quite a difference between religion and spirituality. It seems to me that I was elevated beyond "religion." By that I mean, religion is a tool used to climb the ladder, so to speak, to reach the higher level of spirituality.

In my experience so far with organized religion, it often fails to bring about this higher level of spirituality by concentrating on rules and regulations and inter-denominational conflicts. I am in no way degrading any religion as I feel they all play an important role in providing the people with spiritual nourishment.

In my instance, however, I feel that I am looking down from a higher perch somewhere in our spiritual development and that I have already received my college degree in "religion" even though I have not comprehended all the religious teachings of the Bible. The knowledge flows through my consciousness instinctively and I am able to recognize what is true and what is not. I did not feel this way prior to the experience.

BETTER SELF-IMAGE

Before my experience, I guess I was like most people struggling with a better self-image. But I really *experienced* how precious and how loved I am by God—the light—and I am constantly reminded of that in my daily life. I often think, "If He values me so much (as I experienced it that January day), then no matter what bad thoughts I may think about myself—I HAVE to be a worthwhile person." There's no ifs, ands, or buts.

You see, with all my faults and I have them—He still chose to give me this life-changing experience. Not because I deserved it in any way or initiated it on my own. But for some reason unknown to me, I am worthy in His eyes. Believing that, then in my own eyes, I AM!

NO LONGER FEAR DEATH

I am no longer afraid of death. The dying process, yes, for I do not look forward to the pain and suffering that might accompany the death process. But death itself I do not fear. In fact, odd as it may sound, I look forward to death for I know I will be reunited with the light source, God, and there is NOTHING in this world—riches, fame, power, or even life itself—that I would desire more than to be united once again with Him.

QUEST FOR KNOWLEDGE

I have noticed a great desire to learn about spiritual matters (Biblical and other) and also to learn about psychic phenomena. I read and search out everything I can. I don't know why I seem to feel as if I'm preparing myself in some way for something greater. Knowledge seems to be very, very important but I don't know why I feel so compelled to learn. I have increased psychic abilities following my experience.

MY GOAL IN LIFE IS TO HELP OTHERS

The most important goal in my life is to use my experience in a positive meaningful way to help others. My greatest problem is determining in what capacity I can best serve. It is my sincere hope that I will be able to link up with someone who will be able to advise and help me. There is no doubt in my mind that I will accomplish my mission on this earth. I firmly believe that this experience was given as a gift to me to be shared with others. I WILL make a meaningful contribution to the research and the application of the life after death phenomenon regardless of the skepticism I shall encounter from those I reach out to. This work is far too important for my own personal feelings to be considered.

I am motivated only by the gratitude I feel in being a recipient of this experience. For giving me a glimpse for a few moments of a life beyond the present one, I owe it to my fellow man to lovingly share this great truth with them.

When I ultimately make my transition to the next world and meet Him again I'll say, "Lord, for the precious gift you gave to me while I lived on the earth, I did my very best work for you. This is MY gift in return to you."

You can easily imagine my enormous delight at receiving such a letter. Quite apart from the very beautiful sentiments it conveys, it reflects virtually every major aftereffect of NDEs I was at pains to document in my earlier chapters. For a letter out of the blue like this to arrive with such exquisite timing seemed almost providential. I could hardly have asked for a more ideal illustration of the composite NDEr I have been sketching in this book.

Except for one thing.

Nancy Clark did *not* have an NDE.

And the reason that I quoted her account of the aftermath of her experience at such length (and without, by the way, omitting even a word) was to demonstrate something quite different from what I may have so far implied. Nancy Clark's letter is valuable chiefly not because it so well exemplifies the typical life transformations in NDErs *but because it shows that these same transformations do not depend on having NDEs*.

What kind of experience did Nancy undergo, then?

A few days before it took place, Nancy had a premonition in a dream of the death of a very close friend—a premonition that she later learned came true within an hour of her dream. Her friend had died in a plane crash that same night.

Several days later, on January 29, 1979, Nancy was preparing to give a eulogy at her friend's funeral service. Somehow—although this did not make sense to her—she felt her deceased friend's "presence" to her right. Nevertheless, she dismissed this thought from her mind and began her eulogy. At this point, she says:

I was addressing the audience with the eulogy and I spoke perhaps three sentences when all of a sudden I became aware of a brilliant white light coming from the left rear of the chapel at ceiling level. I did not see this light with my eyes, but, rather, from some other unexplainable source. It was more of an "inner awareness." I find this very difficult to describe. I could see but it definitely was not through my human eyes.

Upon seeing this light, there was immediate recognition on my part that it was God. I felt I was in the presence of my creator, a very exhilarating, spiritual feeling. I can't explain how I knew or how I recognized God's presence. The best I can do is to say that there was a transference of knowledge placed directly into my consciousness. In other words, I was being fed the information that I was supposed to receive.

The light completely surrounded me. I felt as if I had merged completely with the light and "belonged" to it. I felt a greater sense of reality and truth in this state. I felt as if I was "home."

The love that was emanating from the light is by far the most difficult aspect of my experience to relate to others. I feel so inadequate to speak of this love. Not because I am not a scholar, a theologian, a scientist or someone who can dissect it and analyze it. I am limited simply by being human! It was not a human kind of love. It was not within the framework of our human experiences. Therefore, it defies human explanation. I can only say that it is because of this love that was channeled to me that I am able to remain strong and travel down life's highway knowing that a great truth has occurred.

I wanted to remain in the presence of this light forever! I felt as if I was in a state of grace. All my sins were forgiven and I felt perfectly and totally FREE. If I had somehow been asked at that moment if I wanted to go with this light and leave my earthly life behind, I would not have hesitated and I would have chosen to go. Not because earthly life is so bad, but, rather, that's how incredibly beautiful the light was.

Following this, Nancy received what she described as "a direct communication from Him (God, the light)." As to the form of that communication, she says, "I did not hear the words with my human ears, but rather, the thoughts were placed directly in my consciousness."

Just what the light conveyed to Nancy is, however, something I wish to withhold for the time being, but only because I feel it would be better to divulge it in the next chapter, by which point we will have established a more meaningful context for the message Nancy was given.

Nancy concluded her account of her experience with these words:

After the communication ended, the light disappeared and my friend's "presence" was gone. This entire experience lasted several minutes and was occurring simultaneously while I was delivering this eulogy. I was completely aware at all times of my surroundings and the eulogy that I was delivering.

Clearly, Nancy was having an experience that in form and feeling is virtually identical to the NDEs described in this book. Yet, obviously, there was no near-death crisis involved here. Indeed, Nancy also mentions in her letter that at the time she was healthy, was not taking any medication, and was not in an abnormal state of mind. Throughout this experience, as she says, she was fully conscious of her physical environment. She also indicated that in 1979 she had no knowledge of the work of Kübler-Ross or Moody and had never heard of NDEs.

In short, we seem to be confronted with an instance of a person's having had an NDE and undergoing all the typical aftereffects but without the usual precipitating factor of a near-death incident. Just what is the significance of this?

In these closing chapters we are, of course, going to return to some of the questions that prompted this inquiry in the first place. And of these, the most fundamental was, "What is the meaning of these NDEs?" But the meaning of these experiences must ultimately be grounded in the interpretation we give to them, and it is to the issue of the *interpretation* of NDEs, prior to our final effort to grasp their deepest meaning, that this chapter is directed.

Nancy Clark's letter gives us our first clue as to the kind of interpretation we must seek.

The reason that Nancy's letter is so pertinent is probably obvious by now. It is simply this: Are there more Nancys out there? Are there more people who have also undergone ND-like experiences and their aftereffects without themselves having experienced a near-death crisis?

Of course there are—*lots* of them.

Even in our own IANDS archives, we have more than a hundred letters from people who have written us to the effect, "Well, I was never actually close to death, but I also seem to have had what you call a near-death experience. . . ." Then these correspondents typically relate an incident in their lives—during meditation, childbirth, a personal crisis, a church service, or, in many cases, seemingly spontaneously—in which they, too, seem to have been touched by much the same thing that NDErs come to know during a near-death crisis.

Of course, the information contained in our IANDS archives hardly constitutes a unique collection of these kinds of experiences. Readers familiar with the voluminous literature on mystical and religious experience[1] will already have recognized the significant parallels between experiences of this kind and NDEs. Even a recent informal study conducted by a University of Connecticut graduate student, Pamela Rivard, can illustrate this thesis. In brief, Rivard was interested in interviewing persons who claimed to have undergone a significant religious awakening in the recent past. Her findings demonstrate unequivocally that there are many points of obvious overlap between the religious experiences of her respondents and NDEs, both in phenomenology and transformative effects.[2]

Such convergences serve to buttress a point that is often overlooked in discussion of NDEs but that is crucial to any attempt to explain them: *What occurs during an NDE has nothing inherently to do with death or with the transition into death*. In my opinion, this point cannot be emphasized too strongly, and the failure to do so has led to a serious distortion in our understanding of the NDE. What happens to an individual during an NDE is *not* unique to the moment of apparent imminent death. It is just that coming close to death is one of the very reliable triggers that sets off this kind of experience. The reason that this has been lost on many professionals and the public alike is that the current wave of research has fastened on the NDEr as an exemplar of this variety of transcendental experience. In our collective fascination with the drama of death, we have come nearly to equate what we have called the NDE with the moment of death itself and have failed to recognize that dying is only one, albeit a common one, of the circumstances that tends to be conducive to this kind of experience.

The NDE, then, should be regarded as one of a family of related mystical experiences that have always been with us, rather than as a recent discovery of modern researchers who have come to investigate the phenomenology of dying.

To support further this claim of the generality of (what I will persist, for now, in labeling) the NDE, consider this summary, provided by psychiatrist Stanley Dean, of the characteristics of what he calls "ultraconsciousness" and its effects.[3] "Ultraconsciousness" is a term coined by Dean, but it is virtually synonymous with an older, more familiar term, cosmic consciousness. Incidentally, Dean's summary was first published in 1974, before the explosion of interest in near-death phenomena. Here is Dean's list:

1. The onset is ushered in by an awareness of dazzling light that floods the brain and fills the mind. In the East it is called the "Brahmic Splendor." Walt Whitman speaks of it as ineffable light—"light rare, untellable, lighting the very light—beyond all signs, descriptions, languages. Dante writes that it is capable of "transhumanizing a man into a god. . . ."
2. The individual is bathed in emotions of supercharged joy, rapture, triumph, grandeur, reverential awe, and wonder—an ecstasy so overwhelming that it seems little less than a sort of superpsychic orgasm.
3. An intellectual illumination occurs that is quite impossible to describe. In an intuitive flash one has an awareness of the meaning and drift of the universe, an identification and merging with Creation, infinity, and immortality, a depth beyond depth of revealed meaning—in short, a conception of the Over-Self so omnipotent that religion has interpreted it as God. . . .
4. There is a feeling of transcendental love and compassion for all living things.
5. Fear of death falls off like an old cloak; physical and mental suffering vanish. There is an enhancement of mental and physical vigor and activity, a rejuvenation and prolongation of life. . . .
6. There is a reappraisal of the material things in life, an en-

hanced appreciation of beauty, a realization of the relative unimportance of riches and abundance compared to the treasures of the ultraconscious.

7. There is an extraordinary quickening of the intellect, an uncovering of latent genius. Far from being a passive, dreamlike state, however, it can endow an individual with powers so far-reaching as to influence the course of history.

8. There is a sense of mission. The revelation is so moving and profound that the individual cannot contain it within himself but is moved to share it with all fellowmen.

9. A charismatic change occurs in personality—an inner and outer radiance, as though charged with some divinely inspired power, a magnetic force that attracts and inspires others with unshakable loyalty and faith.

10. There is a sudden or gradual development of extraordinary psychic gifts such as clairvoyance, extrasensory perception, telepathy, precognition, psychic healing, etc. . . ."[4]

I have abridged some of Dean's statements, but I think the overall pattern is clear. And do we not recognize who is being described in this composite of the individual who has attained cosmic consciousness? Do not our own core experiencers of Chapter 3 seem to fit the mold Dean has constructed? And are not the aftereffects he has described those, by and large, of our NDErs, too? I am not claiming a *complete* identity between the configuration Dean has drawn and the one I have so far sketched, but I feel there can be no doubt of their significant overlap. What many—not necessarily all—NDErs encounter while close to death is akin to what others have called cosmic consciousness, and the residues of this experience are also similar to those that affect the lives and personalities of individuals who have been vouchsafed a taste of cosmic consciousness, however it may have been brought about.

This being so, one fact now becomes undeniably plain. Any interpretation that purports to explain NDEs must also be capable of accounting for the *general family* of transcendental experiences—and their aftereffects—of which the classic NDE is but one member. In this view, any interpretation that strives to explain the NDE as an isolated phenomenon uniquely linked to near-death crisis conditions is bound to fall short of the mark.

Accordingly, we must now ask: Do we have an explanatory framework available to us that is sufficiently broad to encompass the NDE and its effects in this larger context?

In my opinion, we do. I believe that there is a *biological* basis for NDEs, but I must hasten to add that the interpretation I will advance fully honors rather than explains away the transcendental features and effects of the phenomenon.

One other, but important, caveat must also be entered here. When I say that I believe we have a suitable explanatory framework for the NDE, I mean that a *case can be made for it*, not that I think the case has been established. Indeed, at the present time, we lack most of the data we need to decide the issue, so all I can legitimately do here is offer this framework as a hypothesis. Further research will be necessary to evaluate the hypothesis itself, but I hope my outlining this framework now will serve as a spur to others to undertake the line of investigation that will test its utility.

What, then, is the possible biological basis that underlies NDEs and the larger family of transcendental experiences?

I propose that all these phenomena may be the outcome of a biological transformation of the human organism that is induced by the release of an energy long known to adepts but only recently studied by scientists interested in transcendental experience. This energy is still called by its Sanskrit name, kundalini.

The Kundalini Hypothesis

Although the literature on kundalini is now extensive,[5] the term is still unfamiliar to many people, and the process it represents remains outside the accepted theories of science. Nevertheless, the *effects* of this process—whatever it be called—have now been widely recognized and, like the NDE itself, can no longer be disregarded even if, again like the NDE, they cannot be easily explained by reference to conventional theories of biology. So we must begin this section with a brief exposition of the essentials of the kundalini hypothesis and of the experiences said to occur when this energy becomes active. What follows, then, is kundalini in a nut-shell.

In Sanskrit, kundalini means "coiled up" (like a serpent). The term represents a postulated, subtle form of bioenergy said to lie latent, like a sleeping serpent, at the base of the spine. Under certain circumstances, however, this energy can be activated, and when it is, it is said to travel upward through the spine (in a special channel). As it travels, it affects certain energy centers (called chakras in the yogic tradition) and may induce explosive and de-stabilizing energy transformations that are experienced both psychologically and physically. The way this energy is experienced by the individual varies, but typically its manifestations are extremely disruptive to one's equilibrium even when—as sometimes is the case—the initial experience is itself one of supreme rapture.[6] In many instances, the physical and psychological concomitants of this awakening are very unpleasant and frightening.

Nevertheless, however the actual process of kundalini arousal may be experienced, it is held that this energy it draws upon has the *capacity* to catapult the individual into a higher state of consciousness. In full awakenings, a state of cosmic consciousness can be attained and, under certain circumstances, maintained. The flow of energy is said to transform the nervous system and the brain to enable them to operate at an entirely new and higher level of functioning. Metaphorically speaking, kundalini appears to throw the nervous system into overdrive, activating its latent potentials and permitting the individual to experience the world and perform in it in extraordinary fashion.

Thus kundalini theorists (who usually have had profound kundalini awakenings themselves) argue that the activation of this energy is responsible for genius, psychic abilities of various kinds, and, ultimately, the varieties of mystical and religious experience that have been reported throughout the ages. The idea that this energy, which is held to be both divine *and* divinizing, is responsible for humanity's evolution toward higher consciousness is called *the kundalini hypothesis*.

As I have already said, this hypothesis has been advanced by various theorists, but, despite the interest of an increasing number of scientists and scholars, it can hardly be said to have been demonstrated. Indeed, the hypothesis can scarcely even be tested scientifically at the present time both because of the lack of appropriate instruments and the uncertainty about what to measure. In this regard, all we have is the provocative research of pioneers such as Itzhak Bentov[7] and Hiroshi Motoyama,[8] both of whom have devised apparatus designed to detect energies presumably indicative of kundalini arousal, but even here their techniques and findings need to be crossvalidated by other investigators. As a result, as with the NDE, what is left for us to draw from in the kundalini literature are the *experiences* of individuals who have clearly undergone something characterized by a pronounced and distinctive pattern. And these people generally refer to a very definite awareness of an energy that has been aroused within them.

But granted that this may be so, just what is the connection between these kundalini experiences and NDEs?

In full kundalini awakenings, *what* is experienced is significantly similar to what many NDErs report from their experiences. And more than that: The aftereffects of these deep kundalini awakenings seem to lead to individual transformations and personal world views essentially indistinguishable from those found in NDErs. That these obvious parallels exist does not, of course, prove that they stem from a common cause, but it does at least suggest the possibility that there may be a general biological process that underlies them both—as well as transcendental experiences at large.

In any case, these parallels are both too evident and too intriguing to be disregarded. Kundalini, then, is a second clue (the first being Nancy Clark's letter) concerning the form that our overall interpretation of NDEs might take. Accordingly, we must next examine more specifically these similarities between kundalini experiences and NDEs.

Kundalini and NDEs: The Parallels

There are already a number of autobiographical accounts of kundalini awakenings in the literature on which we could draw for illustrative and comparative purposes. Perhaps the single best known one is Gopi Krishna's, which is described in full in his book *Kundalini*. In addition, there are a half dozen or so personal narratives in John White's anthology *Kundalini, Evolution and Enlightenment*. Beyond these, there are a few cases I have encountered in my personal correspondence (these have not been published). There are also instances described by physicians interested in the phenomenon, such as the thirteen case histories presented in Lee Sannella's book *Kundalini—Psychosis or Transcendence?* To exemplify possible kundalini-NDE parallels here, however, I have chosen a recent prototypic account provided by scientist Hiroshi Motoyama of what seems to have been a full kundalini awakening.[9] To supplement Motoyama's personal description, I will also refer to some of the more general observations of Gopi Krishna, who is widely accorded to be a leading authority on this subject. Thus, between the specific individual features in Motoyama's experience and the overall characterizations of the phenomenon from Gopi Krishna, we shall have, I think, a sound basis for our later comparisons with the NDE.

Motoyama was introduced to spiritual disciplines at an early age and became an ardent student and practitioner of Yoga. Yoga, of course, is designed to arouse kundalini deliberately through a combination of postures (called *asanas*), breath control (called *pranayama*), and meditations upon the chakras. Motoyama reports that he had his first kundalini experience at twenty-five when

an incredible power rushed through my spine to the top of my head . . . my whole body was burning and a severe headache prevented me from doing anything all day. . . .[10] I felt as if my head would explode with energy.[11]

Not long afterward, Motoyama reports that he began to have prophetic dreams and involuntary ESP experiences such as telepathy. His ESP abilities, he says, continued to develop as he felt his higher chakras beginning to awaken. With the opening of his (so-called) heart chakra—in yogic theory, the fourth of the seven major chakras—his experiences reached a new plateau. At this time he says:

As the kundalini rose from my heart to the top of my head, it became shining white. It left my body through the top of my head and I rose with it into a much higher dimension . . . when I came to myself ten to twenty minutes later, my mother told me that she had seen a golden light shining at the top of my head and at my heart . . . since then, I have been able to do psychic healing [he then gives some examples]. . . . My psychological state also underwent some profound changes with this awakening. Notably, I developed an attitude of non-attachment to worldly things.[12]

Motoyama's progression continued. With the awakening of the fifth (throat) chakra, he claims to have gained the ability to see the past, present, and future in the same dimension. Chronic hearing problems were also relieved, but Motoyama states that it was not just that his physical hearing improved; his "inner" hearing sharpened as well.

It was only with the highest chakras, however, that his experiences culminated and where the similarities to significant NDE phenomena became manifest. When concentrating on the sixth chakra one day, Motoyama relates that

my respiration became so easy and slow that I felt as if I could live without breathing. My body . . . felt as though it disappeared. I was completely immersed in a dark purple light while a bright white light shone from between my eyebrows. I heard a voice call me as if it were echoing in a valley. I was filled with ecstasy. . . . I was simply filled with heavenly calm. . . . I found myself in a state of widened and deepened consciousness, a consciousness of a higher dimension sometimes referred to as superconsciousness. While in this state, the past, present and future are simultaneously knowable.[13]

Continuing his pranayamic practice (which involves, among other things, breath retention), Motoyama experienced the awakening of the seventh (crown) chakra as follows:

. . . a shining golden light began to enter and leave my body through the top of my head. . . . I saw what looked like the head of Buddha, shimmering purple and blue. . . . There was a golden-white light flowing in and out through the gate on top of the Buddha's crown. Gradually, I lost the sensation of my body, but I held a clear awareness of consciousness, of superconsciousness. . . . I was able to hear a powerful, but very tender, Voice resounding through the universe. While listening to the Voice, I realized spontaneously my mission, my previous lives, my own spiritual state, and many other things. Then I experienced a truly indescribable state, in which my entire spiritual existence became totally immersed within an extraordinary calmness. After some time, I felt it imperative that I return to the physical world. I descended, following the same path, and returned to my body through the gate at the top of my head. I consciously had to permeate my whole body with spiritual energy because it was rigid and my extremities were paralyzed. Finally I was able to move my hands and feet a little, and normal sensation gradually returned.[14]

To be sure, differences between Motoyama's cultural and religious traditions and those of Omega NDErs blur the parallels somewhat, and the fact that Motoyama, through a long process of spiritual training, was able to enter into those states consciously and deliberately also sets him apart from our NDErs. Nevertheless, I think it will be apparent that the kind of illumination that core NDEs receive was also experienced by Motoyama. From this account at least it seems that kundalini arousal gives one access to the same (or a similar) dimension of consciousness as does the core NDE.

But how common are these features and outcomes of full kundalini awakenings? Let us now turn to some of the commentary of Gopi Krishna on kundalini.

In one of his books on kundalini—which Gopi Krishna holds to underlie genuine mystical experience—he states that though the latter is

. . . inexpressible, one can convey a distant picture by describing it as the highest perfection of grace, beauty, grandeur, harmony, peace, love, rapture, wonder and happiness, all combined in such an intense degree that the mind may swoon at the stupendous impact of the ecstasy.[15]

The effect of this kundalini-mediated experience is to bring about a permanent

... transforming action on the whole of life. It leads to unshakable belief in the existence of God, even in previously skeptical minds. It also leads to radical change in the pattern of lives formerly devoted to selfish pursuits, resulting in unparalleled acts of altruism, charity and benevolence, heroism, self-sacrifice, and even martyrdom. ... It has conferred unmatched creative powers on the more advanced recipients of the favor and fashioned them into vessels to enlighten humanity.[16]

In addition, as I have already indicated in a previous chapter, Gopi Krishna states that individuals who experience kundalini activation that leads to a higher state of conciousness will be characterized by "genius, psychic talents, lofty traits of character, and an expanded state of consciousness"[17] in which "space and time lose their rigidity, and there is a mingling of the past, the present, and the future."[18]

Furthermore, if one examines Gopi Krishna's writings for their statements concerning the effects of kundalini awakening on one's religious world view and personal values, there are again many parallels with what we have reported for our NDErs. And as to the view of the future that Gopi Krishna seems to have obtained from his own kundalini awakening, it, too, appears to have contained a version of the kind of prophetic vision we have already surveyed in Chapter 8,[19] something that is also suggested in another of Motoyama's books.[20]

None of these similarities between kundalini awakenings and NDEs proves anything, of course, but they do at least permit us to argue that the threads of continuity between them may have some significance for any general interpretation of NDEs. Before we can begin drawing any conclusions here, though, we badly need evidence from another quarter. It is one thing for a researcher like myself to point out a possible kundalini-NDE connection, but what of the views of NDErs themselves? Does that hypothesis make sense to them? And are there any data from NDErs themselves, not yet presented, that square with the hypothesis that kundalini arousal may underlie some NDE phenomena?

Kundalini and NDEs: Views and Data from NDErs

During my interviews with NDErs, my respondents sometimes described for me various energetic phenomena they claimed had occurred in them following their NDE. Many of these energetic discharges struck me as being similar to those reported in the kundalini literature. For example, one of the most common of these phenomena were sensations of heat—something that seems often to be associated with kundalini arousal.

For instance, one woman told me:

You won't believe this, but I get electrical sparks in my hands that drive me crazy . . . it's funny. This energy goes around and around and around; it's like I'll feel a buildup and my hands will start to tingle: They'll actually hurt. [Do they feel hot?] Hot? You can feel the heat pouring out of them! It's just like they are on fire. [Did anything like this occur to you before your incident?] Never. Never . . . It's like an electrical shock going right through you. But powerfully, really powerfully.

Janis also seems to have something like the same energy in her hands, also dating from her NDE:

I've been convinced from the time of my accident that I have a sensitivity in my hands. . . .

Barbara Harris, perhaps more than any other NDEr I know, has had an extraordinary number of kundalini manifestations since her NDE and has sent me voluminous written material (including one fifty-four-page typed letter!) regarding her post-NDE experiences in general and her kundalini symptoms in particular. (She has also shared some of this information in personal interviews.) She, too, has experienced the sensation of heat in many parts of her body on numerous occasions. For example, she once wrote me:

I have pages of notes as I felt symptoms that relate to the physio-kundalini syndrome. The one symptom that is so apparent every day at one time or another is HEAT. I feel heat radiating from isolated parts of my body and [my husband] has felt my hands burning.

Joseph Dippong experienced the heat *immediately* upon regaining consciousness from his NDE. He writes:

I had the feeling that I was burning up. There was a tremendous heat in the central part of my body and along the spinal column. I consumed a prodigious amount of water, and it took several pitchers to quench my thirst. . . . It was as if a biological transformation had occurred in my body.[21]

Intriguingly—and reminiscent of Motoyama's kundalini awakening—Dippong adds that at this time observers said that

. . . there was a kind of glowing light around my head and my face and that I emanated a blissfulness and joy which were beyond words.[21]

In some cases, these apparent kundalini symptoms range far beyond local, if intense, manifestations of extreme heat and come to include many of the typical features of full-fledged kundalini awakenings. For example, in my conversations (mostly informal) with Sonja, she has, over the period of six years since I've known her, described many of these features for me and is convinced, as she put it, that "near-death experiences *activate* the kundalini energy." But perhaps the clearest account of this kind of post-NDE transformation again comes from Barbara Harris.

One night, at about 2:00 or 3:00 A.M., Barbara was lying in bed when she became aware of

. . . a tingling, a tickling in my toe, my left toe, that would move up my left leg. Just a sense of energy, like the energy I was feeling in my hands, coming out from my hands, but this time it was travelling

237 . . .

through my leg and then both legs would start feeling it, both arms and then a tickling at the base of my spine would start moving up. . . .

This happened for several consecutive nights, and then on one subsequent occasion

[the energy] came straight up my spine and somewhere above the heart area [but] then I lost it in the back and it came up almost where I felt a hollow tube travelling into my face. . . . And then I felt this cascade coming over my head [all internally] and I sort of had this feeling of it coming back down and up, like I was recycling it.

In some cases, the sensation of the energy moving through her head was associated with another kundalini phenomenon that Gopi Krishna[22] has stated was a part of his awakening, "the nectar."

. . . while lying curled up in bed one morning, I had the most wonderful sensation of a cascade of "nectar"—sweetness that was thicker than water in feeling [which started] midway across my head (ear to ear over the top of my head) and came down my face. My taste buds said "sweetness" although I don't understand how my taste buds knew.

Barbara also experienced colors:

I started off with a very, very deep red. Now I'm not talking about colors of [ordinary] intensity. . . . Now [at this time] I'm in a totally darkened room and I am seeing light that's red and [then] it was going into oranges and yellows and goldens. Then, this became blatant. It changed to blue and I was getting *blues*—and waves of them. Waves that corresponded to the energy I was feeling . . . and then it turned into the violet. . . .

This, too, is reminiscent of some of the color manifestations that Motoyama had described in conjunction with his kundalini awakening, presumably as a result of the opening of different chakras, each of which is said to be associated with a specific color.

However, not all of Barbara's kundalini related experiences were pleasant. For instance, like many others who have felt kundalini arousal, her early kundalini manifestations were accompanied by terrible headaches, a concomitant that has been observed by other students of the kundalini phenomenon.[23]

On March 26, 1983, Barbara wrote me that her kundalini process seems, at least for now, to have stabilized:

The "pockets of heat" in my body have pretty much subsided and my general overall feeling is one of peace and serenity. I sense strongly that I am part of a much greater "source of energy and wisdom" than just my individual self and that even though I really can't find the right words to explain this—that I am a "Channel" or "Instrument" for this energy.

Elsewhere she has also noted that, in common with other NDErs who have had occasion to comment on the same point, since her NDE she seems to have a lessened requirement for sleep.[24]

I'm back to needing only about 4 hours sleep (a few times when I am enthused about something, I think I don't sleep at all—I just kind of hang there but I feel great the next day; it doesn't bother me) and every so often I get 6 or 7 hours sleep.

In other cases, post-NDE energetic phenomena are experienced primarily in the form of *light*. Consider, for example, the following statement from Nel. You may recall that in 1972 she had her NDE and, upon returning from it, she says she knew that the light would always be with her. And from her subsequent experience, it certainly appears as if it has been. Here is a portion of a brief paper Nel recently sent me that she entitled "The Light/Energy Cycle":

Soothing sensations travel upward through the base of my skull. Every cell is charged, multiplying the energy which now begins to press on the external fringes of my brain. It is painless in its pursuit of a larger area to fill. There is motion which is visual, sensual, gentle, and rhythmical at first. It wells the lightened mass of energy to near-tidal wave proportions. Just as it seems that there is no outlet, I experience an indescribable heave of the internal dimensions of my head. There is an eruption as my cranial cavity takes on a new size and dimension. It becomes as large, as awesome, and as profound as our Capital Rotunda. The Light, with its vast energy potential, fills and illuminates the dome. It directs the thoughts, the ideas, and the visual sensations into an organized, steady flow to be channeled and used. It is rapid and requires my limbs and digits, indeed my whole self, to respond instantly and with precision. The energy pours into the chosen activity.

The Light often emerges before me, in front, as if to lead me. It fills me with total joy and total confidence that "this is right because it feels right." The Light, the energy fills me with love of life, with abounding love for all those I can see and not see, and I want to LIVE! I know that the Light, with its infinite energy is directing me towards ultimate perfection. . . .

The total light/energy package needs to travel the full distance from its resting place inside my chest, up into my skull, and into the dome before it can fully be dissipated and so come to rest again. Once inside the dome, it is not possible to voluntarily make it shut down. It must run its course.

Often my physical body is spent but the light/energy within my head still presses forward and outward. The energy disregards physical fatigue and the body's need for sleep. It surges, with waves of lightened brilliance that demand attention. . . . Although my eyelids are lowered the energy bolts batter their insides illuminating the area between eyelid and eyeball with heavenly light. A painless pressure against my lids makes it difficult to keep them lowered. My facial muscles fight to assist the lids but it is all in vain. I know that in a couple of hours the Light and the energy will rouse me once more and clamor for expression and action.

Nel, too, has visited us at the Near-Death Hotel, and I have been with her on many other occasions as well. Her outward manner and general energy level accord completely with the description she has given of her internal state when she experiences the light.

This internal radiance, described by Gopi Krishna and others as one of the hallmarks of the genuine kundalini experience, is sometimes attested to by other NDErs not yet mentioned in this chapter. As an illustration, let me return to Jayne, whose core NDE we delineated in Chapter 3.

On June 26, 1983, Jayne wrote me a letter and enclosed a little booklet she felt I ought to read. She said it "just blew her away." She had found a number of passages (which she underlined) that were "*absolutely identical* with the feelings I had in the segment of my NDE where I was totally merged with the radiant light. We [meaning the author of this booklet and she] just have to be dipping into the same pool."

The booklet turned out to be one of Gopi Krishna's works,[25] and one of the passages that Jayne had marked for me reads:

I do not claim that I see God, but I am conscious of a Living Radiance both within and outside of myself. In other words, I have gained a new power of perception, not present before. The luminosity does not end with my waking time. It persists even in my dreams. In every state of being—eating, drinking, talking, working, laughing, grieving, walking, or sleeping—I always dwell in a rapturous world of light. It is obvious that the self or observer in me has experienced a change and a new being has been born who is always enwrapped in a health of alluring light.[26]

The similarity between this kind of experience and Nel's is also evident.

Several of the NDErs whose comments I have drawn on here—as well as a few not mentioned—are convinced that the energy they have come to feel they are channeling is a *healing* energy. Indeed, some of these same NDErs have become healers since their NDE, while others have said they believe they now have the capacity to heal others.[27] In this respect, these individuals resemble the fictional heroine of a recent motion picture, *Resurrection*, who, after an NDE (and an initiatory ritual of sorts), develops the gift of healing. The relevance of this to kundalini lies in Motoyama's observation that his experience led to an ability to perform psychic healing and to Gopi Krishna's already cited statement that kundalini awakening elicits a variety of psychic abilities.

In addition to the energetic phenomena we have so far discussed, there is still another characteristic that seems to be found both in some of those who have experienced full kundalini awakenings and in some NDErs. I refer to a marked, perhaps discontinuous change in one's pattern of intellectual functioning, something also mentioned by Dean in his list of the characteristics of ultraconsciousness.

One of the presumed consequences of a complete kundalini awakening is a flowering of a kind of superintelligence. Gopi Krishna, for example, has described this type of development at length in many of his books, and, as modestly as possible, has indicated that he has experienced this change within himself since his kundalini awakening.

Several NDErs have made similar claims for themselves, either spontaneously or in direct response to my inquiries.

Tom Sawyer, for example, has suggested that his mind now operates differently than it did before his NDE, though he doubts a conventional intelligence test would show it (and so do I). Stella—another of our core experiencers—once told me that a psychologist had informed her that her intelligence was now that of a near-genius (though I have only her own personal statement for this and no documentation). And Nel recently wrote me in this regard:

I am able to stimulate the light/energy reaction in order to perform tasks, unpleasant or pleasant. I am able to willfully channel the energy to perform at new and higher levels of efficiency.

Barbara Harris finds the same increased efficiency within herself, but she adds more information concerning just *how* her mind functions now:

[After her NDE, she realized that her] brain was functioning differently and I didn't understand it, but I felt it, I sensed it. It was an ability to absorb knowledge without really studying hard, without cramming. . . . [Later] as the kundalini mechanism has settled in, I have become aware more and more of intuitive knowledge as my basis for functioning holographically. . . . The best word I can come up with is "efficient." Since the NDE, my brain has evolved to a more efficient level. This type of knowledge, by the way, I read about over and over in the kundalini literature and matches it exactly.

Finally, we have the testimony from another NDEr I know personally, Ed Rossiter, who has written me:

Since my experience . . . I notice that I have a much sharper, more acute comprehension of matters I become concerned with. My problem solving abilities have been enhanced. I find I am far better able to grasp pertinent facts and to bring them to reasonable conclusions. . . . I am sure this ability has been enhanced since my experience.

Needless to say, selective and fragmentary data like these must be regarded with extreme tentativeness. My personal impression as a psychologist is that all of the NDErs I've cited here were bright individuals to begin with and, in the absence of any pre- and post-NDE assessment of their style and level of cognitive functioning, it is obviously unwarranted to draw any conclusions even for this small set of NDErs, much less NDErs in general. Furthermore, even if we were to accept those self-reports as accurate, it still would not be clear from them alone whether the enchancement of intellective functions is comparable to what is allegedly triggered by kundalini awakenings.

All we can say from these shards of data is that *perhaps* there might be another parallel here between NDEs and kundalini. In any case, this is one aspect of post-NDE changes that clearly deserves a full investigation. My own data do no more than suggest that the hypothesis of increased or altered intellectual functioning following an NDE might well be worth testing.

Clearly, however, there *are* many other commonalities between aftereffects of full kundalini awakenings and NDEs in values, spiritual perspectives, psychic phenomena, and so on, but since much of our NDE material has already been presented, all we need do here is note those commonalities rather than rehash them.

To complete this section, then, it only remains to survey NDErs themselves concerning the plausibility of the kundalini-NDE link.

Unfortunately, this is not easy to do on the scale one would like. Clearly, most NDErs—like most people everywhere—have never even heard of the term "kundalini," much less understood what it refers to. This necessarily limits our sample severely! Nevertheless, among those who have looked into the matter, I believe it is fair to say that most feel there is some kind of connection. Here I can merely cite those views of NDErs that have so far come to my attention and express the hope that this book will elicit more of them as well as stimulate more research into the possible relationship between kundalini and NDEs.

Some of these opinions we have already acknowledged in passing. For example, I have previously quoted Sonja's judgment that the NDE activates kundalini; I have also mentioned Jayne's strong conviction that her NDE and Gopi Krishna's own experience are drawn from "the same pool." There are two other NDErs, however, who have had cause to dwell on this connection at greater length and to whose views we now must turn.

One of these individuals, not surprisingly, is Barbara Harris, whose post-NDE experiences virtually compelled her, in her opinion, to explore the literature on kundalini to make sense of what was happening to her. As I have already said, she has written extensively to me on this subject, but I will content myself here with this distillation of her search from her most recent statement, written on May 27, 1983. She writes, in part:

Since I started reading the literature on kundalini, I am constantly reading everything I can get my hands on—because it fits. It fits perfectly with the problems and confusions that I felt after the NDE. . . . I could go on and on about the kundalini framework and how it perfectly describes my physical, mental and emotional level of functioning. That was something I never had before the NDE and was what I was searching for. It really was *there* after the NDE. . . .

I *know* that the NDE was the initiation for the kundalini framework. . . . The high levels of consciousness that I am now experiencing are all part of the kundalini flow and are similar if not
identical to what I experienced at moments in the NDE. It's even
hard for me, thinking about it, to separate the NDE now from kundalini. They really contain each other.

The second individual is Joseph Dippong. It will perhaps lessen
the suspense here somewhat when I remind you that Mr. Dippong
is president of the Kundalini Research Institute of Canada! That will
be sufficient, I think, to suggest his overall view on this matter.
Still, it is of interest to describe how he came to his own interpretation and the role he now plays in furthering kundalini research.

In Chapter 5 I quoted a passage from Mr. Dippong in which he
relates how he, like so many other NDErs, was driven to undertake
an intense search for understanding following his experience. What
I did not disclose there, however, was the specific outcome of his
search. It was, of course, kundalini. For Mr. Dippong at least, this
concept and the process it represented explained, as it explained for
Barbara Harris, what his NDE had been about. Specifically, Mr.
Dippong learned

. . . why I, when being suffocated, had had such an overwhelmingly intense experience. I learned that in some very rare instances
when a person is deprived of his supply of oxygen, the life energy
[i.e., kundalini] could actually rush to the brain in order to sustain
life. Unusual as this idea may sound, it has been handed down for
centuries in highly respected Eastern traditions.[28]

This insight provided the spark for Mr. Dippong's future work.
As a businessman and publisher, he has played a leading role in the
West in trying to bring the phenomenon of kundalini to public at-
tention and to encourage scientists to investigate it.

When I wrote him about my hunch that there might be a connection between NDEs and kundalini, I could hardly have received
a more encouraging response:

. . . your letter touched me a great deal and my response to it is Bravo! Bravo! Bravo!—meaning praise to your discovery that the kundalini phenomenon plays the key role in many of the NDEs. To come to such a realization independently is truly a miracle. I'm not trying to butter you up, but rather when you see thousands of people who work and do research in the field of the paranormal who cannot connect the two in spite of ample evidence, it is truly remarkable. . . .

I remember the words of Gopi Krishna whom I met the first time many years ago when I was searching for answers to the meaning of my experience, criss-crossing the globe to soothe my restless soul. This knowledge about kundalini, he said, would totally revolutionize our present concept about the mind and, more importantly, in the next two decades, we would be spending our time rewriting our textbooks, thereby introducing the new phenomenon of kundalini and its exhaustive ramifications into every aspect of human life.

How many NDErs there are who would be as confident as Mr. Dippong about the kundalini-NDE connection I cannot say, but I doubt that I will ever find anyone who would be as inclined as he to agree that the hypothesis I have offered in this chapter is so self-evident!

Kundalini and NDEs: Conclusions

Despite Mr. Dippong's strong endorsement, we must be quick to remind ourselves that scientific truths are not established by testimonials or opinion surveys. To be sure, it would be of interest to know (if it turned out to be true) that NDErs generally found the ideas in this chapter plausible, but from a scientific point of view, that wouldn't prove a thing—any more than the near unanimity of NDErs concerning life after death proves it. As I have repeatedly stated throughout this chapter, the case for the kundalini hypothesis in relation to NDEs must remain conjectural until we can learn much more about both kundalini and NDEs.

Toward that end, however, perhaps I can offer a few concluding suggestions here that might facilitate the search for answers concerning a possible kundalini-NDE connection.

First, we must be clear about the nature of such a connection. There are at least three alternatives.

One possibility is that kundalini is itself the energy released by and that therefore *underlies* the NDE event. This is the position that is suggested by Mr. Dippong's interpretation.

A second possibility is that implied by Sonja's view—that the NDE may lead to a kundalini awakening but does not necessarily involve one. This position would hold, then, that the NDE increases the probability of a subsequent kundalini reaction.

There is, of course, a third possibility, that there is no direct connection between the two phenomena but only an empirical set of commonalities that may stem from one or more other factors. Just as two people can arrive at the same destination by entirely different routes, so kundalini and NDEs could be two completely independent processes leading to a similar outcome.

Only further research can determine which of these interpretations—or possibly some other—is correct (assuming there is at least some commonality).

Second, we must remember that even if kundalini energy underlies NDEs, it may not occur in all cases and it certainly wouldn't be expected to manifest itself to the same degree in different cases. Mr. Dippong's comment on his own experience, for example, implies that his own (kundalini-mediated) NDE was rare, not the rule. However, judging from the change in values that many NDErs report afterward, it seems perfectly plausible to argue that NDEs may well serve to open the heart chakra in these individuals to a variable degree. At least, according to Motoyama,[29] many of the qualities found in NDErs are associated with the activation of this chakra.

Third, this last observation points to specific research issues that would need to be addressed if *empirical* progress is to be made in this area. Clearly, there is a pressing need for comparative research with those who have had kundalini awakenings and those who have had NDEs. If Motoyoma's "chakra machine"—which is designed to measure electrical potentials associated with the different chakras—comes to be accepted as a valid and reliable apparatus, it could be used to establish whether the postulated kundalini activity in NDErs is at all similar to that of those who have had spontaneous kundalini awakenings. Presumably it could also determine which chakras, if any, become active following NDErs and if there is any common pattern among NDErs in that regard. Quite apart from this kind of approach, there is also an obvious requirement for a variety of *psychological* assessments to evaluate just how similar NDEs and kundalini-awakened individuals are in such domains as inner experience, cognitive functioning, personal behavior, and value orientation.

Fourth, we must ask why, theoretically, there should be a connection between kundalini and NDEs at all. Does some common physiological mechanism link them? Here I have one speculation to offer, though I must plainly state at the outset that this speculation, even if it is confirmed, is surely far from the whole story.

We know that, in principle, a great many variables are associated with kundalini awakenings.[30] One of these, however, seems to involve alterations in or even temporary suspensions of the breath. In Yoga, as I have already said, this practice of regulation of the breath—or, more literally, the life force—is called *pranayama* and is one of the traditional eight "limbs" of yoga. You may recall, for instance, that Motoyama, who is a practitioner of Yoga, found in concentrating on the sixth chakra that his breathing had become so slow that he felt as if he could "live without breathing."

If you now think about the usual situation of someone about to undergo an NDE, you can see a possible connection here. Imagine someone, for example, who suffers cardiac arrest. Under such circumstances, there would obviously be an *involuntary* disruption of respiration, followed by a total suspension of breathing, until resuscitation measures reversed the process. Could such typical (for NDEs) conditions trigger a kundalini reaction?

Recall now Mr. Dippong's earlier comment:

I learned that in some very rare instances when a person is deprived of his supply of oxygen, the life energy [i.e., kundalini] could actually rush to the brain in order to sustain life.

Perhaps this state of affairs isn't quite so rare as Mr. Dippong postulated. Oddly enough, in all the theorizing and speculating I have seen in the professional literature concerning interpretations of NDEs, I cannot recall encountering any systematic consideration of the role of respiratory interference in inducing NDEs. If, however, this line of inquiry could be pursued, it might furnish a link that would make sense of the kundalini-NDE connection.

One more word of warning is in order here. It would be a mistake to believe that breath retention *alone* would induce either kundalini awakenings *or* NDEs, even though the former may be associated with the latter. Gopi Krishna is very clear on this issue. He says:

The linkage of diminished breathing and pulse rate, arrested flow of blood, coldness or cataleptic conditions of the body, with the awakening of *kundalini* has been a cause of great misunderstanding and has led to erroneous notions about this power.[31]

Gopi Krishna is implying that individuals such as fakirs and some yogis who may have attained this kind of mastery over their internal states will not necessarily trigger a kundalini reaction simply by resorting to these devices.

While this point should be borne clearly in mind by researchers, it is another question altogether whether, at least in some cases, *involuntary* interruption of respiration, such as occurs in NDEs, may have any direct or ultimate effect on stimulating a kundalini awakening.

Finally, we must return to the beginning theme of this chapter, where evidence was presented that the NDE was one of a family of related transcendental experiences—and that it had nothing *inherently* to do with death. Remember, that position led us to pursue the possibility that a more *general* explanation for NDEs—and not one limited to the special conditions associated with near-death crises—would in the end be justified. In this respect, an explanation that would subsume NDEs as a special case of transcendental experience (along with the common aftereffects of such experience) seemed to be required. The kundalini concept was suggested as a candidate that appeared to have this range and capacity, largely because there is increasing agreement in the field that conventional biologically based theories are incapable of explaining the full range of phenomena and aftereffects reported by NDErs.[32] Of course, it may also prove to be the case that the concept of kundalini itself represents only a limited aspect or understanding of a more general energetic phenomenon that may yet provide a more complete and satisfying explanation for NDEs, but only further research can settle the point. However this may turn out, it is still important to bear in mind that any interpretation of the NDE—assuming that one can be offered by science—must be prepared to come to terms with the fact that the NDE is not unique in the world of transcendental experience.

Evolutionary Implications of Kundalini

Although we have concluded that we cannot say whether kundalini energy does underlie NDEs, we can still ponder some of the implications if a relationship between the two becomes established. To close this chapter, then, and to serve as a bridge to the last chapter in this book, I need to bring out here one class of implications in particular—that which bears on human evolution.

The subtitle of Gopi Krishna's first book is *The Evolutionary Energy in Man,* and clearly it implies that kundalini *is* the mechanism that propels humanity's evolution. Specifically, he has written that "the final target of the [kundalini-mediated] evolutionary processes is to carry the whole of mankind toward a higher dimension of consciousness."[33] This is, of course, the kundalini hypothesis we mentioned earlier. And here we finally begin to see something of the grander sweep of this concept. In Gopi Krishna's view—and in the view of many thinkers—the awakening of kundalini not only accelerates the evolution of one's own consciousness but also that of the human race itself:

Transcendental consciousness . . . is but a step ahead and must be clearly understood as such to chart out the direction in which the evolution of consciousness is taking place before our very eyes.[34]

What is happening to bring about this evolution? If we remain for now with the individual case, we can use this passage from the writings of John White to sum up the implications of this chapter for us:

When properly raised . . . kundalini can result in a figurative death, an ego-death, involving transformation of the nervous system and the experience of divinity. In this experience, the "old Adam" dies, to use St. Paul's phrase, and a new person is born, reborn, as a child of the cosmos, no longer self-centered or even Earth-centered but rather universally centered and cosmically conscious.[35]

Now imagine for a moment the *planetary* implications of such transformations as we move from the individual case to the collective level. This is, of course, a new and sudden leap for us to make, since throughout this book we have been chiefly concerned with patterns of individual experience and transformation. But I am convinced—and I hope to convince you—that only if we begin to examine carefully the collective significance of NDEs will we be able to penetrate into the heart of their meaning.

We are finally ready, then, to revert to the question that initiated this inquiry—the meaning of these NDEs. But to do so we find ourselves having to address this question at a different *level* of analysis from that with which we began. We must be prepared to move from studies of personal transformation to those of planetary scope. Only then will the evolutionary role of NDEs be evident and their higher, global significance made plain.

And only then will we be able to see that we may indeed be heading toward Omega.

CHAPTER 10

· · · · · · ·

NDEs and Human Evolution

∵

Heading toward Omega.

Although I have used this phrase as the title for this book, it has remained in the background, unexplained—until now. Finally it is time that we explore its meaning in the context of near-death experiences and human evolution, the theme of this chapter.

Omega, n. (Gr. *O* + *mega,* great) The twenty-fourth and final letter of the Greek alphabet.

Omega, then, represents an end, as death itself seems to be the end of life. It is in this sense that a well-known journal in the field of thanatology is called *Omega.* Omega means death.

But it also means something else, just as the word "end" similarly has a double meaning. "End" can obviously signify either finality or a goal, and it is Omega as an end *point* that has special meaning to us here. In this sense, Omega stands for the aim of human evolution, the ultimate destination toward which humanity is inexorably bound.

Omega, in this latter sense, is of course associated with a great visionary writer, Pierre Teilhard de Chardin, a Jesuit priest and paleontologist whose celebrated book *The Phenomenon of Man* is one of the twentieth century's landmark contributions to evolutionary thought. In this work, Père Teilhard spoke of the various levels of evolution—matter, life, and consciousness—and argued that human evolution was headed toward a transhuman state he called "noogenesis," the birth of a unified planetary mind aware of its essential divinity. This convergent end state, the culmination of human evolution on earth, Père Teilhard called "The Omega Point."

Teilhard was very clear, however, that this tendency toward planetary consciousness was not likely to reach Omega any time soon. As a paleontologist, Teilhard was accustomed to think in terms of the vast stretches of geologic time during which evolutionary processes slowly manifest themselves. He saw no reason to alter his perspective drastically as he moved from biological evolution to that of the evolution of consciousness and culture. In his work, he forecasted this grand trajectory of our evolutionary destiny while mindful of its aeonic dimensions.

As it had for many, Père Teilhard's thought provided me with an inspiring vision of human evolution when I first encountered it years ago, but while I remained sympathetic to it, it wasn't until 1980 that I began to see a connection between it and the near-death research that was by then central to my life.

In May of that year I happened to attend a conference of the Academy of Religion and Physical Research in Chicago to give an address on my near-death research findings. Immediately after my talk, my good friend John White, a well-known author and lecturer, whose work has always concerned itself with studies in higher consciousness, delivered his prepared lecture to the Academy. I listened with deepening absorption as the relevance of John's ideas for my NDE research sank into my awareness. As reading Moody's *Life After Life* years before had been, hearing John's lecture was catalytic for me—I think I saw in a few moments an entirely new context of meaning for what NDEs might actually represent. And another strong click of recognition went off inside me.

Later in this chapter I will quote from that talk of John's so you can know specifically what he said that so stirred me, but its general effect at the time was to resensitize me to the evolutionary perspective of writers such as Père Teilhard. I suspect that John's talk also reawakened in me the disturbing thought that perhaps my NDE research wasn't finished after all. I think even then I was at least inchoately aware that an *empirical* bridge needed to be constructed to link John's evolutionary framework to NDEs. In any case, not long after listening to John some of the ideas for this inquiry started to gel in my mind and I found myself back in "the near-death business"—and simultaneously setting out to discover whether NDEs would indeed lead to Omega.

Now that I have shared the findings of that journey with you, the time has finally come to explain fully why I believe that my findings strongly suggest we are heading toward Omega. Not, I hasten to qualify, to Teilhard's Omega *point*, but along the same road that ultimately leads there. What I mean to talk about, however, is not merely something that may happen one day. It is happening *now*, in our lifetime. In my opinion, the next stage of our collective journey toward Omega has already come into view.

The Evolutionary Significance of NDEs

Toward the close of the previous chapter I suggested that one could appreciate the full significance of NDEs only by changing levels of analysis from the individual plane to the collective. We have examined many individual cases of personal transformation in this book in our search for patterns, but the *meaning* of those patterns will not be clear until we can see them from a much higher perspective. Toward this end, a few observations are first necessary.

To begin with, recall (from Chapter 2) that according to George Gallup's figures, there may well be eight million adult Americans who have experienced NDEs. Of course, we have no idea how many people in the world may already have had this kind of experience, but it certainly does not seem unreasonable to assume that millions of individuals outside the United States must also have had NDEs. In any event, with resuscitation technology likely to improve and to spread in use around the globe, it appears highly likely that many millions *more* will come to know for themselves what the people described in this book already know.

But, of course, the point is not simply that many millions will know the NDE for themselves but also *how the NDE will transform them afterward*. We have already examined in depth how people's lives and consciousness are affected by NDEs and what values come to guide their behavior. Now, to begin to appreciate the planetary impact of these changes, we must imagine these same effects occurring in millions of lives throughout the world, regardless of race, religion, nationality, or culture.

Yet it is not just NDErs whom we have to visualize on this collective level but also *all* persons who have undergone a similar transformative experience as a result of a deep spiritual awakening. Remember that it has already been established (in Chapter 9) that the NDE is only *one* of a family of related transcendental experiences, and that it appears that most such experiences, however they are brought about, lead to transformations similar to those documented for NDErs. And although there are, to my knowledge, no systematic studies of the incidence of this larger family of transcendental experiences, recent books such as *The Aquarian Conspiracy* and *The Global Brain*[1] have offered evidence that such experiences are widespread, at least in the Western world, and that their number is growing exponentially.[2] NDErs themselves, then, should probably be regarded as one distinct stream feeding into a larger river, with many tributaries, of spiritually transformative experience.

From this perspective we are now finally able to discern the larger meanings of NDEs. May it be that NDErs—and others who have had similar awakenings—*collectively represent an evolutionary thrust toward higher consciousness for humanity at large?* Could it be that the NDE itself is an evolutionary mechanism that has the effect of jump-stepping individuals into the next stage of human development by unlocking spiritual potentials previously dormant? Indeed, are we seeing in such people—as they mutate from their pre-NDE personalities into more loving and compassionate individuals—the prototype of a new, more advanced strain of the human species striving to come into manifestation? No longer *Homo sapiens* perhaps, but tending toward what John White has called *Homo noeticus?* Could NDErs be, then, an evolutionary bridge to the next step in our destiny as a species, a "missing link" in our midst?

These are heady and provocative questions to be sure, but they are not entirely speculative ones. Many other thinkers before me have dreamed and written of the coming of a higher humanity to earth and have attempted to describe the attributes of this more evolved race. Also, though their visions of this higher humanity are of course subjective, the NDErs I have described in this book are real individuals—and they are among us now. We might ask, then: How well do these visions match the characteristics of NDErs?

And here we return to my friend John White, who has been for some years one of the most articulate spokesmen for the view that a new form of human life is appearing on this planet. What he said in Chicago, in part, was:

Homo noeticus is the name I give to the emerging form of humanity. "Noetics" is a term meaning the study of consciousness, and that activity is a primary characteristic of members of the new breed. Because of their deepened awareness and self-understanding, they do not allow the traditionally imposed forms, controls, and institutions of society to be barriers to their full development. Their changed psychology is based on expression of feeling, not suppression. The motivation is cooperative and loving, not competitive and aggressive. Their logic is multilevel/integrated/simultaneous, not linear/sequential/either-or. Their sense of identity is embracing-collective, not isolated-individual. Their psychic abilities are used for benevolent and ethical purposes, not harmful and immoral ones. The conventional ways of society don't satisfy them. The search for new ways of living and new institutions concerns them. They seek a culture founded in higher consciousness, a culture whose institutions are based on love and wisdom, a culture that fulfills the perennial philosophy.[3]

I don't think I will have to resort to any arm-twisting to convince you that John's description of *Homo noeticus* accords pretty well with the general portrait I have drawn of Omega NDErs in this book, especially for those NDErs who seem to have integrated their experience most successfully.

It may be difficult to establish the contention that such individuals constitute a new race per se, but this prototypic description is by no means solely John White's personal vision. As he points out, similar forecasts and characterizations can be found in the writings of other prominent evolutionary thinkers, including R. M. Bucke, Sri Aurobindo, Gopi Krishna, and Ken Wilber,[4] as well as in writings of other, lesser known authors. Interestingly enough, it is also to be found in the work of at least one evolutionary biologist *who has had an NDE*.

Dr. John T. Robinson is professor of zoology at the University of Wisconsin. In 1980 he had a deep NDE as a result of a cardiac arrest following coronary bypass surgery and eventually wrote me about his experience (his wife had earlier sent me an abundance of documented materials concerning his NDE). As usual, a lively correspondence ensued. Dr. Robinson enclosed with one of his letters a couple of papers he had written *prior to* his NDE. Like Nancy Clark, Dr. Robinson did not at the time know that I was working on a new book on NDE, but his materials, like hers, proved remarkably apposite.[5]

It would take too long here to describe Professor Robinson's views in detail, but suffice it to say that in both papers[6] he is concerned with "the evolution of evolution" or "metaevolution," as he terms it. In his second (1980) paper, after considering aspects of physical, biological, and cultural evolution, he speculates that an entirely new stage of evolution, which he calls Phase IV, may already be emerging. Previously, he had argued that successful adaptation to the requirements of Phase III would be promoted by human behavior that is

. . . unselfish, cooperative, altruistic, group-oriented, and does not involve attachment to material possessions.[7]

But about Phase IV he says:

It is tempting to speculate that the strong tendency to generate religious ideas, which seems to have characterized most branches of mankind, stems at least in part from some perception of Phase IV that religions are at best incomplete, and at worst wholly mistaken, attempts to understand the phase of evolution ahead of us.

He goes on to suggest that

. . . it is likely that consciousness will be better developed than in ourselves and the physical even less important. . . . It is also likely that Phase IV would include only fully cooperative beings since full success in Phase III—and thus evolution into Phase IV—could only be gained by having fully learned the necessity for cooperation.[8]

Again, though the characterization is more sketchy here than White's, there appears to be an overlap between Robinson's prototype of Phase IV and NDErs.

Although I have already said that it would be difficult to prove that NDErs (and other individuals who have undergone similar transformations) are truly a new race,[9] it can still be asked: *If* they are, what is the evolutionary mechanism that would theoretically be responsible for giving rise to a new strain of human beings with their attributes?

Presumably it is kundalini—in Gopi Krishna's phrase, "The evolution energy of man." Joseph Dippong states the thesis succinctly:

This [kundalini] awakening is thought to be associated with a biological transformation which allows for the immensely expanded perception that represents the crown of evolution. In this sense it also represents the "birth" of a new human being.[10]

And John White nicely draws out its implications:

The kundalini experience, then, considered from the viewpoint of individual transformation, is said to be a path for enlightenment. But if a large number of enlightened people were to appear in society at the same time, the result could well transform society itself. So the kundalini experience, in its broadest aspect, is evolutionary—a path for the advancement of the entire human race to a higher state.[11]

With this statement, the argument we have been developing over the past several chapters has been brought to completion. But to assemble the various pieces of this hypothesis together in one place, I will simply summarize it here in the following propositions:

1. The NDE represents an experience of higher (transcendental) consciousness.
2. That experience is or may be accompanied by a discharge of subtle biological energy called kundalini.
3. Kundalini may permanently transform the nervous system (including the brain) so as to activate latent spiritual potentials.
4. As the evolutionary mechanism of humanity, kundalini can generate a new type of human being characterized by a noetic understanding of the universe.

5. In recent years, many such people have been "created" through NDEs and other kundalini-mediated spiritual experiences.

6. A new race of human beings is coming into existence which could transform the planet.

7. We are heading toward Omega.

To prevent any misunderstanding of this point, I must not only repeat but also emphasize that nothing in this book *proves* any of these propositions or, of course, the overall thesis that they represent.[12] It is just a framework supported by some of my data and suggested by others. Only further research and the passage of time can demonstrate its validity. I offer it here as one way to understand the deeper meanings of my NDE data and as the outcome of my personal search for understanding of these extraordinary experiences.

But this is not the end of our inquiry by any means; it is only a pause for stock-taking. There are still the views of Omega NDErs on the Omega hypothesis to consider, views that will at least demonstrate that my interpretation is not without support from them. But before we hear one last time from our NDErs, there is a set of related issues that must be addressed first.

For the sake of argument, let us suppose that, however, it may be explained, there is a new spiritual energy manifesting itself through millions of NDErs. Suppose, in short, that we are in some sense heading toward Omega.

These questions then arise: (1) What will the remainder of the journey be like? (2) Will society be transformed in the way suggested by John White's observation? (3) Why are so many people having NDEs and other transformative spiritual experiences at this time in our history?

The answers to these questions will deepen our understanding of the implications of the Omega hypothesis and conclude our inquiry into the significance of NDEs.

Exploring the Omega Hypothesis

Even if we grant that we may be heading toward Omega, there is obviously no guarantee that we will *arrive* there. Here, however, I am not speaking of Omega in the sense of Teilhard's Omega *point* of planetary consciousness but simply the next stage of human evolution toward which NDErs and others, like a kind of species avant-garde, appear to be moving. My understanding of this evolutionary process is that it is a potential that is becoming manifest in some people, not that it is an inevitable destiny—at least in the short term—for our species. Whether humanity as a whole can evolve into *Homo noeticus* and thus transform the world in which we live is a question no one can answer with assurance. Between tendency and realization is a wide gulf of uncertainty, and to bridge it, given the present state of our planetary crisis, will take more than a spirit of optimism toward the future. What might be required to effect this planetary transition we will consider shortly.

But in the meantime, can we perhaps glimpse what form the evolutionary journey will take? Assuming the general course I've suggested, there are obviously several quite different scenarios. One that surfaces immediately comes out of the views of near-death experiencers themselves who claim to have had a prevision of our planetary future. The prophetic visions we surveyed in Chapter 8, if taken literally, indicate that the road to Omega will be built over a ruined earth by the remains of a devastated humanity. This vision of the future implies that only a "planetary near-death experience" can transform human beings to make them fit custodians of the New Age. If their view is correct, our passage to Omega and the next stage of human evolution will take us through Hell.

This is a vision of our probable future that apparently many besides some of our NDErs share, but I reject it. All my studies have led me to the conviction that this scenario need not be and is *not* already set to unfold like a Greek tragedy claiming its victims with the force of fate. I personally believe that the meaning of these visions may be something entirely other than what they seem and that they represent not a vision of our planetary future but, paradoxically, a source of hope. I will spell out this interpretation shortly but for now merely say that I am not one who holds that the road to Omega must necessarily be built upon the blood of the planet. An apocalyptic end to our millennium does not have to be.

But given the current grave situation of our world, you might ask: What hope can there really be that it can be transformed according to the evolutionary drift that NDErs, among others, appear to represent? Even if we assume many millions of persons *are* changing so as to become more loving, compassionate individuals with a deeply inflamed desire to serve others, what can such a relatively small cadre of good-hearted souls do to reverse the tide of human destructiveness and the apparent slow slide toward planetary chaos?

Again, we have a question that beggars any attempt to espouse a cocksure optimism. In our time, there are no guarantees of anything; there is only hope. Human beings live on hope and thrive on possibility and so long as there is any chance at all that humanity may yet be rescued from its descent into the abyss, it will cling to it with all its strength. That being so, I will offer here one possibility that we may grasp onto. It is a slender thread, but at least it is something.

The possibility rests on the work of a young English biologist named Rupert Sheldrake, whose book *A New Science of Life: The Hypothesis of Formative Causation* rocked the English scientific establishment when it was published in 1981 and has remained controversial ever since. According to Sheldrake's hypothesis of formative causation, the characteristic forms and *behavior* of physical, chemical, and biological systems are determined by invisible organizing fields Sheldrake terms *morphogenetic fields*. These fields, which transcend time and space, are said to be without mass or energy and, of course, are not currently recognized by scientists.

Yet there are many anomalies in science, not easily explained or not explainable at all, that Sheldrake's hypothesis allows us to understand. To take one familiar example Sheldrake uses, consider of all improbable things—especially in this context—the maze-swimming behavior of rats.

In 1920, a Harvard psychologist named William McDougall trained a group of rats to swim through a water maze. This these animals learned to do, though, as is the way with rats (and some other creatures), some learned faster than others. And, as is the way of psychologists, McDougall kept track of the number of errors each rat made until the task was mastered.

McDougall continued this experiment by breeding his maze-swimming rats over twenty generations and giving the descendants of the originals the same experimental task. The findings showed that successive generations of rats became progressively *better* at learning to swim throughout the maze; indeed, the last generation learned to do so ten times as fast as the original group. Since parental rats do not send their children to maze-swimming schools, McDougall's findings are puzzling indeed.

But there is more to the story. Other researchers, in Scotland and Australia, attempted to repeat McDougall's work. Astonishingly, in both studies, the first generation of rats learned to negotiate the maze almost as fast as McDougall's last generation. Some of the rats even learned the task immediately and without a single error!

How can such odd findings—and similar ones from other studies Sheldrake cites—be explained? In conventional terms they cannot, but Sheldrake's hypothesis *does* provide a coherent explanation. According to him, McDougall's first generation of rats established a morphogenetic field for that behavior. That field then "guided" the behavior of later rats through a process Sheldrake calls *morphic resonance* so that the task could be learned more quickly.

Sheldrake's basic idea here is that once such fields become established through some initial behavior, that behavior is then facilitated in others through *morphic resonance*. Similarly, once an evolutionary variant occurs in a species, it is likely to spread through the same principle.

At this point you may be wondering about the relevance of all this to NDErs and planetary transformation. But there is a possible connection here stemming from the following observation, which has already been made by a number of others besides myself: *We do not know the limits of Sheldrake's hypothesis*. If it is correct—and it is currently the subject of much excited interest and experimental work—it is distinctly possible that it may also apply to social systems as well. This extrapolation has, in fact, already been made by science writer Peter Russell, whose commentary will make explicit the connection between our concerns here and Sheldrake's work. According to Russell:

Applying Sheldrake's theory to the development of higher states of consciousness, we might predict that the more individuals begin to

raise their own levels of consciousness, the stronger the morphogenetic field for higher states would become, and the easier it
would be for others to move in that direction. Society would gather
momentum toward enlightenment. Since the rate of growth would
not be dependent on the achievements of those who had gone before, we would enter a phase of super-exponential growth. Ultimately, this could lead to a chain reaction, in which everyone
suddenly started making the transition to a higher level of consciousness.[13]

The argument here is clearly similar to the now very popular
idea of "the hundredth-monkey effect," a story whose scientific au-
thenticity now appears doubtful[14] but that has grown to almost
mythic proportions within a very short time. As you probably know,
this tale describes how a new behavior, potato washing by monkeys,
spread to all monkeys on a certain Japanese island—as well as to
monkeys on adjacent islands—once an imaginary "hundredth monkey" indulged in the new ritual. Presumably that was all that was
needed to create a strong enough field for morphic resonance to
occur, turning innovation into custom. The hundredth monkey represented the critical mass sufficient to transform the eating habits of
monkeys in that region.

Although the story itself may be apocryphal, Sheldrake's work
shows that the principle it involves could well be real. Whether
Russell's generalization of Sheldrake's hypothesis to the level of
planetary transformation is warranted only history will tell, but it
already seems clear that "the hundredth-monkey effect" has established itself as a myth of our time. And thus it could be that eight
million NDErs may be to the world what that hundredth monkey
was to his islands. The myth at least gives us hope of possibility and,
if it should become widely enough shared, it could begin to generate
its own reality. Perhaps the conclusions of this book will contribute
just a bit more to the hope that his myth has come to represent for
us and provide a glimpse of an alternate route toward Omega.

And now we come to our last question: *Why* is there such a
seeming profusion of near-death and other transformative experiences in our time? In a sense, this is the key question that will
unlock many levels of meaning for us as our inquiry into NDEs

closes. And here we will find it helpful to cite the views of NDErs as well as others in our attempt to draw out the ultimate significance of these experiences.

So, then, why now?

Let me begin to frame an answer here by quoting a portion of a speculative passage from *Life at Death:*

I think everyone realizes that the closing decades of this century already give us grave cause for uneasiness concerning the destiny of the human race on this planet. Predictions of widespread, even global, calamities are plentiful, and though the scenarios differ, all of us have heard enough of them for them to have become real as *possibilities.* Could it be, then, that one reason why the study of death has emerged as one of the dominant concerns of our time is to help us to become globally sensitized to the experience of death precisely because the notion of death on a *planetary* scale now hangs, like the sword of Damocles, over our heads? Could this be the universe's way of "inoculating" us against the fear of death?[15]

Now it begins to appear that my own speculative musings are shared by at least some core NDErs. For example, in her latest book, *Messengers of Hope,* which is rooted in her NDE and its transformative effect in her life, Carol Parrish-Harra has written:

Is there a logical or spiritual reason for the recent . . . surge of interest in this area [of death and dying]? . . . Could humanity be moving forward to a time when it will need to know that the physical life is only a part of the whole life, and not even the most important part? . . . If humanity's future includes earth changes, social unrest, and perhaps nuclear war, the death and dying movement will be boot camp. This may be the opportunity to "be prepared."[16]

Of course, as Carol herself points out elsewhere in her book, the large numbers of NDErs who are coming forward to tell their stories about what it is like to die are helping the world to understand that, from their collective experience, there *is* no death. Each one may tell his or her story just to a few—or to a few million through television—but the cumulative impact of these testimonies from all over the globe is hard to overestimate. It is, as I asserted in the opening chapter, giving us a new view of death, one that helps to strip away all fear of it.

H. G. Wells wrote that civilization is a race between catastrophe and education. Humanity still seems to be engaged in that race—which we might now rephrase as between catastrophe and *consciousness*—and the pace is increasing along with the consequences. Carol Parrish-Harra is hardly alone among NDErs in her urgency to broadcast the message about death—and what it teaches.[17]

Janis, another core experiencer who, like Carol, returned with intimations of possible planetary cataclysm, told me:

Unless people start working together and stop fighting, they're gonna destroy themselves. . . . Unless people learn to get along and care about each other and care about other life on this planet, there will be no planet. Even during my near-death experience, I had a feeling that there isn't that much time left *here* unless something is done. And that's why I came back because I thought, "Maybe there isn't another chance." There may well not be another chance to come back and do it. . . . There's an urgency about it because there isn't that much time.

Carol's book speaks about NDErs (among others) as "messengers of hope," a phrase I find extremely apt to describe a collective sense of purpose many of them share. Along these lines, perhaps you'll remember that in the previous chapter, when I was discussing Nancy Clark's experience with the Light, I omitted her account of what the Light communicated to her. What she was told sums up as well as any statement I have heard from NDErs the essence of the message of hope they feel they have to give to humanity. Nancy says that the Light told her in these "exact words":

With the gift you have now received, go forth and tell the masses of people that life after death exists; that you shall all experience my PROFOUND LOVE! LOVE is the key to the universe; you must all learn to live in peace and harmony with one another on earth while you have the chance. This will be a very difficult task for you, my child, a huge undertaking, but you shall do it. You are loved.

But what, then, are we finally to make of the dark planetary visions that we have seen swirling around the sun of the near-death experience like clouds of doom threatening to extinguish the light from our world? In what way are these visions part of the message of hope that NDErs presumably have returned from the gates of death to bring us?

One understanding, of course, is that they may not be unconditional forecasts of coming events, but conditional warnings of what may befall us unless we, too, come to hear and heed the timeless but ever so timely message that NDErs have disclosed to us with such uniformity. But there is still another understanding of these visions, compatible with the first yet more in keeping with the evolutionary perspective I have tried to offer here. A succinct statement of this understanding is to be found in the writings of physician W. Brugh Joy:

For me, the cataclysmic prophecies that are rife in current literature foreshadow a revolution of the most astonishing proportions, but instead of being a revolution in the physical plane it is a revolution in consciousness, a revolution of the mental plane. I sense the approach of a psychological earthquake the magnitude of which has not been experienced in the human awareness for millennia and may not have been experienced in the human awareness ever before.[18]

Thus the meaning of these visions may not simply be hortatory but also symbolic of the shift in consciousness that seems to be possible in our time and necessary to avert disaster. And, again, Brugh Joy is not alone in sensing these possibilities. Speaking in the same vein is Peter Russell, who has recently written a book in support of his contention that

Humanity could be on the threshold of an evolutionary leap, a leap that could occur in a flash of evolutionary time, a leap such as occurs only once in a billion years. The changes leading to this leap are taking place right before our eyes—or rather right behind them, within our own minds.[19]

And once more we find NDErs themselves concurring with this view—and with their role in helping to foster the conditions that will bring it about.

One of these persons is writer and lecturer Phyllis M. H. Atwater, herself an NDEr, who is deeply attuned to "New Age" concepts and who, in this vein, recently wrote in part to me:

What does it mean when someone no longer fits the accepted mold for humanhood? What does it mean when someone evolves beyond the accepted norm? I have. I am not an exception. I know many others, Does this make us walk-ins, alien beings just now discovering themselves—or maybe, just maybe, it means we are human beings who through whatever manner or means have shifted gears and projected into our own greater potential. *Anyone* by whatever means can make this shift in consciousness and project into a stepped up or higher version of themselves. *Anyone!* . . . I think there are many ways to step up our vibratory pattern and expand our awareness. I think there are many ways to reach our higher potential and perhaps even operate from the soul level. And it is time. It is time globally for people to transform. As we transform, our earth and its environment will also.

Still another NDEr who shares this transformative vision but who brings a slightly different slant to it is Patricia Bahr, whom I met at a workshop for health professionals during my most recent trip to California. At that workshop, Patricia agreed to share her experience with the audience and, afterward, she wrote me that in her view

[the] main message seems to be to live in love and harmony and trust in the ultimate good within us all. We are headed towards a chance for a quantum leap in consciousness where all beings will remember who they really are and be able to communicate at a level where we'll know the truth of another without ever opening

our mouths. Deceit won't be possible. We'll work toward the ultimate evolvement of all consciousness either through easy lessons or hard ones. But we're the ones doing the choosing.

Carol Parrish-Harra is another NDEr who has also used the same metaphor of "the quantum leap" forward in consciousness and who, like Patricia, has insisted that the choice is ours to continue the movement in this direction. Summing up her own conclusions, Carol has said:

The symbol of a golden age is held before us, encouraging us to believe, hand on, move carefully around the mountain's edge, because one slip and the abyss awaits. The human mind, once animal, received into itself the divine spark and started this ascent. It will not be wiped out. It can be pushed down, tortured, made to wait aeons of time. Humanity has glimpsed divinity. Already some have achieved it. The group mind, collective consciousness, has thrilled with the ecstasy of ascent.[20]

Conclusion

By now, my own conclusions concerning the meaning of the NDE phenomenon will be clear to you. Of course, as was evident at the outset, there are several layers of meaning, each interpenetrating the others, and all of them have been suggested in the closing section of this chapter. From the study of the NDE, we have learned to see death in a new way, not as something to be dreaded but, on the contrary, as an encounter with the Beloved. Those who can come to understand death in this way, as NDErs are compelled to, need never fear death again. And liberated from this primary fear, they too, like NDErs, become free to experience life as the gift it is and to live naturally, as a child does, with delight. Not everyone can have or needs to have an NDE, but everyone can learn to assimilate these lessons of the NDE into his own life if he chooses to.

Beyond this, of course, is the virtual unanimity of Nancy Clark's personal conclusion that, in effect, there is *only* life—life now, and life following what we still presume to call death. This, Nancy says, is the message the Light told her to spread—and it is the universal message of hope, a *cri de coeur,* from all NDErs. None of these persons brings *scientific* proof of life after death, of course. They bring something personally more important: subjective proof. They claim to know in a way and from a source that removes all doubt. Each of us must make of this collective testimony what we will, but it is hard—at least for me—to believe that this is a meaningless consolation given to so many for so many more.

And beyond all this, there is still the profound *evolutionary* meaning of NDEs—that NDErs and others who have had similar awakenings may in some way prefigure our own planetary destiny, the next stage of human evolution, the dazzling ascent toward Omega and the conscious reunion with the Divine.

APPENDIX 1

· · · · · · ·

Interview Schedule

∴

As you know, I am interested to find out some of the things that have happened in your life following your near-death experience in _____. (If respondent has had an NDE which I don't already know about, then say) First of all, though, I wonder if you could give me a brief account of the circumstances which brought you close to death and of the experience you had at the time? (Ask questions of clarification as necessary.)

In this interview what I'd really like to try to get at—at least eventually—is the understanding that you yourself have of your experience. Now it's been _____ years since this experience took place. In that time, I'm sure (I know) that you've had occasion to talk about it with others. (Pause for response) Can you tell me a little concerning how people reacted to learning of your experience? Did talking about it with others help you to gain any clarity about it in your own mind?

In terms of your own understanding of your experience, would you say that it happened to you for a reason? Does that question make sense to you? (If yes, then ask if necessary) What was it (the reason)?

Maybe one way to get at the significance of this kind of experience is to try to determine whether it tended to bring about any changes in your life. Rather than asking you to give a general answer here, though, let me instead ask you a series of related questions along these lines. If, after I've asked them, I've overlooked some things that are significant, you can bring them up then, okay?

First of all, then, did this experience affect in any way your sense of purpose in living? Did it give you any kind of new outlook on life? (Probe as necessary for all these questions)

Second, did it have any effect on the direction of your life? For example, did you change jobs or did your interests change in some specific way that you feel now might have been triggered by your experience?

Did it change your attitudes or feelings about yourself? How so?

Did it affect how you felt about or related to others? (Ask lettered questions below if these issues are not spontaneously brought up by respondent)

 a. Desire to help others?
 b. Compassion for others?
 c. Empathy or understanding for others?
 d. Patience/tolerance for others?
 e. Ability to express love for others?
 f. Acceptance of others AS THEY ARE?

Did it have any effect on your spiritual or religious beliefs or values? (Ask the following questions if not specifically brought up by respondent)

 a. Effect on church/temple attendance?
 b. Feelings about organized religion?
 c. Openness to new religious/spiritual ideas or systems?
 d. Inward feelings about religion, God, etc.?
 e. Fear of death?
 f. Understanding of death?
 g. Attitude toward reincarnation?
 h. Quest for spiritual values/higher consciousness, etc.?

In your opinion, did you experience any changes in your psychic abilities or sensitivities after your near-death experience? (If so) What sorts of changes? Can you give me any examples?

Did you at the time of your near-death episode or afterward get any kind of vision of the future? Or any feeling about what may happen between now and the end of the century? (If so) Did you have any sense of when this was going to take place—or if it was inevitable? Any unusually vivid or recurrent dreams in this connection?

Are there any other things about your near-death episode or its effects upon you that you would be willing to share with me—that we haven't touched upon so far?

All right, now for the $64,000 question. We've talked quite a bit about your experience and the changes that it may have helped to bring about in your life. From your current perspective, then, just what do you *personally* make of this experience? What meaning does it have for you? (Or alternatively) How do you interpret it?

APPENDIX II

· · · · · · ·

Omega Questionnaires

÷

BACKGROUND INFORMATION SHEET

1. NAME _____

2. SEX   M F

3. DATE OF BIRTH_____

4. RACE OR ETHNIC GROUP

___White

___Black

___Hispanic

___(Native American) Indian

___Oriental

___Other (please specify)

5. CURRENT MARITAL STATUS

___Single

___Married

___Remarried

___Separated

___Divorced

___Widowed

6. RELIGIOUS PREFERENCE/AFFILIATION

___Catholic

___Protestant

___Jewish

___Moslem

___Other (please specify)

7. EDUCATIONAL LEVEL

___Grade school

___Some high school

___High school graduate

___Some college or presently attending college

_____College graduate

_____Some post-graduate work

_____Earned advanced degree
(please specify)

8. CURRENT OCCUPATION_____

9. IF YOU HAVE EVER BEEN PHYSICALLY CLOSE TO
DEATH, GIVE APPROXIMATE DATE(S)_____

LIFE CHANGES QUESTIONNAIRE

NAME_____

Year of near-death incident_____

A near-death incident may or may not bring about certain changes
in an individual's life. We would like to know in what ways, if any,
your near-death incident affected your life. In responding to the following items, all you need do is to circle the appropriate alternative,
according to the instructions given below. Each statement should be
understood as beginning with the phrase, "Since my near-death incident in _____ (year of incident)." Consider each statement carefully. For example, consider the following statement:

(Since my near-death incident in _____), my interest in the field of
medicine has . . .

If you felt your interest had *strongly increased*, you would circle *SI*
in the column following this statement. If you felt your interest had
increased somewhat, you would circle *I* next to the statement. If
your interest *hadn't changed*, you would circle *NC*. If your interest
had *decreased somewhat*, you would circle *D*. Finally, if your interest had *strongly decreased*, you would circle *SD*. To summarize:

Strongly increase	= SI	Decrease somewhat	= D
Increase somewhat	= I	Strongly decrease	= SD
No change	= NC		

1. My desire to help others has   SI   I   NC   D   SD
2. My compassion for others has   SI   I   NC   D   SD
3. My appreciation of "the ordinary things of life" has   SI   I   NC   D   SD
4. My ability to listen to others has   SI   I   NC   D   SD
5. My feelings of self-worth have   SI   I   NC   D   SD
6. My interest in psychic phenomena has   SI   I   NC   D   SD
7. My concern with the material things of life has   SI   I   NC   D   SD
8. My tolerance for others has   SI   I   NC   D   SD
9. My interest in creating a "good impression" has   SI   I   NC   D   SD
10. My concern with spiritual matters has   SI   I   NC   D   SD
11. My interest in organized religion has   SI   I   NC   D   SD
12. My understanding of myself has   SI   I   NC   D   SD
13. My desire to achieve a higher consciousness has   SI   I   NC   D   SD
14. My ability to express love for others has   SI   I   NC   D   SD
15. My interest in "living the good life" has   SI   I   NC   D   SD
16. My insight into the problems of others has   SI   I   NC   D   SD
17. My appreciation of nature has   SI   I   NC   D   SD
18. My religious feelings have   SI   I   NC   D   SD
19. My understanding of "what life is all about" has   SI   I   NC   D   SD
20. My personal sense of purpose in life has   SI   I   NC   D   SD
21. My belief in a higher power has   SI   I   NC   D   SD
22. My understanding of others has   SI   I   NC   D   SD

23. My sense of the sacred aspect of life has   SI I NC D SD

24. My ambitions to achieve a high standard of living have   SI I NC D SD

25. My desire for solitude has   SI I NC D SD

26. My sense that there is some inner meaning to my life has   SI I NC D SD

27. My involvement in my family life has   SI I NC D SD

28. My fear of death has   SI I NC D SD

29. My desire to become a well-known person has   SI I NC D SD

30. My tendency to pray has   SI I NC D SD

31. My openness to the notion of re-incarnation has   SI I NC D SD

32. My interest in self-understanding has   SI I NC D SD

33. My inner sense of God's presence has   SI I NC D SD

34. My feelings of personal vulnerability have   SI I NC D SD

35. My conviction that there is life after death has   SI I NC D SD

36. My interest in what others think of me has   SI I NC D SD

37. My concern with political matters has   SI I NC D SD

38. My interest in achieving material success in life has   SI I NC D SD

39. My acceptance of others has   SI I NC D SD

40. My search for personal meaning has   SI I NC D SD

41. My concern with questions of social justice has   SI I NC D SD

42. My interest in issues related to death and dying has

SI   I   NC   D   SD

BEHAVIOR RATING INVENTORY

NAME_____

RELATIONSHIP TO RESPONDENT_____

As one who has known _____ both before and after his/her near-death incident, you can provide us with some very valuable information about how this incident affected this person, if at all. In responding to the questions on this form, we would like you to indicate whether you have become aware of any changes in _____'s behavior or attitudes following his/her near-death incident. All you need do is to circle what *you* feel is the correct response to each statement. If you feel that there has been an *increase* in a given characteristic, just circle the *I* next to the statement; if you feel there has been a *decrease*, circle the *D* next to the statement; if you feel there has been *no* overall *change*, circle *NC*. Please give your own private opinion and, in filling out this form, please do *not* discuss your answers with the person in question. If you would like to make any comments concerning the characteristics listed below, please use the space following each item. At the end of the form, you may wish to express additional comments concerning matters already covered in the questionnaire.

In the years since _____'s near-death incident took place, would you say that his/her

1. interest in spiritual matters has   I D NC

2. tendency to express love openly has   I D NC

3. ability to enjoy "the ordinary things of life"   I D NC
   has

4. fear of death has   I D NC

5. sense of self-worth has   I D NC

6. interest in material things has   I   D   NC

7. tendency to accept others as they are has   I   D   NC

8. closeness to family members has   I   D   NC

9. involvement in religion has   I   D   NC

10. psychic abilities have   I   D   NC

    11. concern with self-understanding has   I D NC

In the space below, please indicate what other significant changes you have become aware of in _____ following his/her near-death incident.

RELIGIOUS BELIEFS INVENTORY

NAME_____

Below you will find a list of statements of religious beliefs. Since your near-death episode, would you say that you are *now* more or less inclined to agree with the following statements or that you hold the same belief as before? If you are now more inclined to *agree* with a given statement, please write in an *M* in the space provided next to the statement; if you are now more inclined to *disagree* with a statement, write in a *D*; if your opinion is the same as before, write in an *S*.

  ___ 1. The essential core of all religions is the same.

  ___ 2. I believe there is a heaven and a hell.

  ___ 3. No matter what your religious belief, there is a life after death.

  ___ 4. It is important to attend church regularly.

___ 5. Private prayer is more important in the religious life of a person than is attendance at public church services.

___ 6. More and more, I feel at home in any church.

___ 7. I find the doctrine of reincarnation—the idea that we come back to earth to live in a physical body again—very implausible.

___ 8. Eternal life is a gift of God only to those who believe in Jesus Christ as savior and Lord.

___ 9. God is within you.

___10. In order to live a truly religious life, the Church or some such other organized religious body is an essential.

___11. The Bible is the inspired word of God.

___12. A universal religion embracing all humanity is an idea which strongly appeals to me.

IANDS RELIGIOUS BELIEFS INVENTORY

Please check your religious affiliation

___ Catholic

___ Protestant (specify: _____)

___ Jewish

___ Eastern religion
(specify: _____)

___ Other specific religion
(specify: _____)

___ No specific religion

___ No religion at all

Please check your "near-death status":

___ have had a near-death experience

___ have come close to death, but have not had a near-death experience

___ have never come close to death

Below is a list of statements of religious beliefs. We are interested in whether you are *now* more or less inclined to agree with each of these statements than you were at some certain time in the past.

If you have had a near-death experience, or have come close to death without having had such an experience, please compare your present beliefs with your beliefs *prior to* that encounter with death. If you have never come close to death, please compare your present beliefs with those you held about ten years ago.

For each statement, please place a mark on the line before the statement to indicate whether you are now *more* inclined to agree with that statement, *less* inclined to agree with it, or whether your view now is the same as it was before.

More inclined to agree	Same	Less inclined to agree	
——	——	——	1. The essential core of all religions is the same.
——	——	——	2. I believe there is a heaven and a hell.
——	——	——	3. No matter what your religious belief, there is life after death.
——	——	——	4. It is important to attend church regularly.
——	——	——	5. Private prayer is more important in the religious life of a person than is attendance at public church services.
——	——	——	6. More and more, I feel at home in any church.
——	——	——	7. I find the doctrine of reincarnation—the idea that we come back to earth to live in a physical body again—very implausible.
——	——	——	8. Eternal life is a gift of God only to those who believe in Jesus Christ as Saviour and Lord.

— — —   9. God is within you.

— — —   10. In order to live a truly religious life, the Church or some such other organized religious body is an essential.

— — —   11. The Bible is the inspired word of God.

— — —   12. A universal religion embracing all humanity is an idea that strongly appeals to me.

PSYCHIC EXPERIENCE INVENTORY

NAME_____

This questionnaire is concerned with whether and to what extent you have had any "psychic experiences." Most questions simply require you to circle the most appropriate alternative. A few questions call for brief written answers. Please answer all questions and consider each one carefully.

1. Psychic phenomena refer to a wide range of events in which people claim either to be aware of or to be able to do things which presumably are impossible, e.g., to "read" another person's thoughts or to separate from one's body. What is your own attitude toward such alleged experiences?

    a. Strongly believe that they occur
    b. Tend to believe that they occur
    c. Don't know or not sure if they occur
    d. Tend to doubt that they occur
    e. Strongly doubt that they occur

2. One type of psychic phenomenon is clairvoyance. This is a term used to describe an awareness of an event which seems to come to you without your usual senses being involved. For example, a mother may suddenly just "sense" or "know" that her daughter, 3,000 miles away, has been seriously injured in an automobile acci-

dent; several hours later, she receives a telephone call confirming her "psychic" impression. With regard to this kind of awareness, would you say that since the time of your near-death incident, it has:

    a. Increased
    b. Decreased
    c. Remained about the same
    d. Not sure if it has changed

3. If you chose alternative "a" in the last question, please describe how your clairvoyant sense has changed. Be as specific as you can and give examples where possible.

4. Telepathy is knowing what somebody else is thinking without that person telling you. Since the time of your near-death episode, would you say that, in general, your telepathic ability has:

    a. Increased
    b. Decreased
    c. Remained about the same
    d. Not sure if it has changed

5. Since the time of your near-death episode, how frequently have you had the experience of seeming to know what somebody will say before he says it?

    a. More frequently, and with regard to casual acquaintances or strangers as well as close friends or relatives
    b. More frequently, but with regard to close friends or relatives only
    c. About the same frequency as before
    d. Less frequently

6. Precognition is knowing when something is going to take place which could not reasonably have been predicted from other information. For example, a person may claim that an airplane is going to crash in the Florida Everglades on a specific date—and it does. Since the time of your near-death episode, do you have:

    a. More precognitive flashes than before

b. Fewer precognitive flashes than before
c. About the same number of precognitive flashes as before

7. If you chose alternative "a" in the last question, do your precognitive flashes usually occur in: (You may check more than one alternative here)

a. Your normal waking state
b. Dreams
c. Relaxed states
d. Other conditions (please describe briefly)

8. Opposite of precognition is retrocognition. This is an experience in which you suddenly become aware of something that has happened in the past although you could not have actually known about it beforehand. Since your near-death episode, have you become:

a. More aware of having these experiences
b. Less aware of having these experiences
c. Equally aware of having these experiences as before
d. I am not aware of ever having had such an experience

9. Déjà vu is a term used to describe an experience which seems like a *re-experiencing* of something that has happened before. For example, you travel for the first time to a remote French village and, suddenly, you "know" that within two streets there will be a tiny church with unusual triangular windows. When you arrive, it's just as you knew it would be—as if you've been there before. Since the time of your near-death episode, have such déjà vu experiences been:

a. More frequent
b. Less frequent
c. As frequent as before
d. Don't know or not sure
e. I am not aware of ever having had such an experience.

10. Related to déjà vu experiences are experiences where you suddenly recognize that some event you are witnessing is one that you

knew was going to happen—as though you "knew" the future all along but only recognized it when it began to unfold. For example, you see a man approach you and you *know* he is going to ask you if you can direct him to a certain address, which he does. Since your near-death episode, have such experiences become:

a. More frequent
b. Less frequent
c. Remained about as frequent as before
d. Don't know or not sure
e. I am not aware of ever having had such an experience

11. Synchronicity is a term used to describe a pattern of events linked more by meaningful connections than by logical causes. For example, you are thinking of a song that you haven't heard in years when you turn on the radio to hear the same song playing. Since your near-death episode, are such synchronistic occurrences:

a. More frequent
b. Less frequent
c. About as frequent as before
d. Perhaps no more frequent than before, but I am more aware of such patterns now

12. Each of us has found himself in situations where things are going badly for us or where we are at a loss as to what to do, when, suddenly, something quite unexpected occurs and rescues us from our plight. Since your near-death episode, have such experiences been:

a. More frequent
b. Less frequent
c. About as frequent as before
d. Not sure

13. Since the time of your near-death episode, do you feel that:

a. You have become more intuitive
b. You have become less intuitive
c. Your intuitive sense has remained about the same
d. You don't know whether your intuitive sense has changed

14. Compared to how you were before your near-death episode, would you say that now you feel you are:

    a. More in touch with an inner source of knowledge or wisdom
    b. Less in touch with an inner source of knowledge or wisdom
    c. As much in touch with an inner source of wisdom or knowledge as I had been before

15. Since the time of your near-death episode, would you say that you are:

    a. More aware of your dreams
    b. Less aware of your dreams
    c. Equally aware of your dreams
    d. No more aware of my dreams, but I pay more attention to them
    e. Not sure if my awareness of dreams has changed

16. Have the contents or the quality of your dreams changed in any significant way since the time of your near-death experience? If so, please indicate in what way(s) in the space below:

17. An out-of-body experience is one where your consciousness or mind seems to function independently of and outside your physical

body. Sometimes during such an episode, you can actually see your own physical body as though a spectator to it. Have you ever had an out-of-body experience?

    a. Yes
    b. No

17a. If so, please answer the following questions:
     Approximate date_____
     Did you actually see your physical body at this time?

    a. Yes
    b. No
    c. Not sure

     Have you had more than one such experience?

    a. Yes
    b. No
    c. Not sure

18. *If* you have had multiple out-of-body experiences, would you say that *after* your near-death episode, they are:

    a. More frequent than before
    b. Less frequent than before
    c. About as frequent as before
    d. Not sure about comparative frequency

19. If you have had one or more out-of-body experiences, please describe the circumstances in the space below. Include in your description date(s), content of experience, how it came about, etc., in as much detail as you care to give. If you have had too many such experiences to list in this way, please try to characterize them in a general way.

20. If you have had one or more out-of-body experiences, did you ever find yourself in what appeared to be "another dimension of reality" as distinct from the physical world? If so, please describe it to the extent you can.

21. *Before* your near-death episode, did you ever sense or feel that you were in touch with "spirits" or "guides" who helped you to understand certain things? If so, please give some specifics in the space below.

22. *After* your near-death episode, have you come to sense or feel you are in touch with "spirits" or "guides" who help you to understand certain things? If so, please give some specifics in the space below:

23. (Answer only if you have replied affirmatively to one or both of the foregoing questions.) Which *one* of the following statements best

describes your "contact" with "spirits" or "guides" since your near-death episode?

    a. Such contact has increased
    b. Such contact has decreased
    c. Such contact has remained about the same
    d. Such contact has remained about the same, but it has become more meaningful to me

24. At the time of your near-death episode or afterward, did you ever sense or know that you had had revealed to you any kind of "vision" of the future? If so, please describe it in as much detail as you can.

25. Would you say that since your near-death episode, your psychic sensitivities have changed in any way not already covered in this inventory? If so, please comment in the space below:

26. In responding to the following concepts, please use this scale:

+2 = strongly believe
+1 = tend to believe
  0 = don't know or not sure
−1 = tend to doubt
−2 = strongly doubt

Use this scale *twice* in responding to the concepts listed below. First indicate your response to the concept in terms of your belief *prior to* your near-death episode. Then make a second set of ratings which reflect your *present* beliefs.

CONCEPT	BEFORE	PRESENT
ASTROLOGY	___	___
LIFE AFTER DEATH	___	___
EXTRA-SENSORY PERCEPTION	___	___
REINCARNATION	___	___
OUT-OF-BODY EXPERIENCES	___	___
SPIRIT GUIDES	___	___
GOD	___	___
PSYCHIC OR SPIRITUAL HEALING	___	___
DEMONIC POSSESSION	___	___

FUTURE SCENARIO QUESTIONNAIRE

Name (optional)_____

Sex_____ Age_____ Highest Grade Completed_____

Occupation_____ Religious Affiliation_____

Have you ever been close to death? Yes_____ No_____

If so, did you ever have a near-death experience?

Yes_____ No_____

This questionnaire is concerned with determining your view of the future, from now to the end of this century. Please be sure to answer all questions. No names (if given) will be used in connection with any publication that might be based on your answers; your identity will remain anonymous.

I. Please place a check mark (x) next to *one* and only one of the following items that most closely reflects your view of the earth's future, from now until the end of this century. *Please read through the entire list first before making your own selection.*

_____ 1. There will be a gradual improvement in world conditions and international relations. No major wars will take place during this time. It will be a period of increasing harmony in the world.

_____ 2. Things will continue pretty much as they are now, with periodic international tensions and ecological stresses, but no *fundamental* changes in the world will occur during this period.

_____ 3. There will be a gradual deterioration in world conditions and international relations. The likelihood of global instability will increase and the prospect of a nuclear war is significant.

_____ 4. There will be many upheavals in the world including an increase in earthquakes, volcanic activity and disruptive weather conditions. International tensions will mount and the threat of a nuclear war will increase.

___ 5. There will be *massive* geophysical changes (i.e., earth-quakes, tidal waves, etc.) including the possibility of a magnetic pole shift, with the result that the earth will experience a tremendous upheaval and widespread destruction of life.

___ 6. There will be all of the events described in #5 and, in addition, a nuclear war will occur.

___ 7. There will be a nuclear war, but it will not be preceded by the massive geophysical changes specified in #5.

___ 8. There will be a period of great stress and turmoil, but before any globally destructive events occur, there will be a supernational intervention of some kind (UFOs, Christ, a new messiah, etc.) that will save the planet.

___ 9. I have no particular view of the earth's future.

___10. My view of the earth's future differs significantly from any of the alternatives listed above.

Ia. If you checked #10, please write a brief description in the space below of the future as you see it.

II. Whatever your view of the future, is it based *primarily* on (check *one*)

___1. Your understanding of information available from books, the media, etc.

___2. An intuitive hunch about future events

___3. A dream, vision, or psychic experience which seemed to disclose the future to you

___4. Other (please specify)

IIa. If you checked #3, would you please describe the circumstances of your dream, vision, or psychic experience (e.g., where and when it occurred) and just *what* was disclosed to you? (Use other side of page if necessary.)

III. Whatever your view of the future, please give a number below (from 0 to 100) which represents your degree of *certainty* that the future you checked in I will actually occur. Use the following chart in choosing a number (but you needn't limit your selection to only those numbers used here as guidelines; choose *any* number from 0 to 100).

  0 = Not certain at all
20 = Not very certain
40 = Somewhat certain

60 = Fairly certain
80 = Quite certain
100 = Completely certain

MY CERTAINTY NUMBER

APPENDIX 3
. . . .

Statistical Data from Omega Study

÷

CHAPTER 5 DATA

FIGURE 1
Appreciation of Life

3. Appreciation of ordinary things

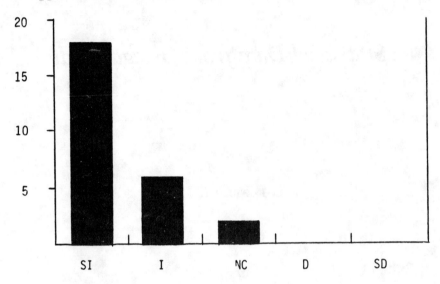

17. Appreciation of nature

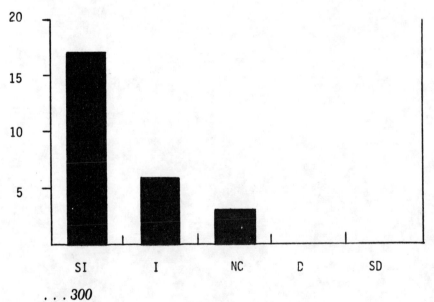

FIGURE 2
Concern for Others

1. Helping others

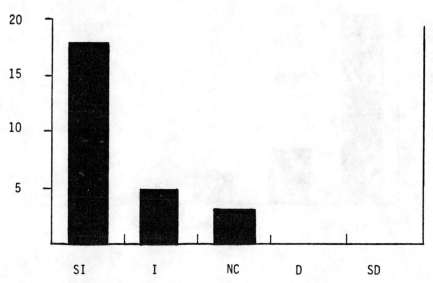

2. Compassion for others

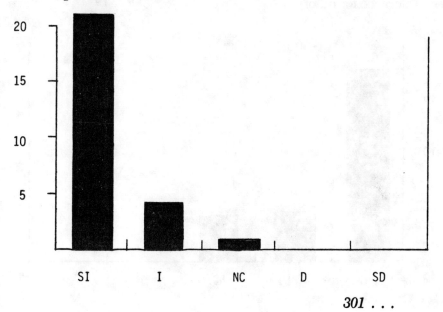

4. Patience for others

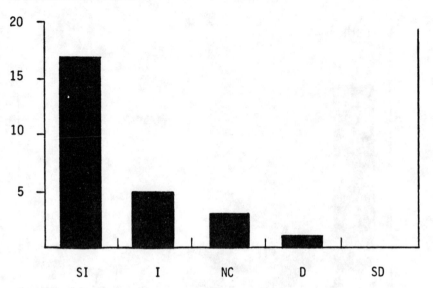

8. Tolerance for others

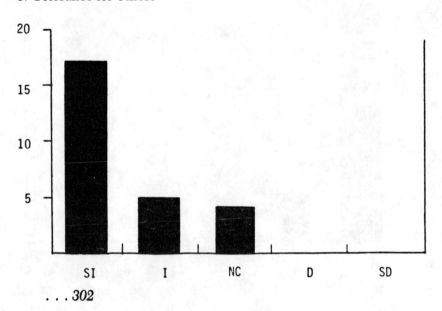

14. Love for others

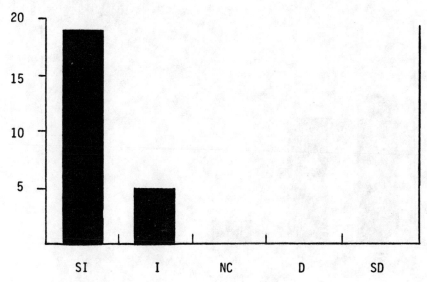

16. Insight into others

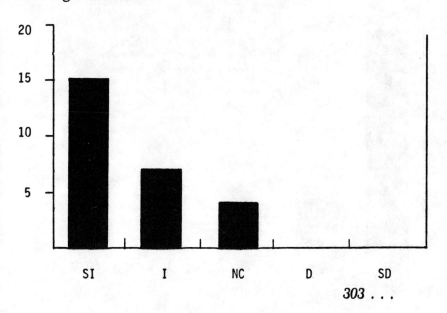

22. Understanding of others

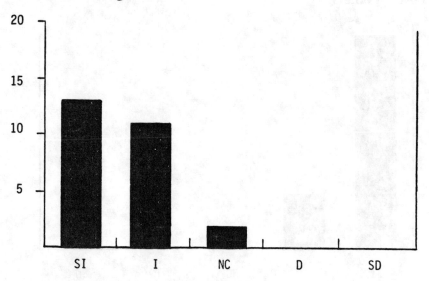

39. Acceptance of others

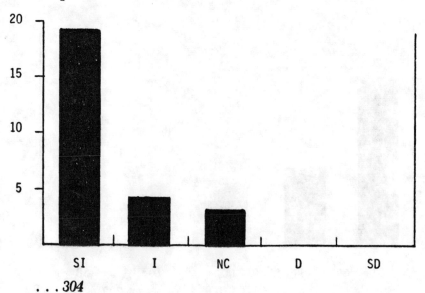

FIGURE 3
Concern with Impressing Others

9. Good impression

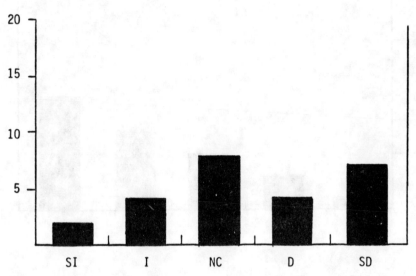

29. Well-known

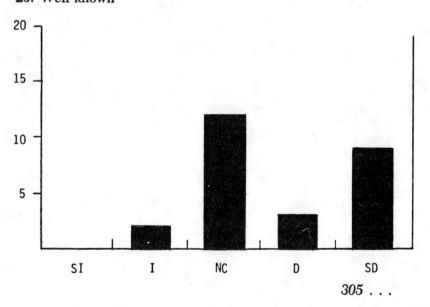

36. What others think

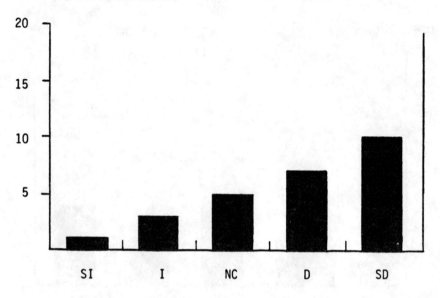

FIGURE 4
Materialism

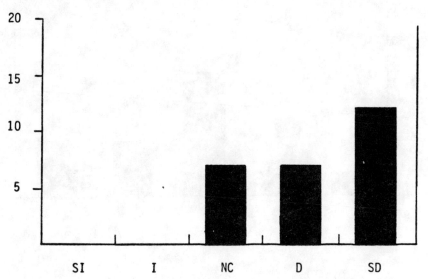

7. Material things

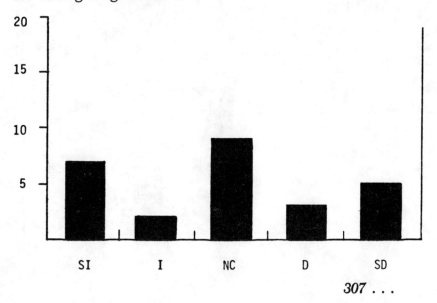

15. "Living the good life"

24. High standard of living

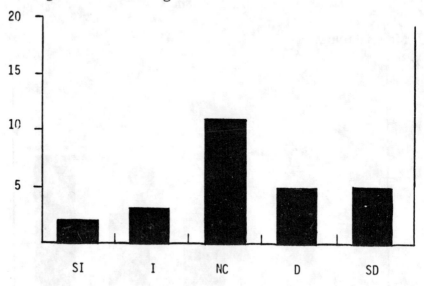

38. Material success

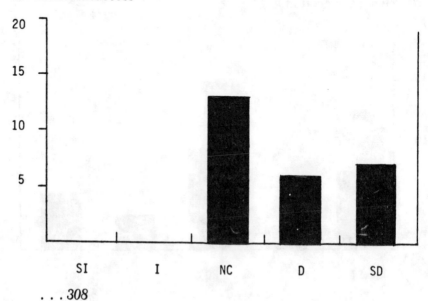

FIGURE 5
Quest for Meaning

13. Higher consciousness

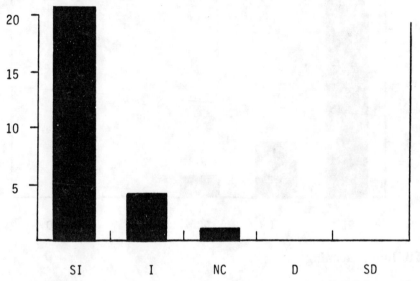

19. "What life is all about"

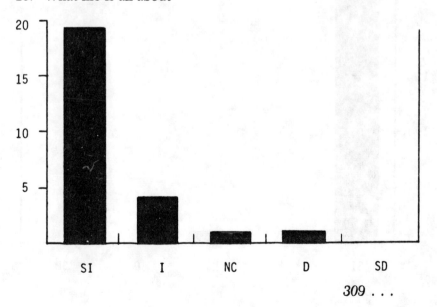

20. Purpose

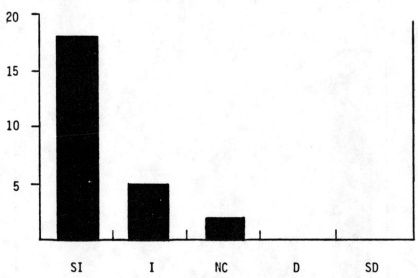

26. Inner meaning

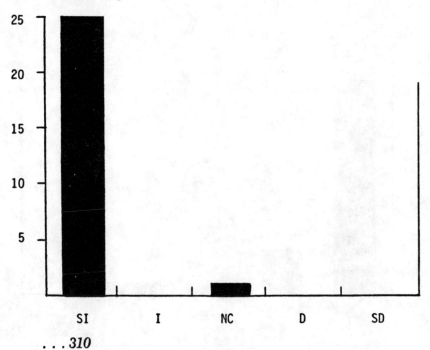

32. Self-understanding

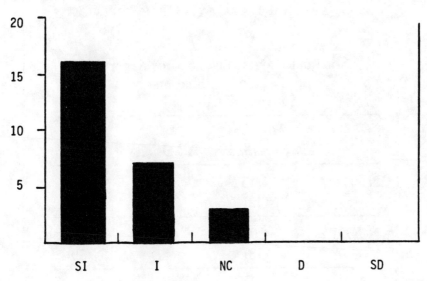

40. Personal meaning

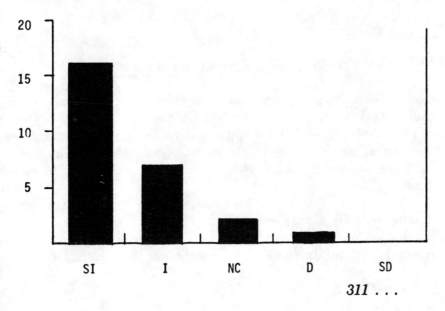

CHAPTER 6 DATA AND COMMENTARY

Table 1
Spiritual Universalism Scores According
to Religious Affiliation and
Near-Death Status

	Mainline Christians	All Others	Average
NDErs	4.45 (42)	7.56 (34)	5.84 (76)
N-NDErs	4.92 (13)	4.00 (17)	4.30 (30)
Others	4.41 (29)	3.41 (37)	3.85 (66)
	4.51 (84)	5.12 (88)	

TECHNICAL COMMENTARY ON TABLE 1

Fractional figures within each cell represent the average (net) shift toward spiritual universalism on the part of individuals in that cell. The integers within parentheses stand for the number of persons in that category. Finally, the fractional figures *outside* the table itself are the weighted averages for their respective rows or columns.

The spiritual universalism index for each respondent was derived by calculating the following double difference score. The number of items relating to spiritual universalism with which the respondent showed decreased agreement was first subtracted from the number of such items with which he or she showed increased agreement. The same procedure was then followed for conventional items. The absolute difference between these scores gives the net shift toward spiritual universalism for that respondent; of course, a positive value indicates a shift in the direction of spiritual universalism. Algebraically, the formula here is:

$$U_s = |\Sigma(U_a - U_d)| - |\Sigma(C_a - C_d)|$$

U_s = shift toward spiritual universalism
U_a = increased agreement with item relating to spiritual universalism
U_d = decreased agreement with item relating to spiritual universalism
C_a = increased agreement with conventional item
C_d = decreased agreement with conventional item

The following hypothetical example will illustrate how this index would be calculated in an individual case. Suppose, for instance, that a respondent's RBI answers were as follows (where + = more agreement, − = less agreement, and 0 = no change):

Item	2	3	4	5	6	7	8	9	10	11	12
Response	+	−	+	−	+	0	−	−	+	−	+	−

We first divide the items into our two basic categories, universal and conventional:

Universal							*Conventional*					
Item	1	3	5	6	9	12	2	4	7	8	10	11
Response	+	+	+	0	+	−	−	−	−	−	−	+

For the universal cluster, our formula gives us (4-1) = 3, while for the conventional cluster, we have (1-5) = −4. When we take the absolute difference *between* these different scores, we obtain /3/ − / − 4/ = 7.

Thus this individual would show a pattern of responses that indicates a tendency to be more in agreement with items relating to spiritual universalism and more in disagreement with conventional ones, resulting in a net shift toward spiritual universalism of $+7$.

Now that these explanations are out of the way, we are in a position to understand just what these figures tell us. There are several points worth noting here. We will take them in order.

First we can see from the cell values in the table that all categories of respondents are now more inclined to endorse statements favoring spiritual universalism than they once were. Given that virtually all respondents are members of IANDS, however, this result is not particularly unexpected. For our purposes, though, it is the *difference* among categories that are of principal interest to us. Let us look at those next.

Second, then, observe the averages for each of the rows (to the right of Table 1). There you will see that NDErs of all groups show the greatest tendency toward spiritual universalism, followed by near-death survivors and others, in that order. This difference is statistically significant (p <.05). In short, NDErs tend to be particularly likely to agree with statements favoring spiritual universalism compared to other groups. The difference in column averages (between mainline Christians and all others) is not significant, however.

Finally, look closely once again at the individual cell values. If you focus on the one in the upper right-hand corner of the table itself, you will be able to discover the most important finding of this analysis and that which significantly qualifies the conclusion stated in the preceding paragraph. Plainly, it is the NDErs who are *not* mainline Christians who show an extremely strong proclivity to endorse statements favoring spiritual universalism. In fact (looking down the column for mainline Christians) we can easily see that mainline Christians—NDErs or not—reveal shifts toward spiritual universalism of about the same magnitude, between 4.4 and 4.9 points. Non-NDErs who are not mainline Christians report an average shift somewhat smaller in magnitude, between 3.4 and 4.0. But the NDEr who is not or is no longer a mainline Christian evinces a tremendous leap toward spiritual universalism. (The interaction here is significant: F = 4.12, p <.05.)

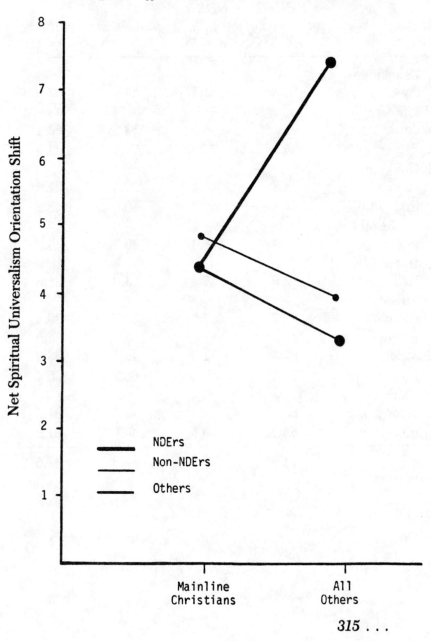

FIGURE 6
*Spiritual Universalism Orientation Shift as a Function of
Religious Affiliation and Near-Death Status*

Table 2

Percent Agreement with Universalistically Spiritual Sentiments on
RBI by Near-Death Status

RBI Item	NDErs (others only) n = 34	NDErs (all) n = 76	Non-NDErs n = 30	Others n = 66
1. Religions same	85.3	71.1	40.0	47.0
3. Life after death	91.2	85.5	53.3	62.1
5. Prayer	85.3	77.6	70.0	43.9
6. Home in church	38.2	43.4	20.0	31.8
9. God within	94.1	80.3	60.0	48.5
12. Universal religion	79.4	68.4	46.7	40.9
2. Heaven / Hell	52.9	47.4	33.3	31.8
4. Attend church	67.7	55.3	56.7	39.4
7. Reincarnation	67.7	51.3	46.7	43.9
8. Jesus Christ	79.4	65.8	66.7	36.4
10. Church membership	85.3	71.1	73.3	51.5
11. Bible	55.9	39.5	40.0	21.2
Mean % Agreement	73.5	63.1	50.6	41.5

Table 3
Frequency Counts for Omega NDErs on Selected LCQ Items

LCQ Item	SI	I	NC	D	SD
10. Spiritual matters	22	0	4	0	0
11. Organized religion	4	7	7	3	5
18. Religious feelings	15	7	2	2	0
21. Higher power	23	2	0	0	0
23. Sacredness of life	19	4	3	0	0
30. Prayer	11	9	3	3	0
31. Reincarnation	10	7	6	1	2
33. God's presence	20	5	1	0	0
35. Life after death	23	1	2	0	0

CHAPTER 7 DATA

Table 4
Concept Changes and Averages for PEI Items
(n = 25)*

Concept	Increase	No Change	Decrease	$\overline{X}$
God	15	10	0	2.00
Life after death	24	1	0	1.92
ESP	16	9	0	1.92
OBEs	23	2	0	1.80
Psychic/spiritual healing	21	3	1	1.52
Spirit guides	17	8	0	1.08
Reincarnation	15	6	4	0.32
Demonic possession	9	10	6	0.04
Astrology	8	10	7	−0.36

*One respondent misinterpreted the instructions here; thus her answers were eliminated from the analysis in this table.

Table 5
Selected Comparisons from Greyson's Study of Psychic Phenomena

Variable	Percent Reporting Before NDE	Percent Reporting After NDE	p*
Waking ESP experiences	24.6	55.1	<.0001
ESP dreams	18.8	33.3	NS
OBEs	11.6	43.5	.0001
Encounters with apparitions	13.0	44.9	.0001
Perception of auras	11.6	33.3	.0015
Communication with the dead	11.6	27.5	NS
Déjà vu	48.5	60.3	NS
Mystical experiences	23.2	59.4	<.0001
Weekly dream recall	36.8	63.2	<.0021
Meditation	21.7	50.0	.0026

*The values in this column refer to the probability that the associated difference could have occurred by chance. For example, a p = .0001 means that such a difference would occur by chance only once in ten thousand times. NS means the difference *could* have occurred by chance often enough that it cannot be regarded statistically as a likely *true* difference.

Table 6
Selected Comparisons from Kohr's Study of Psychic
Phenomena

Variable	NDErs	Near-Death Survivors	Others	Significance
Types of psi/psi-related experiences	7.20	5.95	5.51	Yes
Total number of psi/psi-related experiences	34.80	27.38	25.00	Yes
Frequency of mystical experiences	3.27	2.84	2.52	Yes
Frequency of unusual dream states*	9.30	10.29	9.97	Yes
Frequency of meditation*	1.83	2.20	2.13	Yes

*On these variables, a low score indicates a high frequency.

APPENDIX 4
. . . .

The International Association for Near-Death Studies (IANDS)

÷

Since its inception in December 1980, IANDS has been a center for the study of near-death experiences and related phenomena. Located at the University of Connecticut, IANDS was formed to serve the interests of professional and laypersons alike who are concerned with the study of NDEs and with the judicious application of knowledge based on such study in appropriate settings. The principal objectives of IANDS are:

1. To impart knowledge concerning NDEs and their implications.
2. To encourage and support research dealing with NDEs and related phenomena.
3. To further the utilization of NDE research findings in such settings as hospitals, hospices, nursing homes, and funeral establishments and in death education programs.
4. To form local chapters and support groups for NDErs, their families, and others interested in NDEs.
5. To sponsor international symposia, conferences, and other programs concerned with NDEs and their implications.
6. To maintain a library and archives of materials pertaining to NDEs.

More than seven hundred persons representing virtually every state in the United States and many countries throughout the world are members of IANDS and participate in its activities. IANDS publishes a quarterly newsletter, *Vital Signs*, for its membership and also publishes semiannually a scholarly journal, *Anabiosis—The*

Journal for Near-Death Studies, for persons interested in the field of near-death studies.

If any reader is interested in joining IANDS or in finding out more about its work, please write for free literature to:

IANDS
Box U-20
University of Connecticut
Storrs, CT 06268

If you prefer, you may call IANDS directly at (203) 486-4170.

Notes

CHAPTER 1

1. K. Ring, *Near-Death Studies: A New Area of Consciousness Research*.
2. G. Gallup, Jr., *Adventures in Immortality*.
3. NDE is the commonly used abbreviation for the phrase "near-death experience," and I will use it henceforth throughout this book.
4. This assertion is so far based mainly on informal research studies and other anecdotal evidence. Research is being planned, however, to assess more carefully the magnitude of this effect.
5. The "being of light" is the term coined by Raymond Moody in his pioneering book *Life After Life* to refer to a luminous, seemingly omniscient presence encountered by some near-death experiencers. The being of light seems to be a major constituent of the new archetypal imagery of death deriving from near-death research.
6. I use this term to refer to all persons who have come close to death, whether or not they report an NDE. Those who remember an NDE will be called near-death experiencers, or NDErs for short.
7. In *Life at Death* I use the term "core experience" to refer to what I here call simply a near-death experience. Also in that book I delineated the core experience by reference to its five major stages of sequential development.
8. The problem of representative sampling of NDErs has been troublesome to all near-death researchers beginning with Moody, but evidence presented in the next chapter strongly suggests that despite this limitation, the major findings of near-death studies have now been amply validated.

CHAPTER 2

1. K. Ring, *Near-Death Studies: A New Area of Consciousness Research*
2. S. Vicchio, "Near-Death Experiences: A Critical Review of the Literature and Some Questions for Further Help."
3. B. Greyson, "Near-Death Studies, 1981—1982: A Review."
4. Information on this journal and where it may be obtained is given in Appendix IV.
5. Ring, *Life at Death*, p. 34.
6. There are some investigators (such as thanatologist Elisabeth Kübler-Ross and cardiologist Fred Schoonmaker) who, among them, have interviewed thousands of near-death survivors but who unfortunately have not yet published any systematic accounts of their work along these lines.
7. See Chapter 4.
8. Moody, *Life After Life*.
9. Ring, *Life at Death*, pp. 102—3.
10. Moody, *Life After Life*, pp. 23—24.
11. Sabom, *Recollections of Death;* see especially Chapter 7.
12. Research on negative NDEs is beginning, however. The first systematic study of them to be undertaken is one that IANDS director Nancy Evans Bush has planned for 1983.
13. K. Ring and S. Franklin, "Do Suicide Survivors Report Near-Death Experiences?" B. Greyson, "Near-Death Experiences and Attempted Suicide."
14. Gallup, *Adventures in Immortality*, pp. 198—200.
15. Sabom, p. 59.
16. Ring, pp. 131—32. A suggestion of a possible but negligible correlation between age and NDE status in my study was *not* upheld by Gallup's and Sabom's work and so seems to have been a sampling error.
17. S. Twemlow, G. Gabbard, and F. Jones, "The Out-of-Body Experience: A Phenomenological Typology Based on Questionnaire Responses."
18. John Audette, personal communication (1981).
19. See, e.g., J. C. Hampe, *To Die Is Gain* and P. Giovetti, "Near-Death and Deathbed Experiences: An Italian Survey."
20. K. Osis and E. Haraldsson, *At the Hour of Death*.

CHAPTER 3

1. Excerpts from my interview with Joe in this and the next chapter are taken from Andrew Silver's film *Prophetic Voices,* a twenty-minute documentary featuring interviews with four NDErs. The videotape of *Prophetic Voices* is available through IANDS.
2. I will describe and try to evaluate this purportedly precognitive aspect of Janis's experience and other such NDE-related "life previews" in Chapter 7.
3. We will be discussing kundalini energy in relation to NDEs in some detail in Chapter 9.
4. Before this experience, however, he states that he was "an atheist almost all my life" and thought of himself as one at the time of his NDE. Several other individuals whose NDEs are cited in this chapter also characterized their religious views as weak or absent at the time of their experience.
5. See Chapter 8.
6. Olfactory sensations are, however, extremely rare even in core NDErs; this, then, is *not* a typical experience.
7. It has since been published, and I highly recommend it. Called *A New Age Handbook on Death and Dying,* it was published by Devorss and Co. in 1982.
8. This aspect of core NDEs would be even more obvious if I had quoted each account in full.

CHAPTER 4

1. Beginning here I will no longer give pseudonyms to or biographical details about NDErs whose accounts I cite unless their experience receives extended treatment.
2. A bed in the shape of a ferris wheel for persons who have had spinal fusion operations.
3. Readers familiar with the work of Czech psychiatrist Stanislav Grof, particularly his book *Realms of the Human Unconscious,* will recognize Barbara's description as resembling the emergence of what Grof calls a COEX system, a process that lies at the core of psychodynamic experience and often heralds a major therapeutic breakthrough.
4. See, for example, the already noted book by Grof, *Realms of the Human Unconscious,* for some compelling examples.

5. Nevertheless, she is one of the two core experiencers I mentioned earlier whose NDE suggested—at least to me—this identity for the being of light.
6. The conversations in this section have been checked by Tom for their accuracy, and he is satisfied that they are virtually if not absolutely verbatim. He has also stated to me that all the facts and events relating to him are correct in their essential details.
7. Greek alphabetical symbols are also used to denote numerals.
8. Here, of course, I am recounting only what Tom told me; I do not present this as *evidence* of any kind of paranormal cognition. Obviously, Tom might be mistaken about his prior knowledge of this quotation—which I've seen cited elsewhere—or could be the victim of cryptoamnesia, which is often a "culprit" in cases of this type.
9. Synchronicity—a concept popularized by the writings of the great psychiatrist C. G. Jung—refers to a pattern of meaningful "coincidences" that take place with no apparent causal link among them.

CHAPTER 5

1. Here is one of those instances where it would have been desirable to have had control groups of near-death survivors and those persons who have never been close to death take the LCQ also. Regrettably, it was not possible to arrange to obtain data on the LCQ from demographically comparable control groups (though this was possible with the other questionnaires used in this research—see Chapters 6 and 8—and with the relevant questionnaires of other research—see Chapter 7).
2. The exact breakdown here for those interested is as follows:

Interviewees—no LCQ	24
Interviewees—completed LCQ	18
LCQ respondents only	7
Correspondents	62
Total	111

3. Because of the nonrepresentativeness of this sample (see comments, Chapter 1, page 29), however, no formal tests of statistical significance are appropriate here; nevertheless, *within* this sample, the strong value shifts are evident by inspection.

4. Mr. Dippong is correct, in my judgment, in distinguishing between his core NDE and most others of the kind I emphasized in *Life at Death*.

CHAPTER 6

1. Actually, two functionally equivalent forms of the RBI were used in my research, as will be explained shortly. Both versions are reproduced in Appendix II.
2. In the case of NDErs and near-death survivors, they are asked to respond wiith their present views with reference to their views *before* their near-death incident. For respondents who have never been close to death, their present views are to be compared to those of ten years ago.
3. These labels are my own, however, and were chosen for their descriptive value only; no judgment is implied.
4. I am very grateful to Dr. Greyson for his invaluable assistance in making the necessary arrangements to obtain these data as well as to the members of the IANDS' research pool for their willingness to fill out the RBI for me.
5. Comparison of RBI data from my own sample of twenty-six NDErs with that from IANDS NDErs revealed that the two samples were indistinguishable. It was therefore permissible to combine them, as I have done in this table. It should further be noted that the comparability of these two samples of NDErs provides indirect support for the assumption that my own small sample of twenty-six NDErs *may* be representative of larger groups of NDErs on other variables besides those measured by the RBI. (See Chapter 5, for example.) Of course, at the same time it must be borne in mind that IANDS NDErs themselves probably are *not* representative of NDErs in general, at least in some characteristics.
6. The reason for this seemingly indiscriminate second category—as well as the basic division *between* categories—has to do with the relative uniformity of RBI scores within category subgroups.
7. See technical commentary on Table 1 for the derivation of this index.
8. A chi-square test with 2 df was used to evaluate this difference ($X^2 = 18.21$, p $<.0005$).
9. Previous research (e.g., Ring, 1980; Sabom, 1982) has shown that such statements are made significantly more frequently by NDErs than by near-death survivors.

10. Please be careful to note that I did not say that they became *converted* to this doctrine; it is only that they appeared to become more receptive to it.

11. For example, Gallup has reported that whereas 23 percent of his national sample subscribe to a belief in reincarnation, fully 31 percent of his NDErs do. Though Gallup doesn't say, the difference would appear to be statistically significant. Gallup, ibid., p. 141.

12. Only twenty-five cases—rather than the usual twenty-six—were available here for analysis because one respondent misunderstood the instructions for this section of the PEI, invalidating her answers.

13. For example, Twemlow, Gabbard, and Jones in their major study of OBEs found for a small subsample of NDErs that following the experience there was a drop in affiliation with Catholic and Protestant religions and a corresponding increase of affiliation with "unusual and Eastern faiths."

CHAPTER 7

1. Bhikku Nanamoli, *Vissuddhimagga* (1956).
2. Goleman, "The Buddha on Meditation and States of Consciousness."
3. Goleman, p. 218.
4. Goleman, p. 219.
5. Swami Prabhavananda and Christopher Isherwood, *How to Know God: The Yoga Aphorisms of Patanjali,* (1969).
6. Prabhavananda and Isherwood, p. 134.
7. Prabhavananda and Isherwood, p. 126—27.
8. Motoyama, *Science and the Evolution of Consciousness*, pp. 47—48, 51.
9. Motoyama, p. 50.
10. Motoyama, p. 67.
11. Gopi Krishna, *The Secret of Yoga*.
12. Ibid., p. 195.
13. Gopi Krishna, *Higher Consciousness*.
14. Ibid., p. 117.
15. These key items were 2, 4, 5, 6, 8, 9, 10, 11, 12, 13, 14, 15, 18, and 23.
16. Becker, "Out of Their Bodies or Out of Their Minds? On the Extrasomaticity of OBEs."
17. Pasarow, "Death—My Luminous Journey."
18. Greyson, "Increase in Psychic and Psi-Related Phenomena Following Near-Death Experiences."

19. Kohr, "Near-Death Experience and Its Relationship to Psi and Various Altered States.
20. Ibid., p. 51.
21. *Life at Death;* "Paranormal and Other Non-ordinary Aspects of Near-Death Experiences"; and "Precognitive and Prophetic Visions in Near-Death Experiences."
22. Moody, *Life After Life;* Noyes, "Panoramic Memory."
23. Other persons who have had NDE-related PFs in childhood have also claimed that they were aware of devices then of which they only later learned the names.
24. Belle said that *after* meeting Moody she realized that the man she had sometimes noticed jogging must have been Moody, but she had never paid much attention to him or glanced at his face.
25. It was unusual for Avery to introduce himself in this fashion. According to Belle's account:

    . . . What was even stranger . . . was that he gave me his full name. They said he never gives his full name. Raymond Avery Moody, the third. This was the first time he had ever given out the full name. And that was my signal and his father immediately appeared in my mind and I knew who he was and that it was time to talk to him, to give him certain information.

    From my own knowledge of the Moody family, I can also attest to the fact that their son Avery is always referred to by that name.
26. Personal communication (June 1, 1981).
27. "Precognitive and Prophetic Visions in Near-Death Experiences."

CHAPTER 8

1. This study, coauthored with physician Michael Gulley, is currently being prepared for journal publication.
2. See my article, "Precognitive and Prophetic Visions in Near-Death Experiences."
3. I have heard of still others but have lacked the time and resources to investigate these cases directly.
4. It is my impression that an unusually high proportion of respondents reporting PVs have had particularly deep or prolonged NDEs. In addition, virtually all of them have related an encounter with a "higher being" or beings of some kind, which is not typical of most NDEs.

5. This, of course, is probably the view of most persons at this time in history. The near-death experiencers differ here only in their claim that they have already had a *vision* of these developments.

6. A few observations about this case are in order here. This man—whom I'll call Cliff—was interviewed jointly by Raymond Moody and me on November 19, 1981. On this occasion, Cliff described a series of precognitive dreams he had had following his NDE, in which he had seen scenes of events that later came to pass. He believes that what appeared to him in these dreams were scenes he *originally* saw during his NDE. Since his "track record" with previous dreams was so accurate, his series of dreams about a nuclear war are naturally extremely disquieting to him. He seems to believe that the Olympics year in question is 1984. Interestingly enough, Cliff, at the time of this NDE, chose to "override" the decision of the luminous beings he encountered. They said that they wanted him to go with them "because we don't want you to see and experience things that will happen otherwise that will hurt you a great deal." Cliff insisted on returning, however.

7. Most (though not all) of my sample are Christians.

8. This quotation is from the book *Beyond Coincidence* by a well-known psychic, Alex Tanous, whom I also interviewed for this project. In it he states that his vision came to him in the fall of 1967, well before many of the "signs" that have now occurred took place. The quote is from his chapter "Three Days of Darkness" (pp. 165—69), which describes his vision in detail. In his 1982 interview with me he stated that his initial understanding of his vision has only been reinforced by recent events.

9. Two excellent source books for detailed presentations of some of the main theories of precognition are J. White and S. Krippner, eds., *Future Science,* and D. Zohar, *Through the Time Barrier* (see the Bibliography).

10. Zohar, p. 118.

11. Zohar, p. 145.

12. Consider the cases presented in Chapter 7, for instance, where the course of a "future event" was altered by direct action following a precognitive flash.

13. It might seem that the highly positive final outcome stated or implied in PVs could represent a projection of the tremendous peace individuals often experience while on the threshold of death, but the fact that my respondents typically report that their feelings of peace and well-being *preceded* their PV militates against this interpretation.

14. J. Perry, *The Far Side of Madness.*

15. Ibid.

16. S. Grof, *Realms of the Human Unconscious*.
17. See, for example, J. Goodman, *We Are the Earthquake Generation;* J. White, *Pole Shift;* and W. Martin, "Waiting for the End."
18. The expression (p <.02) means that fewer than two times in a hundred could such a difference arise by chance. Similarly (p <.05) means such a difference occurs by chance fewer than five times in a hundred instances.
19. Tanous, p. 165.
20. For a readable discussion of this topic, intended for the layman, see Zukav.
21. Everett, "'Relative State' Formulation of Quantum Physics."

CHAPTER 9

1. This literature is so vast that there is no way I can adequately reference it here. Suffice it to say that it is represented by such classic works as R. M. Bucke's *Cosmic Consciousness* and William James's *The Varieties of Religious Experience*.
2. P. Rivard, "A Comparison of Near-Death Experience and Religious Experience."
3. S. Dean, "Metapsychiatry: The Confluence of Psychiatry and Mysticism."
4. Ibid, pp. 87–88.
5. For a good introduction to it, see John White's anthology *Kundalini, Evolution and Enlightenment*.
6. For a gripping example of this kind of kundalini awakening and its aftermath, see Gopi Krishna's autobiographical volume *Kundalini*.
7. Bentov, *Stalking the Wild Pendulum*.
8. Motoyama, *Science and the Evolution of Consciousness*.
9. Motoyama's narrative will be found in Chapter 9 of his book *Theories of the Chakras*, specifically pp. 238–57.
10. Sensations of extreme heat or cold and severe headaches are commonly reported in conjunction with kundalini arousal and can be explained by reference to the principles of Yoga.
11. Motoyama, *Theories of the Chakras*, p. 241.
12. Ibid., pp. 247–48.
13. Ibid., pp. 251–52.
14. Ibid., pp. 253–54.
15. Gopi Krishna, *Higher Consciousness*, p. 28.
16. Ibid., p. 29.

17. Ibid., p. 117.
18. Gopi Krishna, *The Awakening of Kundalini*, p. 126.
19. For example, in *The Awakening of Kundalini* he writes: "The entry into the higher dimension of consciousness gives to the mind an acuity of perception into the future. What it discloses is a picture so awful that I wish with all my heart that by some act of grace mankind might be saved the horror of it," p. 30.
20. See Motoyama, *Science and the Evolution of Consciousness*, p. 28.
21. Joseph Dippong, "Dawn of Perception," p. 36.
22. Gopi Krishna, *Kundalini*.
23. See note 10 for this chapter. For a specific reference here, see M. McCleave, "Kundalini, Headaches and Biofeedback."
24. My informal observations here should—and could easily—be followed up by more systematic investigation, but my impression is that many NDErs, because of an apparent (possibly kundalini-mediated) increased level of energetic arousal seem to need less sleep than most individuals require for optimal functioning.
25. Gopi Krishna, *The Real Nature of Mystical Experience*.
26. Ibid., p. 28.
27. Again, this is an area that demands systematic investigation before we can begin to know with any reliability how common this kind of development is and what factors underlie it. For example, the NDE may establish a potential for some individuals to become healers, but whether that potential is activated may depend largely on events subsequent to the NDE itself.
28. Dippong, "Dawn of Perception."
29. Motoyama, *Science and the Evolution of Consciousness*, p. 89.
30. For a good overview of these, see Swami Rama, "The Awakening of Kundalini" in John White, ed., *Kundalini, Evolution and Enlightenment*, pp. 27–47.
31. Gopi Krishna, *Higher Consciousness*, p. 16.
32. This issue has been extensively addressed in the near-death studies literature. See, e.g., the discussions in Moody, *Life After Life*, Chapter 5; Ring, *Life at Death*, Chapter 11; Grosso, "Toward an Explanation of Near-Death Phenomena"; and Sabom, *Recollections of Death*, Chapter 10.
33. Gopi Krishna, *Higher Consciousness*, p. 186.
34. Gopi Krishna, *The Awakening of Kundalini*, p. 43.
35. John White, ibid., p. 367.

CHAPTER 10

1. M. Ferguson, *The Aquarian Conspiracy;* P. Russell, *The Global Brain.*
2. See Peter Russell, *The Global Brain,* Chapter 11.
3. John White, "Jesus, Evolution, and the Future of Humanity," p. 14.
4. R.M. Bucke, *Cosmic Consciousness;* Sri Aurobindo, *Mind of Life;* Gopi Krishna, *Higher Consciousness;* and Ken Wilber, *Up from Eden.*
5. Curiously enough, some time after receiving these papers from Dr. Robinson, I learned that he had been personally acquainted with Père Teilhard and deeply influenced by him. Still later, Dr. Robinson wrote me a long letter of personal reminiscences of Teilhard, which I greatly enjoyed.
6. J.T. Robinson, "Man, Evolution and Society" and "Man, Morals and Metaevolution."
7. J.T. Robinson, "Man, Evolution and Society," p. 18.
8. J.T. Robinson, "Man, Morals and Metaevolution," p. 85.
9. Even John White allows that the difference between *Homo noeticus* and *Homo sapiens* is primarily one of consciousness, not outward form. It is, nevertheless, my intention to initiate soon a new research project to determine whether a significant proportion of NDErs are differentiated from other human beings on certain easily measurable *biological* characteristics. By taking into account anthropological criteria used to define major racial groupings, it may be possible to provide preliminary data (based on physical attributes and physiological functioning) to evaluate the *Homo noeticus* hypothesis.
10. Joseph Dippong, "Dawn of Perception," p. 36.
11. John White, *Kundalini, Evolution and Enlightenment,* p. 17.
12. One important qualification should be noted here. As Lee Sanella and Caroline Myss have reminded me, personal transformation indicative of higher consciousness does not necessarily *guarantee* that the individual will become more loving, compassionate, ethical, or spiritually minded; it only affords an increased opportunity for such growth. Of course, the data presented in this book suggest that NDEs by and large *do* promote this kind of development, but the effects of other avenues leading to personal transformation need to be more carefully assessed. I hope that this book will encourage such research.
13. Russell, *The Global Brain,* p. 129
14. See *Investigations,* p. 8.
15. Ring, *Life at Death,* p. 257.

16. Carol Parrish-Harra, *Messengers of Hope*, pp. 159–60.
17. Shortly after the first draft of this book was completed, I received a copy of a master's thesis reporting the results of an investigation of NDEs in an English population. In her discussion of the implications of her findings, the author, Margot Grey, seems to come to conclusions that are indistinguishable from my own and those of Carol Parrish-Harra. Ms. Grey, for example, writes in part: "That NDEs are occurring with ever increasing frequency seems to me to be directly related to the evolutionary process, which many enlightened beings are becoming ever more aware of, whereby higher consciousness is attempting to alert us on a collective level to the urgent need for a universal brotherhood, based on love and goodwill, manifesting in compassion. . . Do we have to wait until the planet itself is in a life-threatening situation of such magnitude that we are all imperilled and could it be that only when the planet experiences a sufficiently acute near-death episode on a universal scale that the collective consciousness of the planet will experience a shift to a higher level that will enable the entire human family to live in love and peace?" (pp. 78–79)
18. W. Brugh Joy, *Joy's Way*, p. 281.
19. Russell, *The Global Brain*, p. 7.
20. Carol Parrish-Harra, *Messengers of Hope*, pp. 176–77.

Bibliography

Aurobindo, S. *The Mind of Light*. New York: E.P. Dutton, 1971.

Becker, C. "Out of Their Bodies or Out of Their Minds? On the Extrasomaticity of OBE's," Part I. *Journal of Religion and Psychical Research* 6 (1983): 86–93.

Bentov, I. *Stalking the Wild Pendulum*. New York: E.P. Dutton, 1977.

Bucke, R. *Cosmic Consciousness*. New York: E.P. Dutton, 1969.

Dean, S. "Metapsychiatry: The Confluence of Psychiatry and Mysticism." In S. Dean (ed.), *Psychiatry and Mysticism*. Chicago: Nelson-Hall, 1975, pp. 3–18.

Dippong, J. "Dawn of Perception." *CHIMO* 8 (1982): 31–37.

Everett, H., III. "'Relative State' Formulation of Quantum Mechanics." *Reviews of Modern Physics* 29 (1957): 454–62.

Ferguson, M. *The Aquarian Conspiracy*. Los Angeles: J.P. Tarcher, 1980.

Gallup, G., Jr. *Adventures in Immortality*. New York: McGraw-Hill, 1982.

Giovetti, P. "Near-Death and Deathbed Experiences: An Italian Survey." *Theta* 10 (1982): 10–13.

Goleman, D. "The Buddha on Meditation and States of Consciousness." In C. Tart (ed.), *Transpersonal Psychologies*. New York: Harper & Row, 1975, pp. 203–30.

Goodman, J. *We Are the Earthquake Generation*. New York: Berkley, 1979.

Grey, M. "Beyond Death: The Near-Death Experience." Master's thesis in humanistic psychology, Antioch University (England), 1983.

Greyson, B. "Near-Death Experiences and Attempted Suicide." *Suicide and Life Threatening Behavior* 11 (1981): 10–16.

————. "Near-Death Studies, 1981–1982: A Review." *Anabiosis* 2 (1982)· 150–58.

————. "Increase in Psychic and Psi-Related Phenomena Following Near-Death Experiences." *Theta* (in press).

Grof, S. *Realms of the Human Unconscious*. New York: Viking, 1975.

Grosso, M. "Toward an Explanation of Near-Death Phenomena." *Journal of the American Society for Psychical Research* 75 (1981): 37–60.

Hampe, J. *To Die Is Gain*. Atlanta: John Knox, 1979.

Investigations 1 (1983).

James, W. *The Varieties of Religious Experience*. New York: Mentor, 1958.

Joy, W. *Joy's Way*. Los Angeles: J.P. Tarcher, 1979.

Kohr, R. "Near-Death Experience and Its Relationship to Psi and Various Altered States." *Theta* 10 (1982): 50–53.

Krishna, G. *Kundalini*. Berkeley, Calif.: Shambhala, 1970.

————. *The Secret of Yoga*. New York: Harper & Row, 1972.

————. *Higher Consciousness*. New York: Julian Press, 1974.

————. *The Awakening of Kundalini*. New York: E.P. Dutton, 1975.

————. *The Real Nature of Mystical Experience*. New York: New Concepts Publishing, 1978.

Martin, W. "Waiting for the End." *The Atlantic Monthly* (June 1982), pp. 31–37.

McCleave, M. "Kundalini, Headaches and Biofeedback." *Spiritual India and Kundalini* 2 (1978): 19–24.

Moody, R., Jr. *Life After Life*. Atlanta: Mockingbird Books, 1975.

Motoyama, H. *Science and the Evolution of Consciousness*. Brookline, Mass.: Autumn Press, 1978.

————. *Theories of the Chakras*. Wheaton, Ill.: Theosophical Publishing House, 1981.

Nanamoli, B. (tr.). *Visuddhimagga*. Kandy, Sri Lanka: Buddhist Publication Society, 1975.

Noyes, R., Jr. "Panoramic Memory." *Omega* 8 (1977): 181–93.

Osis, K., and Haraldsson, E. *At the Hour of Death*. New York: Avon, 1977.

Parrish-Harra, C. *A New Age Handbook on Death and Dying*. Marina del Rey, Calif.: DeVorss, 1982.

———. *Messengers of Hope*. Black Mountain, N.C.: New Age Press, 1983.

Pasarow, R. "Death—My Luminous Journey." *Fate* 35 (August 1982), pp. 65–69.

Perry, J. *The Far Side of Madness*. Englewood Cliffs, N.J.: Prentice-Hall, 1974.

Prabhavananda, S. and Isherwood, C. (trs.). *How to Know God: The Yoga Aphorisms of Patanjali*. New York: Mentor, 1969.

Rama, "The Awakening of Kundalini." In J. White (ed.), *Kundalini, Evolution and Enlightenment*. Garden City, N.Y.: Anchor Books, 1979, pp. 27–47.

Ring, K. *Life at Death*. New York: Coward, McCann & Geoghegan, 1980.

———. "Paranormal and Other Non-ordinary Aspects of Near-Death Experiences." *Essence* 5 (1981): 33–51.

———. "Precognitive and Prophetic Visions in Near-Death Experiences." *Anabiosis* 2 (1982): 47–74.

———. *Near-Death Studies: A New Area of Consciousness Research*. Storrs, Conn.: International Association for Near-Death Studies, 1982.

———. and Franklin, S. "Do Suicide Survivors Report Near-Death Experiences?" *Omega* 12 (1981–82): 191–208.

Rivard, P. "A Comparison of Near-Death Experience and Religious Experience." Storrs, Conn.: University of Connecticut term paper.

Robinson, J. "Man, Evolution and Society." *Indiana Historical Society Lectures, 1973–1974*. Indianapolis: Indiana Historical Society, 1974.

———. "Man, Morals and Metaevolution." *Central Issues in Anthropology* 2 (1980): 69–87.

Russell, P. *The Global Brain*. Los Angeles: J.P. Tarcher, 1983.

Sabom, M. *Recollections of Death*. New York: Harper & Row, 1982.

Sannella, L. *Kundalini: Psychosis or Transcendence?* San Francisco: H.S. Dakin, 1976.

Tanous, A. *Beyond Coincidence*. Garden City, N.Y.: Doubleday, 1976.

Teilhard de Chardin, P. *The Phenomenon of Man*. New York: Harper & Row, 1959.

Twemlow, S.; Gabbard, G.; and Jones, F. "The Out-of-Body Experience: A Phenomenological Typology Based on Questionnaire Responses." *American Journal of Psychiatry* 139 (1982): 450–55.

Vicchio, S. "Near-Death Experiences: A Critical Review of the Literature and Some Questions for Further Help." *Anabiosis* 1 (1981): 66–87.

White, J. *Pole Shift*. Garden City, N.Y.: Doubleday, 1980.

———. "Jesus, Evolution, and the Future of Humanity," Part I. *Science of Mind* (September 1981): 8–17.

———. (ed.). *Kundalini, Evolution and Enlightenment*. Garden City, N.Y.: Anchor Books, 1979.

——— and Krippner, S. (eds.). *Future Science*. Garden City, N.Y.: Anchor Books, 1977.

Wilber, K. *Up from Eden*. Garden City, N.Y.: Anchor Books, 1981.

Zohar, D. *Through the Time Barrier*. London: Heinemann, 1982.

Zukav, G. *The Dancing Wu-Li Masters*. New York: Morrow, 1979.

INDEX

339 . . .

INDEX

INDEX